Dimensional Data Warehousing with MySQL

A Tutorial

Djoni Darmawikarta

Dimensional Data Warehousing with MySQL: A Tutorial

First Edition: May 2007

ISBN-13: 978-0-9752128-2-0
ISBN-10: 0-9752128-2-6

Book and Cover Designer: Mona Setiadi

Technical Reviewer: Paul Deck
Indexer: Chris Mayle

Warning and Disclaimer
Every effort has been made to make this book as accurate as possible. The author and the publisher shall have neither liability nor responsibility to any person or entity with respect to any loss or damages arising from the information in this book

Table of Contents

Introduction

Welcome to *Dimensional Data Warehousing with MySQL: A Tutorial.*

Data warehousing enables unified information delivery by collecting data from various operational and administrative information systems already in operation and possibly from external data sources. The data from these sources are integrated, cleaned and transformed, and stored for easier access than if the data has to be read directly from the sources.

The data structure in a data warehouse allows you to store current and historical data. Current information is needed for operational activities, mostly for producing regular hardcopy or online reports. Historical data, unlikely to be readily available from the source, provides the business with information for time-based analysis such as tracking, trend analysis, and comparison, all of which are important for long-term planning and strategic decision-making.

Integrating data from multiple sources, storing and accumulating the data regularly, and providing fast access to it require design and development techniques that are different from techniques used in operational and administrative systems. This book is all about data warehousing design and development techniques. It covers most commonly used techniques in the phases of building a data warehouse. More important, this book provides an easy to follow tutorial for developing a real world data warehouse.

What This Book Is About and What It Is Not

Dimensional Data Warehousing with MySQL is a practical book. You will use MySQL, but this book is not about MySQL. The book does not discuss hardware infrastructural aspects either.

The focus of this book is on data warehouse design and development techniques. The book however is not about techniques on managing development projects, development methodologies, or leading developments.

The book uses an example data warehouse development to show the implementation of the techniques. The data model and the SQL scripts are included and can be adapted to be used in real-world data warehouse development. The scripts have been tested on MySQL 5.0.21 running on Windows XP Professional SP2.

In addition, this book does not specifically discuss the following topics.

- The concepts of data warehousing
- SQL
- MySQL

Who This Book Is For

Data warehousing is applicable to all types of organizations and businesses, from government agencies and non-profit organizations to schools, from manufacturers to retail stores, from financial institutions to health services, from brick-and-mortar to dotcom businesses.

This book is primarily for data warehouse developers. However, IT managers and other IT professionals, especially those interested in MIS (management reporting) and DSS (decision support application), will find this book useful too. In general, this book is for those responsible for or involved in preparing data for analytical applications and/or delivering information as printed or online reports.

This book is also for data warehousing beginners. It will, directly and instantly, be beneficial to those who are currently planning to develop their first data warehouse.

Teachers and students can use this book along with their text books to confirm their understanding of the concept and theory of data warehousing. Most chapters can be tailored and used for lab exercises.

Prerequisite Skills

This book is not for IT novices. To benefit from this book, you must have some system development experience. However, no prior data warehousing experience is necessary.

Those who will try the examples must have RDBMS and SQL hands-on skills.

What You Will Get from This Book

You will use only one example, a data warehouse that initially stores sales data, and by doing so, sharpen your data warehousing knowledge and practical skills. The example is a scaled down and simplified version of a real world data warehouse found in many types of businesses.

You will develop the example sales data warehouse on a MySQL database, step by step by using the techniques introduced in this book. These are techniques for resolving problems most commonly encountered in data warehouse development. By the time you finish reading this book and doing all the exercises, you will have acquired a working experience and be ready to get involved in your first real-world data warehousing project.

Chapters Overview

This book consists of 25 chapters and one appendix. The chapters are organized into four parts. Part I covers data warehousing basics. Part II explains the moving of data from the source to the data warehouse database. Part III talks about the techniques to handle growth. Part IV deals with some advanced dimensional techniques. The following section provides an overview of each chapter.

Part I: Fundamentals

Part I, covering the fundamentals of dimensional data warehouse, has four chapters.

Chapter 1, "Basic Components" introduces the star schema (a database schema that has a fact table surrounded by dimension tables) and explains the basic components of the schema.

Chapter 2, "Dimension History" discusses the use of surrogate keys for maintaining dimension history.

Chapter 3, "Measure Additivity" covers one of the most fundamental characteristics of a dimensional data warehouse, namely the additivity of measurement stored in the data warehouse fact tables.

Chapter 4, "Dimensional Queries" introduces a type of SQL query that is most suitably applied to a star schema. A dimensional query is a way to prove the two most fundamental design points of a dimensional data warehouse: simplicity and performance.

Part II: Extract, Transform, and Load

All five chapters in Part II deal with data population and the fact and dimension tables.

Chapter 5, "Source Extraction" explains the various types of data extraction.

Chapter 6, "Populating the Date Dimension" covers the three most common techniques for populating the date dimension.

Chapter 7 , "Initial Population" and Chapter 8, "Regular Population" deal with the two types of population techniques: initial and regular.

Chapter 9, "Regular Population Scheduling" concludes Part II by providing step-by-step instructions to schedule regular population using Windows Task Manager.

Part III: Growth

Part III presents the various techniques for resolving problems associated with the growth of a successful dimensional data warehouse. There are ten chapters in Part III.

Chapter 10, "Adding Columns" deals with the techniques for adding columns to tables in the existing dimensional data warehouse.

Chapter 11, "On-Demand Population" covers the on-demand population technique.

Chapter 12, "Subset Dimensions" explains the techniques for helping users with subset dimensions.

Chapter 13, "Dimension Role Playing" is about using a dimension more than once in a fact table.

Chapter 14, "Snapshots" helps you deliver fast performance queries for users that need to work out summarized data.

Chapter 15, "Dimension Hierarchies" and Chapter 16, "Multipath and Ragged Hierarchies" are about single and multipath hierarchical techniques, respectively. These techniques help users with grouping and drilling analysis.

Chapter 17, "Degenerate Dimensions" shows you how to reduce the complexity of a data warehouse schema by applying the dimension degeneration technique.

Chapter 18, "Junk Dimensions" is about the junk dimension, a technique for selecting seemingly unrelated analytical pieces of data often required by users and organizing them dimensionally.

Chapter 19, "Multi-Star Schemas" shows you how to add more starts to your schema.

Part IV: Advanced Techniques

There are six chapters in this part.

Chapter 20, "Non-Straight Sources" explains how to deal with data sources whose structures do not map directly to the target tables in the data warehouse.

Chapter 21, “Factless Facts” helps you build an analytical aid, a factless fact table, for your users on data that does not have measure from its source.

Chapter 22, “Late Arrival Facts” covers a technique that you use when source data, particularly facts, does not come all together at its scheduled population time.

Chapter 23, “External Data Sources and Dimension Consolidation” covers two topics: handling external data sources and the technique for consolidating scattered attributes in multiple dimensions into one dimension.

Chapter 24, “Accumulated Measures” discusses two related topics: computed measures and non-additivity of the accumulated measures.

Chapter 25, “Band Dimensions” explains a technique that helps users with their needs to analyze data on continuously valued attributes.

Appendix

Appendix A, “Flat File Data Sources” presents instructions on how to use the flat file data sources used in the book examples.

Code Download

The program examples accompanying this book can be downloaded from http://jtute.com.

Part I
Fundamentals

You implement a dimensional data warehouse using a relational database. Two types of relational tables, the fact table and the dimension table, make up the basic components and form the schema of a data warehouse. You will build these basic components in a MySQL database in the first part of this book.

More specifically, Part I covers the following five primary topics:

- The star schema
- Surrogate keys
- Dimension history
- Fact table measure additivity
- Dimensional queries

Chapter 1
Basic Components

There are two topics you learn in this chapter, the star schema and the surrogate key. The star schema is the database structure of a dimensional data warehouse. A surrogate key is a column you add to a data warehouse table that acts as the primary key for that table.

In this chapter you begin a long journey building a real-world data warehouse. Here are the tasks you will perform in this chapter.

- Creating a database user
- Creating a relational database for the data warehouse and another one for the source database
- Creating database tables for the data warehouse
- Generating surrogate keys.

You need to create a source database because you don't have a source for your data warehouse yet. In the real world, this is not necessary because your data warehouse is based on an existing source. You will start using the source database in Part II of this book.

The Star Schema

A good dimensional data warehouse has a simple database structure. Technically, a simple structure means faster queries. In a dimensional data warehouse, the implementation relational database has two types of tables, the fact table and the dimension table. The fact table consists of the facts (or measures) of the business. Dimension tables contain descriptions for querying the database.

Note

You will have better understanding of the fact table and the dimension table after reading the first two chapters of this book.

The tables in a data warehouse are related such that the schema looks like a star, hence the term star schema.

Note

In addition to the star structure, the snowflake structure could also be used in a data warehouse. However, it is more difficult to model than the star structure. As well, the snowflake structure is not that easy to understand and implement and the performance of its queries is slower than that of the star structure. These drawbacks make the snowflake structure unsuitable for dimensional data warehousing.
This book covers the star structure only.

A star consists of a fact table surrounded by two or more dimension tables. A one-star structure has one fact table only. A multi-star structure has multiple fact tables, one for each star. In addition, dimension tables may be shared among multiple fact tables. This chapter covers the one-star structure; you learn the multi-star structure in Chapter 19, "Multi-Star Schemas."

Figure 1.1 shows a one-star dimensional schema of the sales order data warehouse we will develop in this book.

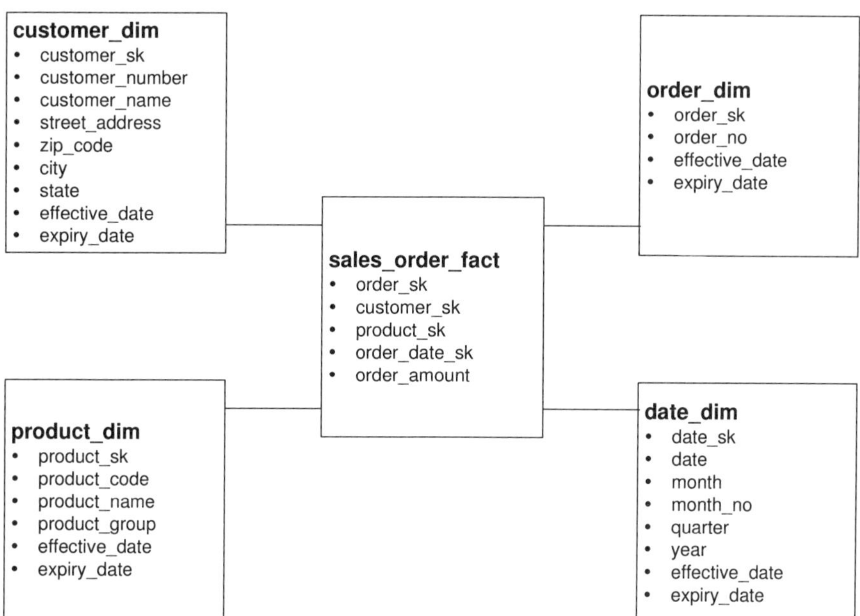

Figure 1.1: A one-star dimensional schema

The fact table name is usually suffixed **fact** and the suffix **dim** (short for dimension) is normally added to the name of a dimension table. It should be clear that the schema in Figure 1.1 has one fact table (**sales_order_fact**) and four dimension tables (**customer_dim**, **order_dim**, **product_dim**, and **date_dim**). The fact table contains one or more measurable facts (a measurable fact is called a measure, for short). Dimension tables categorize measures.

Every dimension table has exactly one surrogate key column. A surrogate key column is suffixed **sk**. Every surrogate key column in a dimension table has a similarly-named column in the fact table to make querying the database easier. However, the **sk**-suffixed columns in the fact table are *not* referred to as surrogate key columns.

The lines connecting the **sales_order_fact** table to the four dimension tables in Figure 1.1 indicate the joins for querying the tables. These joins are on the dimension tables' surrogate key columns.

When building a dimensional data warehouse, you have to generate the surrogate key values within your data warehouse yourself; they do not come from the data source. Surrogate key values are sequential numbers.

Note
The section "Surrogate Keys" later in this chapter explains surrogate keys in detail.

Now that you already know the definitions of the star schema and the fact and dimension tables, let's look at an example. Let's say we're interested in order amounts and decide that the **order_amount** column in the **sales_order_fact** table in Figure 1.1 is the measure. Table 1.1 contains a sample row from the **sales_order_fact** table.

customer_sk	product_sk	date_sk	order_sk	order_amount
1	1	1	1	1000

Table 1.1: A sample row from the fact table

Related dimensions that correspond to the data in Table 1.1 are given in Tables 1. 2 to 1.5.

customer_sk	customer_no	customer_name
1	1	Dons Limited

Table 1.2: The related row in the customer_dim table

product_sk	product_code	product_name
1	1	Cangcung Hard Disk

Table 1.3: The related row in the product_dim table

date_sk	date
1	2007-02-01

Table 1.4: The related row in the date_dim table

order_sk	order_number
1	1

Table 1.5: The related row in the order_dim table

The row from the fact table specifies a sales order value of $1,000. This is the measure of the fact. The value 1 in the **customer_sk** column in the **sales_order_fact** table corresponds to the same value (in this case, 1) in the

customer_sk column in the **customer_dim** table. This relationship reveals that the consumer that placed the order is Dons Limited. By using the value of the **product_sk** column in the **sales_order_fact** table, you can trace the product information in the **product_dim** table. By joining the **sales_order_fact** table and the **date_dim** table on the **date_sk** column, you'll get the order date. And by joining the fact table and the **order_dim** table on the **order_sk** column, you obtain the order number.

Surrogate Keys

The surrogate key column in a dimension table is the primary key of the dimension table. The values of a surrogate key are usually sequential numbers having no business significance. By contrast, many keys from the source data have business meaning.

You generate surrogate key values from within your data warehouse; you do not get surrogate key values from the source data. I cover the purpose of having surrogate keys in Chapter 2, "Dimension History."

In MySQL you generate surrogate key values by setting the **AUTO INCREMENT** attribute of the column. Passing NULL to an AUTO INCREMENT column inserts an incremented integer.

Enough theory. Let's now start building our data warehouse. The following section, "Tasks" elaborate the steps you need to perform in this chapter.

Tasks

There are four tasks you perform in this chapter:

1. Creating a database user
2. Creating the data warehouse database and the source database.
3. Creating data warehouse tables.
4. Generating surrogate keys.

Each task is explained in a separate subsection.

Creating a Database User Id

The first step is to create a database user that you'll use to access the data warehouse and the data source. Before you start, make sure you store all scripts accompanying this book in the **scripts** directory of your MySQL installation. For example, my installation directory is **C:\mysql**, so I stored all my scripts in the **C:\mysql\scripts** directory.

Let's start by logging on to MySQL as root by typing the following command.

```
C:\>mysql -uroot -p
```

You'll be prompted to enter the password.

```
Enter password: ********
```

If you typed in the correct password, you'll see a greeting message similar to this on the console.

```
Welcome to the MySQL monitor.  Commands end with ; or \g.
Your MySQL connection id is 6 to server version: 5.0.21-community-nt

Type 'help;' or '\h' for help. Type '\c' to clear the buffer.

mysql>
```

The lines after the password prompt are a typical response from MySQL when a root user logs in to the MySQL monitor.

The **create_user_id.sql** script in Listing 1.1 creates a user id **dwid** with password **pw**.

Listing 1.1: Creating dwid user id

```
/**********************************************************************/
/*                                                                    */
/* create_user_id.sql                                                 */
/*                                                                    */
/**********************************************************************/

GRANT ALL ON *.* TO dwid@localhost IDENTIFIED BY 'pw'
;

/* end of script                                                      */
```

Run the script by typing the following command.

```
mysql> \. c:\mysql\scripts\create_user_id.sql
```

You will see this response after you press Enter.

```
Query OK, 0 rows affected (0.03 sec)
```

You can confirm that the user **dwid** has been successfully created using the **show grants** command. You might need to include your MySQL host name.

```
mysql> show grants for dwid@localhost;
```

If the user **dwid** was created, you will see

```
Grants for dwid@localhost
GRANT ALL PRIVILEGES ON *.* TO 'dwid'@'localhost' IDENTIFIED BY
      PASSWORD '*D821809F681A40A6E379B50D0463EFAE20BDD122'
1 row in set (0.00 sec)
```

Note
The PASSWORD portion displayed on your monitor may be different from that shown above.

You now need to log off and log back in as **dwid**. To log off, type the **exit** command:

```
mysql> exit
```

To log on as dwid, use this command:

```
c:\>mysql -udwid -p
```

Then, enter the password for **dwid**. Remember the password is **pw**.

Creating the Databases

There are two databases you need to create, **source** and **dw**. The source database stores your data, namely the data that will be the source of your data warehouse. The **dw** database is for the data warehouse.

You create the databases using the **create_databases.sql** script in Listing 1.2.

Listing 1.2: Creating dw and source databases

```
/******************************************************************/
/*                                                                */
/* create_databases.sql                                           */
/*                                                                */
/******************************************************************/
CREATE DATABASE dw
;
CREATE DATABASE source
;
```

Here is the command to run the **create_databases.sql** script.

```
mysql> \. c:\mysql\scripts\create_databases.sql
```

On your console, you'll see

```
Query OK, 1 row affected (0.00 sec)
Query OK, 1 row affected (0.00 sec)
```

You can confirm that the command was executed successfully by using the **show databases** command. To confirm that the **dw** database has been successfully created, use this command.

```
mysql> show databases like 'dw';
```

The response should look something like the following.

```
+---------------+
| Database (dw) |
+---------------+
| dw            |
+---------------+
1 row in set (0.00 sec)
```

To confirm that the source database has been successfully created, use this command.

```
mysql> show databases like 'source';
```

The response should be

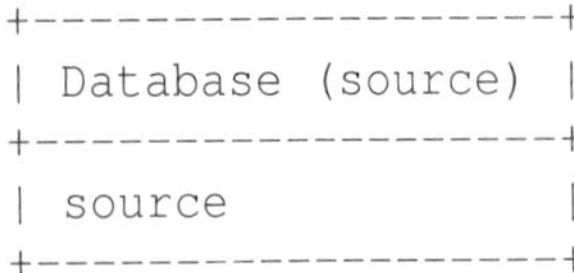

```
+-------------------+
| Database (source) |
+-------------------+
| source            |
+-------------------+
```

```
1 row in set (0.00 sec)
```

Creating Data Warehouse Tables

The next step is to create data warehouse tables in the **dw** database. You can use the **create_dw_tables.sql** script in Listing 1.3 to create the **sales_order_fact** table and the four dimension tables shown in Figure 1.1.

Listing 1.3: Creating data warehouse tables

```
/**********************************************************************/
/*                                                                    */
/* create_dw_tables.sql                                               */
/*                                                                    */
/**********************************************************************/
/* default to dw database                                             */

USE dw;

/* creating customer_dim table                                        */

CREATE TABLE customer_dim
( customer_sk INT NOT NULL AUTO_INCREMENT PRIMARY KEY
, customer_number INT
, customer_name CHAR(50)
, customer_street_address CHAR(50)
, customer_zip_code INT(5)
, customer_city CHAR(30)
, customer_state CHAR(2)
, effective_date DATE
, expiry_date DATE )
;

/* creating product_dim table                                         */
CREATE TABLE product_dim
( product_sk INT NOT NULL AUTO_INCREMENT PRIMARY KEY
, product_code INT
, product_name CHAR(30)
, product_category CHAR(30)
, effective_date DATE
, expiry_date DATE )
;

/* creating order_dim table                                           */
```

```
CREATE TABLE order_dim
( order_sk INT NOT NULL AUTO_INCREMENT PRIMARY KEY
, order_number INT
, effective_date DATE
, expiry_date DATE )
;

/* creating date_dim table                                              */
CREATE TABLE date_dim
( date_sk INT NOT NULL AUTO_INCREMENT PRIMARY KEY
, date DATE
, month_name CHAR(9)
, month INT(1)
, quarter INT(1)
, year INT(4)
, effective_date DATE
, expiry_date DATE )
;

/* creating sales_order_fact_table                                      */
CREATE TABLE sales_order_fact
( order_sk INT
, customer_sk INT
, product_sk INT
, order_date_sk INT
, order_amount DECIMAL(10,2) )
;
```

Now run the **create_dw_tables.sql** script.

```
mysql> \. c:\mysql\scripts\create_dw_tables.sql
```

You'll see something similar to this on your console:

```
Database changed
Query OK, 0 rows affected (0.13 sec)

Query OK, 0 rows affected (0.12 sec)

Query OK, 0 rows affected (0.12 sec)

Query OK, 0 rows affected (0.10 sec)

Query OK, 0 rows affected (0.11 sec)
```

You can confirm a table has been created correctly using the **show create table** command. For example, to verify that the **customer_dim** table has been created successfully, use this command.

```
mysql> show create table customer_dim \G
```

On you console, you'll see

```
*************************** 1. row ***************************
       Table: customer_dim
Create Table: CREATE TABLE `customer_dim` (
  `customer_sk` int(11) NOT NULL auto_increment,
  `customer_number` int(11) default NULL,
  `customer_name` char(50) default NULL,
  `customer_street_address` char(50) default NULL,
  `customer_zip_code` int(5) default NULL,
  `customer_city` char(30) default NULL,
  `customer_state` char(2) default NULL,
  `effective_date` date default NULL,
  `expiry_date` date default NULL,
  PRIMARY KEY  (`customer_sk`)
) ENGINE=InnoDB DEFAULT CHARSET=latin1
1 row in set (0.00 sec)
```

Using the same command, you can verify the other four tables were created successfully.

Generating Surrogate Keys

The last task in this chapter is to generate surrogate keys using the **customer_sk.sql** script in Listing 1.4. This script inserts three records into the **customer_dim** table.

Listing 1.4: Generating customer surrogate key values

```
/*****************************************************************/
/*                                                               */
/* customer_sk.sql                                               */
/*                                                               */
/*****************************************************************/
/* default to dw                                                 */

USE dw;
```

```
INSERT INTO customer_dim
( customer_sk
, customer_number
, customer_name
, customer_street_address
, customer_zip_code
, customer_city
, customer_state
, effective_date
, expiry_date )
VALUES
  (NULL, 1, 'Big Customers', '7500 Louise Dr.', '17050',
       'Mechanicsburg', 'PA', CURRENT_DATE, '9999-12-31')
, (NULL, 2, 'Small Stores', '2500 Woodland St.', '17055',
       'Pittsburgh', 'PA', CURRENT_DATE, '9999-12-31')
, (NULL, 3, 'Medium Retailers', '1111 Ritter Rd.', '17055',
       'Pittsburgh', 'PA',  CURRENT_DATE, '9999-12-31')
;

/* end of script                                                 */
```

Before you run the **customer_sk.sql** script, however, you must set your MySQL date to February 1, 2007. This is because the **CURRENT_DATE** function used in the **customer_sk.sql** script uses the operating system date to populate the **effective_date** column and I ran the **customer_sk.sql** script on my computer on that date. You can change the MySQL date by setting the date of the computer running the MySQL to the specified date.

Note

Bear in mind that you change the MySQL date so that you have a smooth learning experience. In production environment, you do not change your MySQL or system date before or after running a script. In fact, you schedule your scripts to run regularly in your data warehouse production environment. Regular scheduling is discussed in Chapter 8, “Regular Population.”

Note

Your MySQL monitor might lose its connection to the server after the system date is modified. To ensure you don’t get any problem when running the script, run a simple command such as **use dw;** right after adjusting the date. You might still get an error message, but your monitor should be back. You can confirm that it’s connected to the server by running the **use dw** command once more. This time you should not get any more error message.

Now that you've changed your MySQL date to February 1, 2007, run the script in Listing 1.4 by using this command.

```
mysql> \. c:\mysql\scripts\customer_sk.sql
```

You'll see this on your MySQL console.

```
Database changed
Query OK, 3 rows affected (0.06 sec)
Records: 3  Duplicates: 0  Warnings: 0
```

Query the table and you will see that the script has inserted the surrogate key correctly.

```
mysql> select * from customer_dim \G
```

```
*************************** 1. row ***************************
            customer_sk: 1
        customer_number: 1
          customer_name: Big Customers
customer_street_address: 7500 Louise Dr.
      customer_zip_code: 17050
          customer_city: Mechanicsburg
         customer_state: PA
         effective_date: 2007-02-01
            expiry_date: 9999-12-31
*************************** 2. row ***************************
            customer_sk: 2
        customer_number: 2
          customer_name: Small Stores
customer_street_address: 2500 Woodland St.
      customer_zip_code: 17055
          customer_city: Pittsburgh
         customer_state: PA
         effective_date: 2007-02-01
            expiry_date: 9999-12-31
*************************** 3. row ***************************
            customer_sk: 3
        customer_number: 3
          customer_name: Medium Retailers
customer_street_address: 1111 Ritter Rd.
      customer_zip_code: 17055
          customer_city: Pittsburgh
```

```
         customer_state: PA
         effective_date: 2007-02-01
            expiry_date: 9999-12-31
3 rows in set (0.00 sec)

mysql>
```

Now add more rows by using the **more_customer_sk.sql** script in Listing 1.5.

Listing 1.5: Inserting more customers

```
/**********************************************************************/
/*                                                                    */
/* more_customer_sk.sql                                               */
/*                                                                    */
/**********************************************************************/

USE dw;

INSERT INTO customer_dim (
  customer_sk
, customer_number
, customer_name
, customer_street_address
, customer_zip_code
, customer_city
, customer_state
, effective_date
, expiry_date
)
VALUES
  (NULL, 4, 'Good Companies', '9500 Scott St.', '17050',
       'Mechanicsburg', 'PA', CURRENT_DATE, '9999-12-31')
, (NULL, 5, 'Wonderful Shops', '3333 Rossmoyne Rd.', '17050',
       'Mechanicsburg', 'PA', CURRENT_DATE, '9999-12-31')
, (NULL, 6, 'Loyal Clients', '7070 Ritter Rd.', '17055',
       'Pittsburgh', 'PA', CURRENT_DATE, '9999-12-31')
;
```

Here is how you run the **more_customer_sk.sql** script.

```
mysql> \. c:\mysql\scripts\more_customer_sk.sql
```

This is what you'll see on the console.

```
Database changed
```

```
Query OK, 3 rows affected (0.06 sec)
Records: 3  Duplicates: 0  Warnings: 0
```

Now if you query the **customer_dim** table, you will see six records in it.

```
mysql> select * from customer_dim \G
*************************** 1. row ***************************
            customer_sk: 1
        customer_number: 1
          customer_name: Big Customers
customer_street_address: 7500 Louise Dr.
      customer_zip_code: 17050
          customer_city: Mechanicsburg
         customer_state: PA
         effective_date: 2007-02-01
            expiry_date: 9999-12-31
*************************** 2. row ***************************
            customer_sk: 2
        customer_number: 2
          customer_name: Small Stores
customer_street_address: 2500 Woodland St.
      customer_zip_code: 17055
          customer_city: Pittsburgh
         customer_state: PA
         effective_date: 2007-02-01
            expiry_date: 9999-12-31
*************************** 3. row ***************************
            customer_sk: 3
        customer_number: 3
          customer_name: Medium Retailers
customer_street_address: 1111 Ritter Rd.
      customer_zip_code: 17055
          customer_city: Pittsburgh
         customer_state: PA
         effective_date: 2007-02-01
            expiry_date: 9999-12-31
*************************** 4. row ***************************
            customer_sk: 4
        customer_number: 4
          customer_name: Good Companies
customer_street_address: 9500 Scott St.
      customer_zip_code: 17050
          customer_city: Mechanicsburg
         customer_state: PA
         effective_date: 2007-02-01
```

```
             expiry_date: 9999-12-31
************************** 5. row **************************
             customer_sk: 5
         customer_number: 5
           customer_name: Wonderful Shops
customer_street_address: 3333 Rossmoyne Rd.
       customer_zip_code: 17050
           customer_city: Mechanicsburg
          customer_state: PA
          effective_date: 2007-02-01
             expiry_date: 9999-12-31
************************** 6. row **************************
             customer_sk: 6
         customer_number: 6
           customer_name: Loyal Clients
customer_street_address: 7070 Ritter Rd.
       customer_zip_code: 17055
           customer_city: Pittsburgh
          customer_state: PA
          effective_date: 2007-02-01
             expiry_date: 9999-12-31
6 rows in set (0.01 sec)
```

Do not delete these customers, as you will use them in the next chapters.

Summary

In this chapter you have learned the star schema and the surrogate key. You have also created two databases and a user to access the databases. You will use and expand these database in the next chapters..

Chapter 2
Dimension History

The data values stored in a dimension table are called dimensions. The **product_dim** table in Chapter 1, for example, contains product dimensions.

Most dimensions change over time. Customers change addresses, products get renamed and recategorized, sales orders get corrected, etc. When a dimension changes, such as when a product gets a new category, you must maintain the dimension history. In the event of a product being recategorized, for example, you must maintain the product dimension history. In this case, you must store the product's old category as well as the product's current category in the **product_dim** table. In addition, product category information in old sales orders keep referencing the old category.

Slowly Changing Dimension (SCD) is the technique for implementing dimension history in a dimensional data warehouse. This chapter teaches you how to maintain dimension history using SCD. You will also learn various SCD scripts and test them to prove that they maintain the dimension history correctly.

Slowly Changing Dimension Techniques

There are three variants of the SCD technique: SCD Type 1 (SCD1), SCD Type 2 (SCD2), and SCD Type 3 (SCD3). SCD1 updates dimension records by overwriting the existing data—no history of the records is maintained. SCD1 is normally used to directly rectify incorrect data.

SCD2 maintains dimension history by creating newer 'versions' of a dimension record whenever its source changes. SCD2 does not delete or modify existing data.

SCD3 keeps one version of a dimension record. It keeps history by allocating more than one column for a data unit to maintain its history. For instance, to maintain customer addresses, a **customer_dim** table has a **customer_address** column and a **previous_customer_address** column. SCD3 effectively maintains limited history, as opposed to SCD2's full history. SCD3 is rarely used. It is only used in situations where you have a database space constraint and your data warehouse users can live with limited dimension history.

Note
This book covers SCD1 and SCD2.

Slowly Changing Dimension Type 1 (SCD1)

You use SCD1 if you do not need to maintain dimension history. When source data changes, you update the existing data in the corresponding dimension table.

As an example, I will apply SCD1 to the **customer_dim** table created and populated in Chapter 1. Recall that the table has six records as shown in Table 2.1.

customer_number	customer_name	customer_street_address	customer_zip_code	customer_city	customer_state
1	Big Customers	7500 Louise Dr.	17050	Mechanicsburg	PA
2	Small Stores	2500 Woodland St.	17055	Pittsburgh	PA
3	Medium Retailers	1111 Ritter Rd.	17055	Pittsburgh	PA
4	Good Companies	9500 Scott St.	17050	Mechanicsburg	PA
5	Wonderful Shops	3333 Rossmoyne Rd.	17050	Mechanicsburg	PA
6	Loyal Clients	7070 Ritter Rd.	17055	Pittsburgh	PA

Table 2.1: The customer_dim table before changes are applied

Suppose customer details have changed and now the content of the customer table in the source is as presented in Table 2.2.

customer _number	customer _name	customer _street _address	customer _zip _code	customer _city	customer _state
1	**Really Large Customers**	7500 Louise Dr.	17050	Mechanicsburg	PA
2	Small Stores	2500 Woodland St.	17055	Pittsburgh	PA
3	Medium Retailers	1111 Ritter Rd.	17055	Pittsburgh	PA
4	Good Companies	9500 Scott St.	17050	Mechanicsburg	PA
5	Wonderful Shops	3333 Rossmoyne Rd.	17050	Mechanicsburg	PA
6	Loyal Clients	7070 Ritter Rd.	17055	Pittsburgh	PA
7	**Distinguished Partners**	**9999 Scott St.**	**17050**	**Mechanicsburg**	**PA**

Table 2.2: The revised customer details

As you can see, the name of the first customer has changed and there is now one more customer, customer number 7.

You can apply SCD1 to the **customer_dim** table in the data warehouse by running the script in Listing 2.1, which assumes that the new customer information has been uploaded to a staging (temporary) table named **customer_stg**.

Listing 2.1: Applying SCD1 to the customer names in customer_dim

```
/******************************************************************/
/*                                                                */
/* scd1.sql                                                       */
/*                                                                */
/******************************************************************/

/* default database to dw                                         */
```

```
USE dw;

/* update existing customers                                          */

UPDATE customer_dim a, customer_stg b
SET a.customer_name = b.customer_name
WHERE     a.customer_number = b.customer_number
      AND a.expiry_date = '9999-12-31'
      AND a.customer_name <> b.customer_name
;

/* add new customers                                                  */

INSERT INTO customer_dim
SELECT
  NULL
, customer_number
, customer_name
, customer_street_address
, customer_zip_code
, customer_city
, customer_state
, CURRENT_DATE
, '9999-12-31'
FROM customer_stg
WHERE customer_number NOT IN (
  SELECT b.customer_number
  FROM customer_dim a, customer_stg b
  WHERE a.customer_number = b.customer_number )
;

/* end of script                                                      */
```

The script in Listing 2.1 contains two SQL statements, an Update statement and an Insert statement. The Update statement copies the value of the **customer_name** column in the staging table to the **customer_name** column in the **customer_dim** table. The Insert statement inserts the record in the staging table that is not yet present in the **customer_dim** table. Running the script updates the name of the first customer and inserts the seventh customer in the staging table to the **customer_dim** table.

Before you run the script file, however, note that we don't have a staging table yet, but we have the content of the current customer table (from the source database) in a **customer.csv** file. As such, applying SCD1 to the **customer_dim** table consists of two steps:

1. Creating the staging table **customer_stg** and uploading the content of the **customer.csv** file into it.
2. Running the script in Listing 2.1.

These steps are explained in the subsections below.

Creating and Loading the Customer Staging Table

The **customer.csv** file contains the current customer information and can be found in the zip file accompanying this book. Its content is as follows.

```
CUSTOMER NO,CUSTOMER NAME,STREET ADDRESS,ZIP CODE,CITY,STATE
1,Really Large Customers,7500 Louise Dr.,17050,Mechanicsburg,PA
2,Small Stores,2500 Woodland St.,17055,Pittsburgh,PA
3,Medium Retailers,1111 Ritter Rd.,17055,Pittsburgh,PA
4,Good Companies,9500 Scott St.,17050,Mechanicsburg,PA
5,Wonderful Shops,3333 Rossmoyne Rd.,17050,Mechanicsburg,PA
6,Loyal Clients,7070 Ritter Rd.,17055,Pittsburgh,PA
7,Distinguished Partners,9999 Scott St.,17050,Mechanicsburg,PA
```

The script in Listing 2.2 creates the **customer_stg** table in the data warehouse database (*dw*), and loads the **customer.csv** source file to the **customer_stg** table.

Listing 2.2: Creating and loading the customer_stg table

```
/******************************************************************/
/*                                                                */
/* create_customer_stg.sql                                        */
/*                                                                */
/******************************************************************/

/* default database to dw                                         */

USE dw;

/* create customer_stg table                                      */

CREATE TABLE customer_stg
(customer_number INT
```

```
, customer_name CHAR(30)
, customer_street_address CHAR(30)
, customer_zip_code INT(5)
, customer_city CHAR(30)
, customer_state CHAR(2) )
;

/* clean up customer_stg table and load customer.csv                 */

TRUNCATE customer_stg;

LOAD DATA INFILE 'customer.csv'
INTO TABLE customer_stg
FIELDS TERMINATED BY ','
OPTIONALLY ENCLOSED BY '"'
LINES TERMINATED BY '\r\n'
IGNORE 1 LINES
( customer_number
, customer_name
, customer_street_address
, customer_zip_code
, customer_city
, customer_state )
;

/* end of script                                                     */
```

Run the script in Listing 2.2 by using this command:

```
mysql> \. c:\mysql\scripts\create_customer_stg.sql
```

Applying SCD1

Now you're ready to run the SCD1 script in Listing 2.1. Before you do that, set your MySQL date to February 2, 2007 (a date later than the one you set in Chapter 1) to help you easily identify the newly added customer). After you set the date, run the **scd1.sql** script:

```
mysql> \. c:\mysql\scripts\scd1.sql
```

Now confirm that the script in Listing 2.1 was executed successfully by querying the **customer_dim** table:

```
mysql> select * from customer_dim \G
```

You should see the following result.

```
************************** 1. row **************************
             customer_sk: 1
         customer_number: 1
           customer_name: Really Large Customers
customer_street_address: 7500 Louise Dr.
       customer_zip_code: 17050
           customer_city: Mechanicsburg
          customer_state: PA
          effective_date: 2007-02-01
             expiry_date: 9999-12-31
************************** 2. row **************************
             customer_sk: 2
         customer_number: 2
           customer_name: Small Stores
customer_street_address: 2500 Woodland St.
       customer_zip_code: 17055
           customer_city: Pittsburgh
          customer_state: PA
          effective_date: 2007-02-01
             expiry_date: 9999-12-31
************************** 3. row **************************
             customer_sk: 3
         customer_number: 3
           customer_name: Medium Retailers
customer_street_address: 1111 Ritter Rd.
       customer_zip_code: 17055
           customer_city: Pittsburgh
          customer_state: PA
          effective_date: 2007-02-01
             expiry_date: 9999-12-31
************************** 4. row **************************
             customer_sk: 4
         customer_number: 4
           customer_name: Good Companies
customer_street_address: 9500 Scott St.
       customer_zip_code: 17050
           customer_city: Mechanicsburg
          customer_state: PA
          effective_date: 2007-02-01
             expiry_date: 9999-12-31
************************** 5. row **************************
             customer_sk: 5
         customer_number: 5
```

```
           customer_name: Wonderful Shops
customer_street_address: 3333 Rossmoyne Rd.
       customer_zip_code: 17050
           customer_city: Mechanicsburg
          customer_state: PA
          effective_date: 2007-02-01
             expiry_date: 9999-12-31
************************** 6. row **************************
             customer_sk: 6
         customer_number: 6
           customer_name: Loyal Clients
customer_street_address: 7070 Ritter Rd.
       customer_zip_code: 17055
           customer_city: Pittsburgh
          customer_state: PA
          effective_date: 2007-02-01
             expiry_date: 9999-12-31
************************** 7. row **************************
             customer_sk: 7
         customer_number: 7
           customer_name: Distinguished Partners
customer_street_address: 9999 Scott St.
       customer_zip_code: 17050
           customer_city: Mechanicsburg
          customer_state: PA
          effective_date: 2007-02-02
             expiry_date: 9999-12-31
7 rows in set (0.00 sec)
```

Analyzing the Result

The query's output shows that:

- The name of first customer has changed to 'Really Large Customers'. This is the only name for the first customer, which means that no history is maintained for this customer. The effective and expiry dates of the first six customers do not change; only the name of the first customer changed.
- Customer 7 is added with an effective date of 2007-02-02 (the date you ran the script).

Slowly Changing Dimension Type 2 (SCD2)

I discussed the surrogate key in Chapter 1, "Basic Components" and up to now it's probably still not clear to you why you ever need one at all. You might still be wondering why you need another key when you already have the data source's key (also called the natural key). You will soon learn that you use a surrogate key (as well as the effective date and the expiry date) to maintain dimension history using SCD2.

You cannot use a source key to implement SCD2. The source key of the product dimension, for example, is stored in the **product_code** column. In SCD2 if the product name changes, to maintain history you must keep the previous record and add a new record with the new name. However, you can't have two records with the same key, the product code. That's why you need a surrogate key.

The effective and expiry dates define the validity of a record. When a new version of an existing dimension record gets created, you expire the existing record by changing its expiry date to one day prior to the effective date of the new record. For instance, if the effective date of the new record is January 19, 2008, you set the expiry date of the existing record to January 18, 2008. You also set the expiry date of the new record to 9999-12-31. By contrast, SCD1 does not use effective dates and expiry dates.

The script in Listing 2.3 applies SCD2 to the **product_dim** table. As such, whenever there is a change in the **product_name** or **product_category** columns, SCD2 expires the existing row and adds a new row that describes the same product. Note that the script in Listing 2.3 assumes that new product information is available in a staging table called **product_stg**.

Listing 2.3: Applying SCD2 to product_name and product_category in the product_dim table

```
/**********************************************************************/
/*                                                                    */
/* scd2.sql                                                           */
/*                                                                    */
/**********************************************************************/

/* default database to dw                                             */
```

```
USE dw;

/* expire the existing product                                    */

UPDATE
  product_dim a
, product_stg b
SET
  expiry_date = SUBDATE(CURRENT_DATE, 1)
WHERE
    a.product_code = b.product_code
AND (   a.product_name <> b.product_name
     OR a.product_category <> b.product_category )
AND expiry_date = '9999-12-31'
;

/* add a new row for the changing product                         */

INSERT INTO product_dim
SELECT
  NULL
, b.product_code
, b.product_name
, b.product_category
, CURRENT_DATE
, '9999-12-31'
FROM
  product_dim a
, product_stg b
WHERE
    a.product_code = b.product_code
AND (   a.product_name <> b.product_name
     OR a.product_category <> b.product_category )
AND EXISTS
( SELECT * FROM product_dim x
  WHERE   b.product_code = x.product_code
      AND a.expiry_date = SUBDATE(CURRENT_DATE, 1) )
AND NOT EXISTS
( SELECT *
  FROM product_dim y
  WHERE     b.product_code = y.product_code
        AND y.expiry_date = '9999-12-31' )
;

/* add new product                                                */
```

```
INSERT INTO product_dim
SELECT
  NULL
, product_code
, product_name
, product_category
, CURRENT_DATE
, '9999-12-31'
FROM product_stg
WHERE product_code NOT IN(
SELECT y.product_code
FROM product_dim x, product_stg y
WHERE x.product_code = y.product_code )
;

/* end of script                                                */
```

Note

In a production environment you schedule this script and related scripts to run regularly within the data warehouse load cycle. (Regular loading is discussed in Chapter 8, "Regular Population.")

Before you can run the script in Listing 2.3, you need to prepare the data first and create the **product_stg** table. In fact, there are two stages of preparation. The first stage is comprised of three steps:

1. Preparing the product source file.
2. Creating the **product_stg** table and loading the product source file by running the **create_product_stg.sql** script (given in Listing 2.4) and the **load_product_stg.sql** script (shown in Listing 2.5).
3. Running the **scd2.sql** script to initially populate the **product_dim** table

The second stage consists of two steps:

1. Changing the product source file and loading it into its staging
2. Applying SCD2 by running the **scd2.sql** script again and confirming SCD2 has been applied correctly.

All the steps are discussed in the following subsections.

Preparing the Product Source File

You will load two products into the **product_dim** table from a fixed-width text file named **product.txt** included in the zip file accompanying this book. Here is the content of the file.

```
PRODUCT CODE      PRODUCT NAME      PRODUCT GROUP
1                 Hard Disk         Storage
2                 Floppy Drive      Storage
```

All you need to do is copy this file to the **c:\mysql\data\dw** directory. In fact, you will need to copy all flat files to this directory.

Creating the Staging Table and Loading Data

You create the **product_stg** table using the script in the **create_product_stg.sql** script in Listing 2.4.

Listing 2.4: Creating the product_stg table

```
/**********************************************************************/
/*                                                                    */
/* create_product_stg.sql                                             */
/*                                                                    */
/**********************************************************************/

/* default database to dw                                             */

USE dw;

CREATE TABLE product_stg
( product_code INT
, product_name CHAR(30)
, product_category CHAR(30))
;

/* end of script                                                      */
```

Now run the **create_product_stgsql** script.

```
mysql> \. c:\mysql\scripts\create_product_stg.sql
```

Next, you use MySQL's **LOAD DATA INFILE** command to load the content of a flat file into a MySQL table. The **load_product_stg.sql** script in Listing 2.5 loads the **product.txt** file to the **product_stg** table.

Listing 2.5: Loading products to its staging table

```
/**********************************************************************/
/*                                                                    */
/* load_product_stg.sql                                               */
/*                                                                    */
/**********************************************************************/

/* default database to dw                                             */

USE dw;

/* clean up the staging table                                         */

TRUNCATE product_stg;

/* use LOAD DATA INFILE                                               */

LOAD DATA INFILE 'product.txt'
INTO TABLE product_stg
FIELDS TERMINATED BY ''
OPTIONALLY ENCLOSED BY ''
LINES TERMINATED BY '\r\n'
IGNORE 1 LINES
( product_code
, product_name
, product_category )
;

/* end of script                                                      */
```

You can run the script in Listing 2.5 by using this command.

```
mysql> \. c:\mysql\scripts\load_product_stg.sql
```

The response should be similar to the following.

```
Database changed
Query OK, 1 row affected (0.09 sec)

Query OK, 2 rows affected (0.09 sec)
Records: 2  Deleted: 0  Skipped: 0  Warnings: 0
```

Next, query the **product_stg** table to confirm that you have loaded the two products successfully.

```
mysql> select * from product_stg;
```

Here is how the content of the **product_stg** table should look like.

```
+--------------+--------------+------------------+
| product_code | product_name | product_category |
+--------------+--------------+------------------+
|            1 | Hard Disk    | Storage          |
|            2 | Floppy Drive | Storage          |
+--------------+--------------+------------------+
2 rows in set (0.00 sec)
```

Running the Initial Population

Set your operating system date to February 3, 2007, then run the **scd2.sql** script in Listing 2.3 to initially populate the **product_dim** table with the two products.

```
mysql> \. c:\mysql\scripts\scd2.sql
```

You should see this on your console.

```
Database changed
Query OK, 0 rows affected (0.16 sec)
Rows matched: 0  Changed: 0  Warnings: 0

Query OK, 0 rows affected (0.02 sec)
Records: 0  Duplicates: 0  Warnings: 0

Query OK, 2 rows affected (0.06 sec)
Records: 2  Duplicates: 0  Warnings: 0
```

Then, query the **product_dim** table to confirm that you have loaded the two products successfully.

```
mysql> select * from product_dim \G
```

You should see the following response.

```
*************************** 1. row ***************************
      product_sk: 1
    product_code: 1
    product_name: Hard Disk
```

```
product_category: Storage
  effective_date: 2007-02-03
     expiry_date: 9999-12-31
*************************** 2. row ***************************
      product_sk: 2
    product_code: 2
    product_name: Floppy Drive
product_category: Storage
  effective_date: 2007-02-03
     expiry_date: 9999-12-31
2 rows in set (0.00 sec)
```

Changing the Product Source File

Next, using a text editor, update the **product.txt** file you used earlier. You need to change the name of product code 1 into "Hard Disk Drive" and add product code 3.

```
PRODUCT CODE,PRODUCT NAME,PRODUCT GROUP
1          Hard Disk Drive               Storage
2          Floppy Drive                  Storage
3          LCD Panel                     Monitor
```

Applying SCD2

Set your MySQL date to February 5, 2007. This is necessary to simulate a later date than the date of the previous (initial) product population (February 3, 2007).

Now, run the **load_product_stg.sql** script in Listing 2.5 one more time and then run the **scd2.sql** script in Listing 2.3.

```
mysql> \. c:\mysql\scripts\load_product_stg.sql
```

Here is what you should see on your console.

```
Database changed
Query OK, 2 rows affected (0.11 sec)

Query OK, 3 rows affected (0.06 sec)
Records: 3  Deleted: 0  Skipped: 0  Warnings: 0

mysql> \. c:\mysql\scripts\scd2.sql
```

```
Database changed
Query OK, 1 row affected (0.43 sec)
Rows matched: 1  Changed: 1  Warnings: 0

Query OK, 1 row affected (0.08 sec)
Records: 1  Duplicates: 0  Warnings: 0

Query OK, 1 row affected (0.05 sec)
Records: 1  Duplicates: 0  Warnings: 0
```

To confirm SCD2 has worked correctly, query the **product_dim** table.

```
mysql> select * from product_dim \G
*************************** 1. row ***************************
      product_sk: 1
    product_code: 1
    product_name: Hard Disk
product_category: Storage
  effective_date: 2007-02-03
     expiry_date: 2007-02-04
*************************** 2. row ***************************
      product_sk: 2
    product_code: 2
    product_name: Floppy Drive
product_category: Storage
  effective_date: 2007-02-03
     expiry_date: 9999-12-31
*************************** 3. row ***************************
      product_sk: 3
    product_code: 1
    product_name: Hard Disk Drive
product_category: Storage
  effective_date: 2007-02-05
     expiry_date: 9999-12-31
*************************** 4. row ***************************
      product_sk: 4
    product_code: 3
    product_name: LCD Panel
product_category: Monitor
  effective_date: 2007-02-05
     expiry_date: 9999-12-31
4 rows in set (0.00 sec)
```

Analysing the Result

The following analysis on the **product_dim** table proves that SCD2 has been applied correctly.

- Product 1 has two rows. One of the two rows (whose **product_sk** is 1) has expired. Its expiry date is February 4, 2007, that is one day earlier than the date you applied SCD2 (February 5, 2007). The other row (whose **product_sk** is 3) has a new name. Its effective date is February 5, 2007. Its expiry date is 9999-12-31, which means it has not expired.
- The new product with product code 3 is added, its effective date is February 5, 2007.

Summary

In this chapter you learned what dimensions and dimension history are, and why you need to maintain dimension history. You learned the SCD (Slowly Changing Dimension) techniques and applied SCD1 and SCD2 to customer and product dimensions respectively.

In Chapter 7, "Initial Population" and Chapter 8, "Regular Population" you begin to include these techniques in your data warehouse initial and regular population, respectively. However, before that you need to learn an important characteristic of a fact table (measure additivity) in the next chapter

Chapter 3
Measure Additivity

A measure always has numeric values. One of the most important characteristics of a fact table pertaining to measures is measure additivity. With regard to additivity, a measure may be fully-additive or semi-additive. If you can sum the values of a measure in all situations, the measure is fully-additive. If you can only add up its values in some situations, it is semi-additive. Understanding measure additivity is key to selecting a data item as a measure in a fact table. The **order_amount** measure in the **sales_order_fact** table, for example, is fully-additive because you can correctly add up this measure across any one and all of its dimensions. This means, you can correctly sum the **order_amount** measure in your **sales_order_fact** table any time, for any product, any customer, and any order.

This chapter covers fully-additive measures. Semi-additive measures are explained in Chapter 24, "Accumulated Measures."

Fully-Additive Measures

A measure is fully additive if the total of its individual values across any one dimension is the same as the total across any other dimension and across any combination of some or all dimensions.

This section explains fully additive measures by using the **order_amount** measure in the **sales_order_fact** table. I show that this measure is fully-additive by querying the **sales_order_fact** table across all dimensions and the combinations of some dimensions. When you design a fact table and want to make sure its measures are fully-additive, you should test every measure using this type of query.

However, before you start, you need to add data to the **order_dim**, **date_dim**, and **sales_order_fact** tables because they are empty. You already have three products in the **product_dim** table and seven customers in the **customer_dim** table, so you don't need to add data to these tables.

You can use the script in Listing 3.1 to add data. This script inserts ten rows into the **order_dim** table, one row into the **date_dim** table, and ten rows into the **sales_order_fact** table.

Listing 3.1: Inserting data to demonstrate fully-additive measures

```
/**********************************************************************/
/*                                                                    */
/* additive_data.sql                                                  */
/*                                                                    */
/**********************************************************************/

USE dw;

INSERT INTO order_dim VALUES
  (NULL, 1, CURRENT_DATE, '9999-12-31')
, (NULL, 2, CURRENT_DATE, '9999-12-31')
, (NULL, 3, CURRENT_DATE, '9999-12-31')
, (NULL, 4, CURRENT_DATE, '9999-12-31')
, (NULL, 5, CURRENT_DATE, '9999-12-31')
, (NULL, 6, CURRENT_DATE, '9999-12-31')
, (NULL, 7, CURRENT_DATE, '9999-12-31')
, (NULL, 8, CURRENT_DATE, '9999-12-31')
, (NULL, 9, CURRENT_DATE, '9999-12-31')
, (NULL, 10, CURRENT_DATE, '9999-12-31')
;

INSERT INTO date_dim VALUES
  (NULL, '2005-10-31', 'October', 10, 4, 2005, CURRENT_DATE,
  '9999-12-31')
;

INSERT INTO sales_order_fact VALUES
  (1, 1, 2, 1, 1000)
, (2, 2, 3, 1, 1000)
, (3, 3, 4, 1, 4000)
, (4, 4, 2, 1, 4000)
, (5, 5, 3, 1, 6000)
, (6, 1, 4, 1, 6000)
, (7, 2, 2, 1, 8000)
, (8, 3, 3, 1, 8000)
, (9, 4, 4, 1, 10000)
, (10, 5, 2, 1, 10000)
```

```
;

/* end of script                                                   */
```

You run the script in the MySQL monitor by entering the script name with its full path as follows:

```
mysql> \. c:\mysql\scripts\additive_data.sql
```

Here is what you should see on the console after you press Enter.

```
Database changed
Query OK, 10 rows affected (0.26 sec)
Records: 10  Duplicates: 0  Warnings: 0

Query OK, 1 row affected (0.09 sec)

Query OK, 10 rows affected (0.11 sec)
Records: 10  Duplicates: 0  Warnings: 0
```

Testing Fully-Additivity

The **order_amount** measure is fully-additive if all query results are the same. To prove that **order_amount** is fully-additive, we use the queries in Listings 3.2, 3.3, 3.4, and 3.5. We will prove that all the four queries produce a total order of 58,000.

The first query, the **across_all_dimensions.sql** script in Listing 3.2, sums the **order_amounts** across all dimensions (adding up the **order_amount** values by selecting all dimensions).

Listing 3.2: Querying across all dimensions

```
/******************************************************************/
/*                                                                */
/* across_all_dimensions.sql                                      */
/*                                                                */
/******************************************************************/

USE dw;

SELECT SUM(order_amount) sum_of_order_amount
FROM sales_order_fact a
```

```
;

/* end of script                                                 */
```

Run the script using this command.

```
mysql> \. c:\mysql\scripts\across_all_dimensions.sql
```

You'll get:

```
Database changed
+---------------------+
| sum_of_order_amount |
+---------------------+
|            58000.00 |
+---------------------+
1 row in set (0.04 sec)
```

The second query, the **across_date_product_order.sql** script in Listing 3.3, sums the **order_amount** values across the date, product, and order dimensions (adding up the **order_amount** values by selecting customers only).

Listing 3.3: Querying across the date, product, and order

```
/*****************************************************************/
/*                                                               */
/* across_date_product_order.sql                                 */
/*                                                               */
/*****************************************************************/

USE dw;

SELECT
  customer_number
, SUM(order_amount) sum_of_order_amount
FROM
  sales_order_fact a
, customer_dim b
WHERE
    a.customer_sk = b.customer_sk
GROUP BY
  customer_number
;

/* end of script                                                 */
```

You run the script in Listing 3.3 using this command.

```
mysql> \. c:\mysql\scripts\across_date_product.sql
```

The result is as follows.

```
Database changed
+-----------------+---------------------+
| customer_number |sum_of_order_amount  |
+-----------------+---------------------+
|               1 |             7000.00 |
|               2 |             9000.00 |
|               3 |            12000.00 |
|               4 |            14000.00 |
|               5 |            16000.00 |
+-----------------+---------------------+
5 rows in set (0.10 sec)
```

The total of the sum of order amounts is 7,000 + 9,000 + 12,000 + 14,000 + 16,000 = 58,000.

The third query, the **across_date_customer_order.sql** script in Listing 3.4, sums the order amounts across the date, customer, and order dimensions.

Listing 3.4: Querying across the date, customer, and order

```
/**********************************************************************/
/*                                                                    */
/* across_date_customer_order.sql                                     */
/*                                                                    */
/**********************************************************************/

USE dw;

SELECT
  product_code
, SUM(order_amount) sum_of_order_amount
FROM
  sales_order_fact a
, product_dim b
WHERE
    a.product_sk = b.product_sk
GROUP BY
  product_code
;

/* end of script                                                      */
```

You can run the script in Listing 3.4 using this command.

```
mysql> \. c:\mysql\scripts\across_date_customer.sql
```

The result is this.

```
Database changed
+--------------+---------------------+
| product_code | sum_of_order_amount |
+--------------+---------------------+
|            1 |            15000.00 |
|            2 |            23000.00 |
|            3 |            20000.00 |
+--------------+---------------------+
3 rows in set (0.09 sec)
```

Again, the query produces a total order amount of 58,000 (15,000 + 23,000 + 20,000).

The fourth query, the **across_date_order.sql** script in Listing 3.4, sums the order amounts across the date and order dimensions.

Listing 3.5: Querying across the date and order

```
/**************************************************************/
/*                                                            */
/* across_date_order.sql                                      */
/*                                                            */
/**************************************************************/

USE dw;

SELECT
  customer_number
, product_code
, SUM(order_amount) sum_of_order_amount
FROM
  sales_order_fact a
, customer_dim b
, product_dim c
WHERE
    a.customer_sk = b.customer_sk
AND a.product_sk = c.product_sk
GROUP BY
  customer_number
, product_code
;
```

```
/* end of script                                                 */
```

Run the script in Listing 3.5 using this command.

```
mysql> \. c:\mysql\scripts\across_date.sql
```

You should see the following on your console.

```
Database changed
+-----------------+--------------+---------------------+
| customer_number | product_code | sum_of_order_amount |
+-----------------+--------------+---------------------+
|               1 |            2 |             1000.00 |
|               1 |            3 |             6000.00 |
|               2 |            1 |             1000.00 |
|               2 |            2 |             8000.00 |
|               3 |            1 |             8000.00 |
|               3 |            3 |             4000.00 |
|               4 |            2 |             4000.00 |
|               4 |            3 |            10000.00 |
|               5 |            1 |             6000.00 |
|               5 |            2 |            10000.00 |
+-----------------+--------------+---------------------+
10 rows in set (0.03 sec)
```

The total is again 58,000 (1,000 + 6,000 + 1,000 + 8,000 + 8,000 + 4,000 + 4,000 + 10,000 + 6,000 + 10,000).

All the four queries produce the same total (58,000), which confirms that this measure is fully-additive.

Summary

In this chapter you learned measure additivity. You proved that the **order_amount** measure of the **sales_order_fact** table is fully additive.

Chapter 4
Dimensional Queries

A dimensional query is a query in a dimensional data warehouse that joins the fact table and the dimension tables on one or more surrogate keys. This chapter teaches you the dimensional query pattern and how to apply it to the three most common query types: aggregation, specific, and inside out.

Aggregate queries aggregate individual facts, for example, by adding up measure values. In a specific query you query the facts of a specific dimension value. While most queries specify one or more dimensions as the selection criteria (constraints), an inside out query's criteria are measure values. Understanding these three most common query types allows you to apply dimensional queries to other query types.

Applying Dimensional Queries

In this section I explain how you can apply dimensional queries on the three most common query types: aggregate, specific, and inside-out queries.

To apply dimensional queries, you first need to add data to your data warehouse by running the script in Listing 4.1. You need this additional data to test the dimensional queries in Listings 4.2 to 4.7.

Listing 4.1: Script for that adds data for testing dimensional queries

```
/**********************************************************************/
/*                                                                    */
/* dimensional_query_data.sql                                         */
/*                                                                    */
/**********************************************************************/

USE dw;

INSERT INTO order_dim VALUES
```

```
  (NULL, 11, CURRENT_DATE, '9999-12-31')
, (NULL, 12, CURRENT_DATE, '9999-12-31')
, (NULL, 13, CURRENT_DATE, '9999-12-31')
, (NULL, 14, CURRENT_DATE, '9999-12-31')
, (NULL, 15, CURRENT_DATE, '9999-12-31')
, (NULL, 16, CURRENT_DATE, '9999-12-31')
;

INSERT INTO date_dim VALUES
  (NULL, '20075-0211-016', 'FebruaryNovember', 112, 41, 20057,
      CURRENT_DATE, '9999-12-31')
;

INSERT INTO sales_order_fact VALUES
  (11, 1, 2, 2, 20000)
, (12, 2, 3, 2, 25000)
, (13, 3, 4, 2, 30000)
, (14, 4, 2, 2, 35000)
, (15, 5, 3, 2, 40000)
, (16, 1, 4, 2, 45000)
;

/* end of script                                                    */
```

Before you start, change your MySQL date to February 6, 2007; and run the script in Listing 4.1 to insert six orders into the **order_dim** table, one date into the **date_dim** table, and six sales orders into the **sales_order_fact** table.

```
mysql> \. c:\mysql\scripts\dimensional_query_data.sql
```

You'll see this on your MySQL console.

```
Database changed
Query OK, 6 rows affected (0.05 sec)
Records: 6  Duplicates: 0  Warnings: 0

Query OK, 1 row affected (0.06 sec)

Query OK, 6 rows affected (0.06 sec)
Records: 6  Duplicates: 0  Warnings: 0
```

Now that you have the necessary data, you're ready to apply dimensional queries to the three types of queries mentioned earlier.

Aggregate Queries

Aggregate queries summarize (aggregate) individual facts. The measure values are typically summed, even though count is also a common aggregate. Two examples are discussed in this section.

Daily Sales Aggregation

The dimensional query in Listing 4.2 gives you the daily sales summary. The aggregation of the order amounts and number of orders is done by date. Note that the join between the **sales_order_fact** table and **date_dim** table is on their surrogate keys.

Listing 4.2: Daily Aggregation

```
/**********************************************************************/
/*                                                                    */
/* daily_aggregation.sql                                              */
/*                                                                    */
/**********************************************************************/

SELECT
  date
, SUM(order_amount)
, COUNT(*)
FROM
  sales_order_fact a
, date_dim b
WHERE
a.order_date_sk = b.date_sk
GROUP BY date
ORDER BY date
;

/* end of script                                                      */
```

Run the query using this command.

```
mysql> \. c:\mysql\scripts\daily_aggregation.sql
```

Here is the output of this query.

```
+---------------+------------------+----------+
| date          | SUM(order_amount) | COUNT(*) |
+---------------+------------------+----------+
| 2007-02-05    |          58000.00 |       10 |
| 2007-02-06    |         195000.00 |        6 |
+---------------+------------------+----------+
2 rows in set (0.03 sec)
```

The query result shows the daily total order amounts (sum) and the number of orders (count) of all orders.

Annual Aggregation

The dimensional query in Listing 4.3 gives you the annual sales summary. The order amounts and the number of orders are not only aggregated by date, but also by product and customer city. The three joins, between the fact table and each of the three dimension tables (date, product, and customer dimensions), are on the surrogate keys.

Listing 4.3: Annual aggregation

```
/******************************************************************/
/*                                                                */
/* annual_aggregation.sql                                         */
/*                                                                */
/******************************************************************/

SELECT year, product_name, customer_city, SUM(order_amount),
  COUNT(*)
FROM
  sales_order_fact a
, date_dim b
, product_dim c
, customer_dim d
WHERE
    a.order_date_sk = b.date_sk
AND a.product_sk = c.product_sk
AND a.customer_sk = d.customer_sk
GROUP BY year, product_name, customer_city
ORDER BY year, product_name, customer_city
;

/* end of script                                                  */
```

Run the script as follows:

```
mysql> \. c:\mysql\scripts\annual_aggregation.sql
```

Here is the output of the query

```
+------+-----------------+--------------+---------------+---------+
| year | product_name    | customer_city |SUM           |COUNT(*) |
|      |                 |              |(order_amount) |         |
+------+-----------------+--------------+---------------+---------+
| 2007 | Floppy Drive    | Mechanicsburg |     70000.00 |       5 |
| 2007 | Floppy Drive    | Pittsburgh   |       8000.00 |       1 |
| 2007 | Hard Disk Drive | Mechanicsburg |     46000.00 |       2 |
| 2007 | Hard Disk Drive | Pittsburgh   |      34000.00 |       3 |
| 2007 | LCD Panel       | Mechanicsburg |     61000.00 |       3 |
| 2007 | LCD Panel       | Pittsburgh   |      34000.00 |       2 |
+------+-----------------+--------------+---------------+---------+
6 rows in set (0.03 sec)
```

The query result presents the annual total order amounts (sum) and number of orders (count) of all orders grouped by years, products, and cities.

Specific Queries

A specific query selects and aggregates the facts on a specific dimension value. The two examples show the application of dimensional queries in specific queries.

Monthly Storage Product Sales

The **monthly_storage.sql** script in Listing 4.4 aggregates sales amounts and the number of orders every month.

Listing 4.4: Specific query (monthly storage product sales)

```
/**********************************************************************/
/*                                                                    */
/* monthly_storage.sql                                                */
/*                                                                    */
/**********************************************************************/

USE dw;
```

```
SELECT
  product_name
, month_name
, year
, SUM(order_amount)
, COUNT(*)
FROM
  sales_order_fact a
, product_dim b
, date_dim c
WHERE
    a.product_sk = b.product_sk
AND a.order_date_sk = c.date_sk
GROUP BY
  product_name
, product_category
, month_name
, year
HAVING product_category = 'Storage'
ORDER BY
  year
, month_name
;

/* end of script                                                   */
```

Run the script using this command.

```
mysql> \. c:\mysql\scripts\monthly_storage.sql
```

Here is the output of the query:

```
Database changed
+-----------------+------------+------+------------------+---------+
| product_name    | month_name | year |SUM(order_amount) | COUNT(*)|
+-----------------+------------+------+------------------+---------+
| Hard Disk Drive | February   | 2007 |         65000.00 |       2 |
| Floppy Drive    | February   | 2007 |         55000.00 |       2 |
| Hard Disk Drive | February   | 2007 |         15000.00 |       3 |
| Floppy Drive    | February   | 2007 |         23000.00 |       4 |
+-----------------+------------+------+------------------+---------+
4 rows in set (0.00 sec)
```

The query result shows the monthly total order amounts (sum) and the number of orders (count), grouped by the individual storage products.

Quarterly Sales in Mechanisburg

The query in Listing 4.5 is another specific query. It produces the quarterly aggregation of the order amounts in Mechanicsburg.

Listing 4.5: Specific query (quarterly sales in Mechanicsburg)

```
/**********************************************************************/
/*                                                                    */
/* quarterly_mechanicsburg.sql                                        */
/*                                                                    */
/**********************************************************************/

USE dw;

SELECT
  customer_city
, quarter
, year
, SUM(order_amount)
, COUNT(order_sk)
FROM
  sales_order_fact a
, customer_dim b
, date_dim c
WHERE
    a.customer_sk = b.customer_sk
AND a.order_date_sk = c.date_sk
GROUP BY
  customer_city
, quarter
, year
HAVING customer_city = 'Mechanicsburg'
ORDER BY
  year
, quarter;

/* end of script                                                      */
```

Run the script using this command.

```
mysql> \. c:\mysql\scripts\quarterly_mechanicsburg.sql
```

Here is the query result.

```
Database changed
```

```
+---------------+---------+------+-----------------+---------------+
| customer_city | quarter | year |SUM(order_amount)|COUNT(order_sk)|
+---------------+---------+------+-----------------+---------------+
| Mechanicsburg |       4 | 2007 |       177000.00 |            10 |
+---------------+---------+------+-----------------+---------------+
1 row in set (0.00 sec)
```

The query result shows the quarterly total order amounts (sum) and the number of orders (count) for Mechanicsburg.

Inside-Out Queries

While the preceding queries have dimensional constraints (the selection of facts is based on dimensions), an inside out dimensional query selects the facts based on one or more measure values. In other words, your query starts from the fact (the centre of the star schema) towards the dimensions, hence the name inside-out query. The following two examples are inside-out dimensional queries.

Product Performer

The dimensional query in Listing 4.6 gives you the sales orders of products that have a monthly sales amount of 75,000 or more.

Listing 4.6: Inside-out – Monthly Product Performer

```
/*****************************************************************/
/*                                                               */
/* monthly_product_performer.sql                                 */
/*                                                               */
/*****************************************************************/

USE dw;

SELECT
  month_name
, year
, product_name
, SUM(order_amount)
, COUNT(*)
FROM
```

```
  sales_order_fact a
, product_dim b
, date_dim c
WHERE
    a.product_sk = b.product_sk
AND a.order_date_sk = c.date_sk
GROUP BY
  month_name
, year
, product_name
HAVING SUM(order_amount) >= 75000
ORDER BY
  month
, year
, product_name
;

/* end of script                                                    */
```

Run the script using this command.

```
mysql> \. c:\mysql\scripts\monthly_product_performer.sql
```

Here is the result of the query:

```
Database changed
+------------+------+--------------+-------------------+----------+
| month_name | year | product_name | SUM(order_amount) | COUNT(*) |
+------------+------+--------------+-------------------+----------+
| November   | 2007 | LCD Panel    |          75000.00 |        2 |
+------------+------+--------------+-------------------+----------+
1 row in set (0.00 sec)
```

The query output shows the total order amounts (sum) and the number of orders (count) for LCD Panel, the only product that has a total order amount that is equal to or greater than 75000.

Loyal Customer

The query in Listing 4.7 is a more complex inside out query than the one in Listing 4.6. If your users would like to know which customer(s) placed more than five orders annually in the past eighteen months, you can use the query in

Listing 4.7. This query shows that even for such a complex query, you can still use a dimensional query.

Listing 4.7: Inside-out (loyal customer)

```
/*****************************************************************/
/*                                                               */
/* loyal_customer.sql                                            */
/*                                                               */
/*****************************************************************/

USE dw;

SELECT
  customer_number
, year
, COUNT(*)
FROM
  sales_order_fact a
, customer_dim b
, date_dim c
WHERE
    a.customer_sk = b.customer_sk
AND a.order_date_sk = c.date_sk
GROUP BY
  customer_number
, year
HAVING
    COUNT(*) > 3
AND (12 -  MONTH(MAX(date))) < 7
;

/* end of script                                                 */
```

Run the script using this command.

```
mysql> \. c:\mysql\scripts\loyal_customer.sql
```

Here is the output of the query:

```
Database changed
+-----------------+------+----------+
| customer_number | year | COUNT(*) |
+-----------------+------+----------+
|               1 | 2007 |        4 |
+-----------------+------+----------+
1 row in set (0.02 sec)
```

The query result shows the number of orders (count) from customer_number 1, the only customer that meets the above selection criteria.

Summary

In this chapter you learned and applied dimensional queries, which are queries that always have joins on surrogate keys. You use dimensional queries further in more complex queries in the next chapters..

Part II
Extract, Transform, and Load

This part, Part II, discusses the process that populates a dimensional data warehouse. This process is known as ETL, short for Extract, Transform, and Load. Extract is getting the data you need for the data warehouse from the source. Transform is the process of preparing the data. And Load is the process of storing the data in the data warehouse.

The E, T, or L is not always a distinct step. For instance, if the source data is in a MySQL database, the ETL can be a single “INSERT SELECT” SQL statement. In other cases, the Transform portion can be quite involved, requiring not only adding surrogate keys and preparing the history maintenance, but also integrating multiple sources, handling data source errors, and aggregating.

This part covers the following topics.

- Extracting source data
- Populating the date dimension
- Initial population
- Regular population
- Regular job and scheduling

Chapter 5
Source Extraction

The first step to populate a data warehouse is extracting data from the source. You do this either by taking (pulling) the data out of the source or by requesting the source to send (push) the data to the data warehouse.

An important factor when extracting data is the volume and the availability of the source data, based on which you either extract the whole source data or just its changes since the last extraction.

This chapter covers the following two data sources extraction topics:

- Which part of a data source do you need to extract and load into your data warehouse? There are two common approaches, whole source and change data capture.
- The direction of data extraction. There are two possible modes, the pull mode (pulled by your data warehouse) and the push mode (pushed by the source).

The following sections explain the various modes of data source extraction briefly mentioned above, and then use sales order extraction as an example to show how a push-by-source and change extraction works.

Whole Source or Change Data Capture (CDC)

You normally extract the whole source data (all file records or all rows of database tables) if the data volume is manageable. This mode is suitable for extraction of reference type data sources, such as postal codes. A reference type data is often the data source for dimension tables.

You may have to extract changes of the source data (only the new and changed data since the last extraction) if the volume of the data source is high and extracting the whole data is inefficient or impossible. This mode of data extraction, known as Change Data Capture (CDC), is usually applied to extract operational transaction data, such as sales orders.

In the following section I explain how push-by-source CDC works on the sales order data extraction. Chapter 8, "Regular Population," covers the other modes.

Pull by Data or Push by Source

You use the pull mode if you want the source data to simply wait for your data warehouse to extract it. You must be sure, however, that the source data is available and ready when your data warehouse is extracting it. When you ran the **scd1.sql** and **scd2.sql** scripts in Chapter 2, "Dimension History," you used this pull mode.

If your data extraction timing is critical and you want the source to send its data as soon as it's ready, then you use push-by-source data extraction mode. A factor that forces you to apply this mode is if the source must be protected and access is prohibited.

Push-by-source CDC on Sales Orders Extraction

I demonstrate in this section how push-by-source CDC works on sales order source data. Push-by-source CDC means the source system extracts only the changes since the last extraction. In the case of sales order source data, the source system is the source database created in Chapter 1, "Basic Components."

The script in Listing 5.1 is a stored procedure that extracts sales order data from the **sales_order** table in the **source** database. The script captures the changes in the table daily (Let's assume you load data daily into your data warehouse).

You compile the stored procedure and store it in the source database. You also run the script daily at the source. In this case, the script runs push-by-source CDC extraction.

Note

The two lines in bold almost towards the end of the script ensure that valid products on the order date will be picked up for the sales orders.

Listing 5.1: Push CDC sales orders

```
/******************************************************************/
/*                                                                */
/* push_sales_order.sql                                           */
/*                                                                */
/******************************************************************/

/* point to source database                                       */

USE source;

DELIMITER // ;

DROP PROCEDURE IF EXISTS push_sales_order //

CREATE PROCEDURE push_sales_order()
BEGIN

INSERT INTO dw.sales_order_fact
SELECT
  a.order_amount
, b.order_sk
, c.customer_sk
, d.product_sk
, e.date_sk
FROM
  sales_order a
, dw.order_dim b
, dw.customer_dim c
, dw.product_dim d
, dw.date_dim e
WHERE
    a.entry_date = CURRENT_DATE
AND a.order_number = b.order_number
AND a.customer_number = c.customer_number
AND a.product_code = d.product_code
AND a.order_date >= d.effective_date
AND a.order_date <= d.expiry_date
AND a.order_date = e.date
;
```

```
END
//

DELIMITER ; //

/* end of script                                                     */
```

To compile and run the stored procedure, use the following command.

```
mysql> \. c:\mysql\scripts\push_sales_order.sql
```

Here is the response on your console.

```
Database changed
Query OK, 0 rows affected, 1 warning (0.08 sec)

Query OK, 0 rows affected (0.05 sec)
```

To confirm that the stored procedure has successfully been created, invoke the **run procedure** command.

```
mysql> show procedure status like 'push_sales_order' \G;
```

You should see this on your console.

```
*************************** 1. row ***************************
           Db: source
         Name: push_sales_order
         Type: PROCEDURE
      Definer: root@localhost
     Modified: 2007-02-05 22:26:56
      Created: 2007-02-05 22:26:56
Security_type: DEFINER
      Comment:
1 row in set (0.00 sec)

mysql>
```

Testing

I show you in this section how to confirm that the stored procedure you already compiled correctly does push-by-source CDC daily extraction from the **sales_order** table in the **source** database and loading the extracted data into the **sales_order_fact** table in the data warehouse.

The first step you need to do is create a **sales_order** table in the **source** database by running the script in Listing 5.2. Then, add some test data (four sales orders and a date) to the data warehouse (**dw**) database by running the script in Listing 5.3.

Listing 5.2: Creating the sales_order table

```
/**********************************************************************/
/*                                                                    */
/* create_sales_order.sql                                             */
/*                                                                    */
/**********************************************************************/

USE source;

CREATE TABLE sales_order
( order_number INT
, customer_number INT
, product_code INT
, order_date DATE
, entry_date DATE
, order_amount DECIMAL(10,2))
;

/* end of script                                                      */
```

Listing 5.3: Data for testing Push mode

```
/**********************************************************************/
/*                                                                    */
/* push_data.sql                                                      */
/*                                                                    */
/**********************************************************************/

USE dw;

INSERT INTO order_dim VALUES
  (NULL, 17, CURRENT_DATE, '9999-12-31')
, (NULL, 18, CURRENT_DATE, '9999-12-31')
, (NULL, 19, CURRENT_DATE, '9999-12-31')
, (NULL, 20, CURRENT_DATE, '9999-12-31')
;

INSERT INTO date_dim VALUES
  (NULL, '2007-02-06', 'February', 2, 6, 2007, CURRENT_DATE, '9999-
      12-31')
```

```
;

/* load sales orders in the source database                                */

USE source;

INSERT INTO sales_order VALUES
  (17, 1, 1, '2007-02-06', '2007-02-06', 1000)
, (18, 2, 1, '2007-02-06', '2007-02-06', 1000)
, (19, 3, 1, '2007-02-06', '2007-02-06', 4000)
, (20, 4, 1, '2007-02-06', '2007-02-06', 4000)
;

/* end of script                                                            */
```

Before you start, you must set your MySQL date to February 7, 2007 (the entry date of the sales order test data) and point to the **source** database (the database where you have the stored procedure).

To use the **source** database, type in the following and press Enter.

```
mysql> use source;
```

MySQL will respond by printing

```
Database changed
```

Next, run the **push_sales_order** stored procedure to populate the sales order fact using this command.

```
mysql> call push_sales_order();
```

The response should indicate that four rows were affected.

```
Query OK, 4 rows affected (0.09 sec)
```

Finally, confirm that only the current sales orders are loaded into the **sales_order_fact** table by querying the table. Recall that you loaded sixteen sales orders in the previous chapters, the last four of which was on February 6, 2007.

Now change the database to dw.

```
mysql> use dw;
```

Then, query the **sales_order_fact** table by issuing this command.

```
mysql> select * from sales_order_fact;
```

The result should be the same as the following.

```
+----------+------------+-----------+------------+-------------+
| order_sk | customer_sk | product_sk |order_date_sk| order_amount |
+----------+------------+-----------+------------+-------------+
|        1 |          1 |         2 |          1 |     1000.00 |
|        2 |          2 |         3 |          1 |     1000.00 |
|        3 |          3 |         4 |          1 |     4000.00 |
|        4 |          4 |         2 |          1 |     4000.00 |
|        5 |          5 |         3 |          1 |     6000.00 |
|        6 |          1 |         4 |          1 |     6000.00 |
|        7 |          2 |         2 |          1 |     8000.00 |
|        8 |          3 |         3 |          1 |     8000.00 |
|        9 |          4 |         4 |          1 |    10000.00 |
|       10 |          5 |         2 |          1 |    10000.00 |
|       11 |          1 |         2 |          2 |    20000.00 |
|       12 |          2 |         3 |          2 |    25000.00 |
|       13 |          3 |         4 |          2 |    30000.00 |
|       14 |          4 |         2 |          2 |    35000.00 |
|       15 |          5 |         3 |          2 |    40000.00 |
|       16 |          1 |         4 |          2 |    45000.00 |
|       17 |          1 |         3 |          3 |     1000.00 |
|       18 |          2 |         3 |          3 |     1000.00 |
|       19 |          3 |         3 |          3 |     4000.00 |
|       20 |          4 |         3 |          3 |     4000.00 |
+----------+------------+-----------+------------+-------------+
20 rows in set (0.00 sec)
```

Note that the last four records are new data.

Summary

In this chapter you learned whole source and CDC approaches as well as pull and push modes of data source extraction. You applied CDC and push modes to extract sales orders data. In the next chapter, you will learn the various techniques to populate the date dimension

Chapter 6
Populating the Date Dimension

A date dimension has a special role in dimensional data warehousing. First and foremost, a date dimension contains times and times are of utmost importance because one of the primary functions of a data warehouse is to store historical data. Therefore, the data in a data warehouse always has a time aspect. Another unique aspect of a date dimension is that you have the option to generate the dates to populate the date dimension from within the data warehouse.

Note

Some data warehouses require both dates and times.

In your data warehouse, you start by creating a **date_dim** table that has a date or datetime column. The values in this table will then become a reference for other tables with date values. In our data warehouse, the **date_dim** table relates to the **sales_order_fact** table through the **date_sk** surrogate key. For instance, all sales order rows in the fact table with February 6, 2007 order dates have a value of 1, because in the **date_dim** table the **date_sk** value for February 6, 2007 is 1. In addition to the date itself, the date dimension has other data, such as the month name and the quarter. Having the surrogate key relationship makes this additional data available to the sales orders. This means you can query the sales orders by month name and by quarter.

This chapter teaches you the three most common techniques for populating the date dimension in a dimensional data warehouse. The three techniques are

- Pre-population
- One date everyday
- Loading the date from the source data

Pre-population

Among the three techniques, pre-population is the easiest one for populating the date dimension. With pre-population, you insert all dates for a period of time. For example, you can pre-populate the date dimension with dates in ten years, such as from January 1, 2005 to December 31, 2015. Using this technique you may pre-populate the date dimension once only for the life of your data warehouse. Alternatively, you may add data as required.

The drawbacks of pre-population are:

- Early disk space consumption
- You might not need all the dates (sparse usage)

Listing 6.1 shows a stored procedure you can use for pre-population. The stored procedure accepts two arguments, **start_dt** (start date) and **end_dt** (end date). The **WHILE** loop in the stored procedure incrementally generates all the dates from **start_dt** to **end_dt** and inserts these dates into the **date_dim** table.

Note

An effective date 0000-00-00 means the dates are effective from anytime in the past. An expiry date of 9999-12-31 means it has not expired.

Listing 6.1: Stored procedure to pre-populate the date dimension

```
/******************************************************************/
/*                                                                */
/* pre_populate_date.sql                                          */
/*                                                                */
/******************************************************************/

USE dw;

DELIMITER // ;

DROP PROCEDURE IF EXISTS pre_populate_date //

CREATE PROCEDURE pre_populate_date (IN start_dt DATE, IN end_dt
       DATE)
BEGIN
       WHILE start_dt <= end_dt DO
```

```
            INSERT INTO date_dim(
              date_sk
            , date
            , month_name
            , month
            , quarter
            , year
            , effective_date
            , expiry_date
            )
            VALUES(
              NULL
            , start_dt
            , MONTHNAME(start_dt)
            , MONTH(start_dt)
            , QUARTER(start_dt)
            , YEAR(start_dt)
            , '0000-00-00'
            , '9999-12-31'
      )
            ;
            SET start_dt = ADDDATE(start_dt, 1);
      END WHILE;
END
//

DELIMITER ; //

/* end of script                                                  */
```

You compile the stored procedure using this command.

```
mysql> \. c:\mysql\scripts\pre_populate_date.sql
```

Confirm the stored procedure has been successfully created in the **dw** database by using the **show procedure** command:

```
mysql> show procedure status like 'pre_populate_date' \G
```

The response from the stored procedure is as follows.

```
*************************** 1. row ***************************
           Db: dw
         Name: pre_populate_date
         Type: PROCEDURE
      Definer: root@localhost
```

```
     Modified: 2007-02-07 22:42:03
      Created: 2007-02-07 22:42:03
Security_type: DEFINER
      Comment:
1 row in set (0.43 sec)
```

Testing Pre-Population

In this section I show you how to verify that the pre-population date stored procedure generates the dates in the **date_dim** table correctly.

Before we start, clear the **date_dim** table using the following command.

```
mysql> truncate date_dim;
```

MySQL will indicate that three rows were deleted.

```
Query OK, 3 rows affected (0.59 sec)
```

Now, run the stored procedure in Listing 6.1 to pre-populate the date dimension for the period of January 1, 2007 to December 31, 2010. It will take a few minutes to insert the 1461 rows, which is the number of dates from January 1, 2007 to December 31, 2010.

```
mysql> call pre_populate_date('2007-01-01', '2010-12-31');
```

To confirm the dates are correctly populated into the **date_dim** table, query the number of rows in the **date_dim**.

```
mysql> select count(0) from date_dim;
```

You should see 1461 as the result.

```
+----------+
| count(0) |
+----------+
|     1461 |
+----------+
1 row in set (0.06 sec)
```

If you query the first ten dates using this command

```
mysql> select * from date_dim limit 10 \G
```

you'll see these records.

```
************************** 1. row **************************
        date_sk: 1
           date: 2007-01-01
     month_name: January
          month: 1
        quarter: 1
           year: 2007
 effective_date: 0000-00-00
    expiry_date: 9999-12-31
************************** 2. row **************************
        date_sk: 2
           date: 2007-01-02
     month_name: January
          month: 1
        quarter: 1
           year: 2007
 effective_date: 0000-00-00
    expiry_date: 9999-12-31
************************** 3. row **************************
        date_sk: 3
           date: 2007-01-03
     month_name: January
          month: 1
        quarter: 1
           year: 2007
 effective_date: 0000-00-00
    expiry_date: 9999-12-31
************************** 4. row **************************
        date_sk: 4
           date: 2007-01-04
     month_name: January
          month: 1
        quarter: 1
           year: 2007
 effective_date: 0000-00-00
    expiry_date: 9999-12-31
************************** 5. row **************************
        date_sk: 5
           date: 2007-01-05
     month_name: January
          month: 1
        quarter: 1
           year: 2007
 effective_date: 0000-00-00
```

```
   expiry_date: 9999-12-31
*************************** 6. row ***************************
       date_sk: 6
          date: 2007-01-06
    month_name: January
         month: 1
       quarter: 1
          year: 2007
effective_date: 0000-00-00
   expiry_date: 9999-12-31
*************************** 7. row ***************************
       date_sk: 7
          date: 2007-01-07
    month_name: January
         month: 1
       quarter: 1
          year: 2007
effective_date: 0000-00-00
   expiry_date: 9999-12-31
*************************** 8. row ***************************
       date_sk: 8
          date: 2007-01-08
    month_name: January
         month: 1
       quarter: 1
          year: 2007
effective_date: 0000-00-00
   expiry_date: 9999-12-31
*************************** 9. row ***************************
       date_sk: 9
          date: 2007-01-09
    month_name: January
         month: 1
       quarter: 1
          year: 2007
effective_date: 0000-00-00
   expiry_date: 9999-12-31
*************************** 10. row ***************************
       date_sk: 10
          date: 2007-01-10
    month_name: January
         month: 1
       quarter: 1
          year: 2007
effective_date: 0000-00-00
   expiry_date: 9999-12-31
```

```
10 rows in set (0.00 sec)
```

If you query the last ten dates using this command

```
mysql> select * from date_dim limit 1451, 1461 \G
```

you'll see these records shown.

```
*************************** 1. row ***************************
        date_sk: 1452
           date: 2010-12-22
     month_name: December
          month: 12
        quarter: 4
           year: 2010
 effective_date: 0000-00-00
    expiry_date: 9999-12-31
*************************** 2. row ***************************
        date_sk: 1453
           date: 2010-12-23
     month_name: December
          month: 12
        quarter: 4
           year: 2010
 effective_date: 0000-00-00
    expiry_date: 9999-12-31
*************************** 3. row ***************************
        date_sk: 1454
           date: 2010-12-24
     month_name: December
          month: 12
        quarter: 4
           year: 2010
 effective_date: 0000-00-00
    expiry_date: 9999-12-31
*************************** 4. row ***************************
        date_sk: 1455
           date: 2010-12-25
     month_name: December
          month: 12
        quarter: 4
           year: 2010
 effective_date: 0000-00-00
    expiry_date: 9999-12-31
*************************** 5. row ***************************
        date_sk: 1456
```

```
           date: 2010-12-26
     month_name: December
          month: 12
        quarter: 4
           year: 2010
 effective_date: 0000-00-00
    expiry_date: 9999-12-31
*************************** 6. row ***************************
        date_sk: 1457
           date: 2010-12-27
     month_name: December
          month: 12
        quarter: 4
           year: 2010
 effective_date: 0000-00-00
    expiry_date: 9999-12-31
*************************** 7. row ***************************
        date_sk: 1458
           date: 2010-12-28
     month_name: December
          month: 12
        quarter: 4
           year: 2010
 effective_date: 0000-00-00
    expiry_date: 9999-12-31
*************************** 8. row ***************************
        date_sk: 1459
           date: 2010-12-29
     month_name: December
          month: 12
        quarter: 4
           year: 2010
 effective_date: 0000-00-00
    expiry_date: 9999-12-31
*************************** 9. row ***************************
        date_sk: 1460
           date: 2010-12-30
     month_name: December
          month: 12
        quarter: 4
           year: 2010
 effective_date: 0000-00-00
    expiry_date: 9999-12-31
*************************** 10. row ***************************
        date_sk: 1461
           date: 2010-12-31
```

```
    month_name: December
         month: 12
       quarter: 4
          year: 2010
effective_date: 0000-00-00
   expiry_date: 9999-12-31
10 rows in set (0.00 sec)
```

One-Date-Every-Day

The second technique for populating the date dimension is one-date-every-day, which is similar to pre-population. However, with one-date-every-day you pre-populate one date every day, not all dates in a period. Using this method, you still have all dates regardless of their usage, but you do not load all the dates at once.

The script in Listing 6.2 loads the current date into the **date_dim** table. You should schedule this script to run everyday. If your data warehouse loading also takes place daily, you can merge this daily date population in its dimension loading part.

Listing 6.2: Daily date population

```
/**********************************************************************/
/*                                                                    */
/* daily_date.sql                                                     */
/*                                                                    */
/**********************************************************************/

USE dw;

INSERT INTO date_dim VALUES
( NULL
, CURRENT_DATE
, MONTHNAME(CURRENT_DATE)
, MONTH(CURRENT_DATE)
, QUARTER(CURRENT_DATE)
, YEAR(CURRENT_DATE)
, '0000-00-00'
, '9999-12-31'
)
;
```

```
/* end of script                                                    */
```

Clear the **date_dim** table and run the **daily_date.sql** script in Listing 6.2.

```
mysql> \. c:\mysql\scripts\daily_date.sql
```

Assuming you run this script after setting your MySQL date to February 7, 2007, you'll get

```
Database changed
Query OK, 1 row affected (0.27 sec)
```

To verify that the **date_dim** table was populated successfully, query the table.

```
mysql> select * from date_dim \G
```

This is the content of the **date_dim** table.

```
*************************** 1. row ***************************
       date_sk: 1
          date: 2007-02-07
    month_name: February
         month: 2
       quarter: 1
          year: 2007
effective_date: 0000-00-00
   expiry_date: 9999-12-31
1 row in set (0.00 sec)
mysql>
```

Loading Dates from the Source

In this section, I explain and present an example of yet another date population technique. Using this technique you populate the date dimension by loading dates from the source.

When you populate the **date_dim** table by loading dates from the source, your **date_dim** table will store only the dates that are used, saving you disk space. Unfortunately, this method is more complex because you must load all dates to the date dimension from your data sources that have dates.

The script in Listing 6.3 loads the sales order dates from the **sales_order** table in the **source** database into the **date_ dim** table. You use the **DISTINCT** keyword in the script to make sure no duplicates are loaded.

Listing 6.3: Loading dates from the source

```
/**********************************************************************/
/*                                                                    */
/* source_date.sql                                                    */
/*                                                                    */
/**********************************************************************/

USE dw;

INSERT INTO date_dim
SELECT DISTINCT
  NULL
, order_date
, MONTHNAME(order_date)
, MONTH(order_date)
, QUARTER(order_date)
, YEAR(order_date)
, '0000-00-00'
, '9999-12-31'
FROM source.sales_order
WHERE order_date NOT IN
(SELECT date FROM date_dim)
;

/* end of script                                                      */
```

Before you run the script in Listing 6.3, truncate the **date_dim** table. Then, run the **source_date.sql** script using this command.

```
mysql> \. c:\mysql\scripts\source_date.sql
```

The response should be similar to this.

```
Database changed
Query OK, 1 row affected (0.23 sec)
Records: 1  Duplicates: 0  Warnings: 0
```

Query the **sales_order** source table and the **date_dim** table to confirm correct population. All source dates must get into the **date_dim** table. You query the source table using this command.

```
mysql> select * from source.sales_order \G
```

The result is as follows.

```
*************************** 1. row ***************************
         order_number: 17
      customer_number: 1
         product_code: 1
           order_date: 2007-02-06
           entry_date: 2007-02-06
         order_amount: 1000.00
*************************** 2. row ***************************
         order_number: 18
      customer_number: 2
         product_code: 1
           order_date: 2007-02-06
           entry_date: 2007-02-06
         order_amount: 1000.00
*************************** 3. row ***************************
         order_number: 19
      customer_number: 3
         product_code: 1
           order_date: 2007-02-06
           entry_date: 2007-02-06
         order_amount: 4000.00
*************************** 4. row ***************************
         order_number: 20
      customer_number: 4
         product_code: 1
           order_date: 2007-02-06
           entry_date: 2007-02-06
         order_amount: 4000.00
4 rows in set (0.05 sec)
```

Now, query the **date_dim** table using this command.

```
mysql> select * from date_dim \G
```

You'll see

```
*************************** 1. row ***************************
      date_sk: 1
         date: 2007-02-06
   month_name: February
        month: 2
      quarter: 1
         year: 2007
```

```
effective_date: 0000-00-00
   expiry_date: 9999-12-31
1 row in set (0.00 sec)
```

You happen to have only one date in this example source data, February 6, 2007, therefore only this date is copied to the **date_dim** table.

Now, add some sales orders by running the script in Listing 6.4, then run the population script (**source_date.sql**) again.

Listing 6.4: Adding more dates from additional sales orders

```
/******************************************************************/
/*                                                                */
/* more_sales_order.sql                                           */
/*                                                                */
/******************************************************************/

USE source;

INSERT INTO sales_order VALUES
  (21, 1, 3, '2007-02-07', '2007-02-07', 1000)
, (22, 2, 3, '2007-02-08', '2007-02-08', 1000)
, (23, 3, 3, '2007-02-09', '2007-02-09', 4000)
, (24, 4, 3, '2007-02-10', '2007-02-10', 4000)
;

/* end of script                                                  */
```

You run the script in Listing 6.4 using this command.

```
mysql> \. c:\mysql\scripts\more_sales_order.sql
```

Then, run the **source_date.sql** script again using this command.

```
mysql> \. c:\mysql\scripts\source_date.sql
```

Finally, confirm that the four dates from the source are correctly loaded into the **date_dim** table.

```
mysql> select * from date_dim \G
```

Here is how your result should look like.

```
*************************** 1. row ***************************
       date_sk: 1
          date: 2007-02-06
```

```
    month_name: February
         month: 2
       quarter: 1
          year: 2007
effective_date: 0000-00-00
   expiry_date: 9999-12-31
*************************** 2. row ***************************
       date_sk: 2
          date: 2007-02-07
    month_name: February
         month: 2
       quarter: 1
          year: 2007
effective_date: 0000-00-00
   expiry_date: 9999-12-31
*************************** 3. row ***************************
       date_sk: 3
          date: 2007-02-08
    month_name: February
         month: 2
       quarter: 1
          year: 2007
effective_date: 0000-00-00
   expiry_date: 9999-12-31
*************************** 4. row ***************************
       date_sk: 4
          date: 2007-02-09
    month_name: February
         month: 2
       quarter: 1
          year: 2007
effective_date: 0000-00-00
   expiry_date: 9999-12-31
*************************** 5. row ***************************
       date_sk: 5
          date: 2007-02-10
    month_name: February
         month: 2
       quarter: 1
          year: 2007
effective_date: 0000-00-00
   expiry_date: 9999-12-31
5 row in set (0.00 sec)
```

Summary

In this chapter, you learned the three most common date population techniques, including their advantages and disadvantages. You also tested some example scripts that perform date dimension population. You will use the pre-population technique in the next chapters.

Chapter 7
Initial Population

In Chapter 6, "Populating the Date Dimension" you learned how to populate the date dimension. In this chapter, you learn how to populate the fact table and the other dimension tables.

Right before the start of your data warehouse operation, you need to load historical data. This historical data is the first set of data you populate the data warehouse with. This first loading is referred to as initial population.

Your data warehouse users determine how much historical data they want to have in the data warehouse. For example, if your data warehouse should start on March 1, 2007 and your user wants to load two years of historical data, you will load the source data dated between March 1, 2005 to February 28, 2007. Then, at the start of the data warehouse on March 1, 2007, you load the March 1, 2007 data.

You must load all dimension tables before you load the fact table, because the fact table needs the dimensions' surrogate keys. This is true not only during the initial population, but also during regular population. (Regular population is discussed in Chapter 8.)

In this chapter I explain the steps to perform initial population, including identifying the source data, developing the initial population script, and testing the script.

Source Data

I explain in this section what key aspects of source data you need to identify before you can begin writing the initial population script.

The first step is to identify what source data is needed and available for every fact and every dimension of the data warehouse. You also need to know the characteristics of the data source, such as its file type, record structure, and accessibility.

A sample document that summarizes the key information of the source data for the sales order data warehouse, including the file types, formats, and data warehouse target tables, is shown in Table 7.1. This type of table is often called the data source map because it maps every data from the source to the target. The activity to produce the table is called data source mapping.

Note

The source data for customer and product dimensions map directly to their target data warehouse tables, the **customer_dim** and **product_dim** tables. On the other hand, the sales order transaction is the source for more than one data warehouse table. You learn a more complex source data in Chapter 20, "Non-Straight Sources."

Source Data	Data Type	File/Table Name	Target Table in Data Warehouse
Customer	CSV text file	customer.csv	customer_dim
Product	Fixed-width text file	product.txt	product_dim
Sales order transaction	MySQL	sales_order in source database	order_dim
			sales_order_fact
			date_dim, if you use "Loading the Date from Source" option, but you'll use pre-population here

Table 7.1: Your data warehouse's data sources

Initial Population Script

Now that you have identified your data sources, it's time to write a script that can be used for initial population. Assuming your data warehouse will start operation on March 1, 2007 and your user wants to load two years of historical data, you need to load the source data dated from March 1, 2005 to February 28, 2007.

The script in Listing 7.1 serves as an example. Note that:

- The customer dimension's and the product dimension's effective date is March 1, 2007. No sales order loaded has an earlier date, meaning no earlier customer and product dimensions are required.
- The effective date of the order dimension is, of course, the order date.
- The surrogate key columns of the sales order fact table are populated from the dimension surrogate keys.
- You need to pre-populate the **date_dim** table separately using pre-population with dates from March 1, 2005 to, say, December 31, 2010.

Listing 7.1: DW initial population

```
/******************************************************************/
/*                                                                */
/* dw_initial.sql                                                 */
/*                                                                */
/******************************************************************/

USE dw;

LOAD DATA INFILE 'customer.csv'
INTO TABLE customer_stg
FIELDS TERMINATED BY ','
OPTIONALLY ENCLOSED BY '"'
LINES TERMINATED BY '\r\n'
IGNORE 1 LINES
( customer_number
, customer_name
, customer_street_address
, customer_zip_code
, customer_city
, customer_state )
;

INSERT INTO customer_dim
SELECT
  NULL
, customer_number
, customer_name
, customer_street_address
, customer_zip_code
, customer_city
, customer_state
, '2005-03-01'
, '9999-12-31'
```

```
FROM
customer_stg
;

LOAD DATA INFILE 'product.txt'
INTO TABLE product_stg
FIELDS TERMINATED BY ''
OPTIONALLY ENCLOSED BY ''
LINES TERMINATED BY '\r\n'
IGNORE 1 LINES
( product_code
, product_name
, product_category )
;

INSERT INTO product_dim
SELECT
  NULL
, product_code
, product_name
, product_category
, '2005-03-01'
, '9999-12-31'
FROM
product_stg
;

INSERT INTO order_dim
SELECT
  NULL
, order_number
, order_date
, '9999-12-31'
FROM
source.sales_order
WHERE order_date >= '2005-03-01'
AND order_date < '2007-02-28'
;

INSERT INTO sales_order_fact
SELECT
  order_sk
, customer_sk
, product_sk
, date_sk
, order_amount
```

```
FROM
  source.sales_order a
, order_dim b
, customer_dim c
, product_dim d
, date_dim e
WHERE
    a.order_number = b.order_number
AND a.customer_number = c.customer_number
AND a.product_code = d.product_code
AND a.order_date = e.date
AND order_date >= '2005-03-01'
AND order_date < '2007-02-28'
;

/* end of script                                              */
```

Running the Initial Population Script

Before you run the initial population script in Listing 7.1, you need to perform the following steps.

- Clearing all the tables, including the staging tables
- Pre-populating the date dimension
- Preparing customer and product test data
- Creating test data in the source database

These steps are discussed in the subsections below.

Clearing the Tables

To clear all tables, use the script in Listing 7.2.

Listing 7.2: Script for truncating the tables

```
/******************************************************************/
/*                                                                */
/* truncate_tables.sql                                            */
/*                                                                */
/******************************************************************/
```

```
USE dw;

TRUNCATE customer_dim;
TRUNCATE product_dim;
TRUNCATE order_dim;
TRUNCATE date_dim;
TRUNCATE sales_order_fact;
TRUNCATE customer_stg;
TRUNCATE product_stg;

USE source;

TRUNCATE sales_order;

/* end of script                                                */
```

You run the script in Listing 7.2 by invoking this command.

```
mysql> \. c:\mysql\scripts\truncate_tables.sql
```

MySQL will respond by telling you how many records are deleted from each table.

```
Database changed
Query OK, 7 rows affected (0.17 sec)

Query OK, 4 rows affected (0.05 sec)

Query OK, 20 rows affected (0.06 sec)

Query OK, 5 rows affected (0.06 sec)

Query OK, 20 rows affected (0.05 sec)

Query OK, 7 rows affected (0.06 sec)

Query OK, 3 rows affected (0.06 sec)

Database changed
Query OK, 8 rows affected (0.07 sec)
```

Pre-populating the Date Dimension

Once all the tables are empty, you can pre-populate the date dimension for the period of March 1, 2005 to December 31, 2010 by executing the

pre_populate_date stored procedure discussed in Chapter 6, "Populating the Date Dimension." Make sure that the current database is **dw** by calling:

```
mysql> use dw;
```

Then, call the stored procedure, passing the start date and the end date as arguments.

```
mysql> call pre_populate_date('2005-03-01', '2010-12-31');
```

Preparing the Customer and Product Test Data

The next step after pre-populating the **date_dim** table is to prepare the customer and product test data. I've prepared the customer data in a CSV file and the product data in a fixed-width text file.

Here is the customer source data.

```
CUSTOMER NO,CUSTOMER NAME,STREET ADDRESS,ZIP CODE,CITY,STATE
1,Really Large Customers,7500 Louise Dr.,17050,Mechanicsburg,PA
2,Small Stores,2500 Woodland St.,17055,Pittsburgh,PA
3,Medium Retailers,1111 Ritter Rd.,17055,Pittsburgh,PA
4,Good Companies,9500 Scott St.,17050,Mechanicsburg,PA
5,Wonderful Shops,3333 Rossmoyne Rd.,17050,Mechanicsburg,PA
6,Loyal Clients,7070 Ritter Rd.,17055,Pittsburgh,PA
7,Distinguished Partners,9999 Scott St.,17050,Mechanicsburg,PA
```

And here is the product data.

```
PRODUCT CODE,PRODUCT NAME,PRODUCT GROUP
1          Hard Disk Drive              Storage
2          Floppy Drive                 Storage
3          LCD Panel                    Monitor
```

Preparing the Sales Orders

The last set of test data you need is sales orders. The script in Listing 7.3 can be used to insert 21 sales orders into the **sales_order** table in the **source** database.

Listing 7.3: Sales orders for testing initial population

```
/*****************************************************************/
```

```
/*                                                              */
/* sales_order_initial.sql                                      */
/*                                                              */
/****************************************************************/

USE source;

INSERT INTO sales_order VALUES
  (1, 1, 1, '2005-02-01', '2005-02-01', 1000)
, (2, 2, 2, '2005-02-10', '2005-02-10', 1000)
, (3, 3, 3, '2005-03-01', '2005-03-01', 4000)
, (4, 4, 1, '2005-04-15', '2005-04-15', 4000)
, (5, 5, 2, '2005-05-20', '2005-05-20', 6000)
, (6, 6, 3, '2005-07-30', '2005-07-30', 6000)
, (7, 7, 1, '2005-09-01', '2005-09-01', 8000)
, (8, 1, 2, '2005-11-10', '2005-11-10', 8000)
, (9, 2, 3, '2006-01-05', '2006-01-05', 1000)
, (10, 3, 1, '2006-02-10', '2006-02-10', 1000)
, (11, 4, 2, '2006-03-15', '2006-03-15', 2000)
, (12, 5, 3, '2006-04-20', '2006-04-20', 2500)
, (13, 6, 1, '2006-05-30', '2006-05-30', 3000)
, (14, 7, 2, '2006-06-01', '2006-06-01', 3500)
, (15, 1, 3, '2006-07-15', '2006-07-15', 4000)
, (16, 2, 1, '2006-08-30', '2006-08-30', 4500)
, (17, 3, 2, '2006-09-05', '2006-09-05', 1000)
, (18, 4, 3, '2006-10-05', '2006-10-05', 1000)
, (19, 5, 1, '2007-01-10', '2007-01-10', 4000)
, (20, 6, 2, '2007-02-20', '2007-02-20', 4000)
, (21, 7, 3, '2007-02-28', '2007-02-28', 4000)
;

/* end of script                                                */
```

Now, run the **sales_order_initial.sql** script by using this command.

```
mysql> \. c:\mysql\scripts\sales_order_initial.sql
```

You'll see that 21 new rows were inserted.

```
Database changed
Query OK, 21 rows affected (0.05 sec)
Records: 21  Duplicates: 0  Warnings: 0
```

Note

The historical data to load is from March 1, 2005. Therefore, the first two orders will not be loaded.

Running and Confirming the Initial Population

Now that the test data is ready, it's time to perform the initial population. First of all, however, you need to set your MySQL date to 28 February, 2007, one day before the start of your data warehouse operation. You run the initial population at the end of the day, when no more data gets in and the source data is ready.

You are now ready to test the initial population. Run the **dw_initial.sql** population script in Listing 7.1 by using this command.

```
mysql> \. c:\mysql\scripts\dw_initial.sql
```

On your console, you should see the following messages.

```
Database changed
Query OK, 7 rows affected (0.06 sec)
Records: 7  Deleted: 0  Skipped: 0  Warnings: 0

Query OK, 7 rows affected (0.06 sec)
Records: 7  Duplicates: 0  Warnings: 0

Query OK, 3 rows affected (0.06 sec)
Records: 3  Deleted: 0  Skipped: 0  Warnings: 0

Query OK, 3 rows affected (0.07 sec)
Records: 3  Duplicates: 0  Warnings: 0

Query OK, 19 rows affected (0.06 sec)
Records: 19  Duplicates: 0  Warnings: 0

Query OK, 19 rows affected (0.10 sec)
Records: 19  Duplicates: 0  Warnings: 0
```

You can use the query in Listing 7.4 to check that nineteen sales orders have been loaded correctly.

Listing 7.4: Query to confirm the sales orders are loaded correctly

```
/**********************************************************************/
/*                                                                    */
/* confirm_initial_population.sql                                     */
/*                                                                    */
/**********************************************************************/
```

```
USE dw;

SELECT
  order_number no
, customer_name
, product_name
, date
, order_amount amount
FROM
  sales_order_fact a
, customer_dim b
, product_dim c
, order_dim d
, date_dim e
WHERE
    a.customer_sk = b.customer_sk
AND a.product_sk = c.product_sk
AND a.order_sk = d.order_sk
AND a.order_date_sk = e.date_sk
;

/* end of script                                                    */
```

Run the query in Listing 7.4 by using this command.

```
mysql> \. c:\mysql\scripts\confirm_initial_population.sql
```

The result should be as follows.

```
Database changed
+--+------------------------+-----------------+-----------+--------+
|no| customer_name          | product_name    | date      | amount |
+--+------------------------+-----------------+-----------+--------+
| 3| Medium Retailers       | LCD Panel       | 2005-03-01| 4000.00|
| 4| Good Companies         | Hard Disk Drive | 2005-04-15| 4000.00|
| 5| Wonderful Shops        | Floppy Drive    | 2005-05-20| 6000.00|
| 6| Loyal Clients          | LCD Panel       | 2005-07-30| 6000.00|
| 7| Distinguished Partners | Hard Disk Drive | 2005-09-01| 8000.00|
| 8| Really Large Customers | Floppy Drive    | 2005-11-10| 8000.00|
| 9| Small Stores           | LCD Panel       | 2006-01-05| 1000.00|
|10| Medium Retailers       | Hard Disk Drive | 2006-02-10| 1000.00|
|11| Good Companies         | Floppy Drive    | 2006-03-15| 2000.00|
|12| Wonderful Shops        | LCD Panel       | 2006-04-20| 2500.00|
|13| Loyal Clients          | Hard Disk Drive | 2006-05-30| 3000.00|
|14| Distinguished Partners | Floppy Drive    | 2006-06-01| 3500.00|
|15| Really Large Customers | LCD Panel       | 2006-07-15| 4000.00|
|16| Small Stores           | Hard Disk Drive | 2006-08-30| 4500.00|
```

```
|17| Medium Retailers       | Floppy Drive    | 2006-09-05| 1000.00|
|18| Good Companies         | LCD Panel       | 2006-10-05| 1000.00|
|19| Wonderful Shops        | Hard Disk Drive | 2007-01-10| 4000.00|
|20| Loyal Clients          | Floppy Drive    | 2007-02-20| 4000.00|
|21| Distinguished Partners | LCD Panel       | 2007-02-28| 4000.00|
+--+-----------------------+-----------------+-----------+--------+
19 rows in set (0.00 sec)
```

Summary

In this chapter you learned source data mapping and the process called initial population to load historical data that your users specified. In the next chapter, you learn regular population that you need to operate your data warehouse.

Chapter 8
Regular Population

This chapter covers regular population. Unlike initial population that you perform once only before the start of your data warehouse operation, you schedule a regular population to load the source data regularly.

In this chapter I show you how to prepare data before running a script that does regular population in our **dw** database.

Identifying Data Sources and Loading Types

The first step to schedule a regular population is identify what source data is needed and available for every fact and every dimension of the data warehouse. Afterwards, you decide the extraction mode and the loading type suitable for the population. A sample document that summarizes this information is shown in Table 8.1.

Source Data	Data Warehouse Table	Extraction Mode	Loading Type
Customer	customer_dim	Whole, Pull	SCD2 on address SCD1 on name
Product	product_dim	Whole, Pull	SCD2
Sales order Transaction	order_dim	CDC (daily), Pull	Unique order number
	sales_order_fact	CDC (daily), Pull	Daily sales orders
n/a	date_dim	n/a	Pre-populate

Table 8.1: Data sources and loading types of regular population

Note

You learned about extraction mode in Chapter 5, "Source Extraction" and SCD in Chapter 2, "Dimension History."

Another aspect of the source data that might have impact on your design is the window of time when a particular data is available for the regular population. This is especially important for transactional source data that is usually large, such as sales orders.

In addition, you need to know the detailed characteristics of every source data, such as its file type and record structure, down to the individual field or column.

Regular Population Script

I use the script in Listing 8.1. to explain how regular population works. You can use it to populate the data warehouse on a daily basis. The extraction mode and loading type used are as follows:

- The **customer.csv** and **product.txt** flat files are loaded into the **customer_dim** and **product_dim** tables through the **customer_stg** and **product_stg** tables, respectively. Loading is achieved through the use of MySQL's **LOAD DATA INFILE** utility.
- SCD2 is applied to customer addresses, product names, and product groups. SCD1 is applied to customer names.
- Only sales orders entered on the current date are loaded to the **order_dim** and **sales_order_fact** tables.

Listing 8.1: Daily dw regular population

```
/**********************************************************************/
/*                                                                    */
/* dw_regular.sql                                                     */
/*                                                                    */
/**********************************************************************/

USE dw;

/* customer dimension loading                                         */

TRUNCATE customer_stg
;

LOAD DATA INFILE 'customer.csv'
INTO TABLE customer_stg
```

```
FIELDS TERMINATED BY ','
OPTIONALLY ENCLOSED BY '"'
LINES TERMINATED BY '\r\n'
IGNORE 1 LINES
( customer_number
, customer_name
, customer_street_address
, customer_zip_code
, customer_city
, customer_state )
;

/* SCD2 on customer street addresses                              */

/* first, expire the existing customers                           */

UPDATE
  customer_dim a
, customer_stg b
SET
  expiry_date = SUBDATE(CURRENT_DATE, 1)
WHERE
    a.customer_number = b.customer_number
AND a.customer_street_address <> b.customer_street_address
AND expiry_date = '9999-12-31'
;

/* then, add a new row for the customer                           */

INSERT INTO customer_dim
SELECT
  NULL
, b.customer_number
, b.customer_name
, b.customer_street_address
, b.customer_zip_code
, b.customer_city
, b.customer_state
, CURRENT_DATE
, '9999-12-31'
FROM
  customer_dim a
, customer_stg b
WHERE
    a.customer_number = b.customer_number
```

```
AND (a.customer_street_address <> b.customer_street_address)
AND EXISTS (
SELECT *
FROM customer_dim x
WHERE
    b.customer_number = x.customer_number
AND a.expiry_date = SUBDATE(CURRENT_DATE, 1))
AND NOT EXISTS (
SELECT *
FROM customer_dim y
WHERE
    b.customer_number = y.customer_number
AND y.expiry_date = '9999-12-31')
;

/* SCD1 on customer name                                          */

UPDATE customer_dim a, customer_stg b
SET a.customer_name = b.customer_name
WHERE     a.customer_number = b.customer_number
      AND a.customer_name <> b.customer_name
;

/* add new customer                                               */

INSERT INTO customer_dim
SELECT
  NULL
, customer_number
, customer_name
, customer_street_address
, customer_zip_code
, customer_city
, customer_state
, CURRENT_DATE
, '9999-12-31'
FROM customer_stg
WHERE customer_number NOT IN(
SELECT y.customer_number
FROM customer_dim x, customer_stg y
WHERE x.customer_number = y.customer_number )
;

/* product dimension loading                                      */

TRUNCATE product_stg
```

```
;

LOAD DATA INFILE 'product.txt'
INTO TABLE product_stg
FIELDS TERMINATED BY ''
OPTIONALLY ENCLOSED BY ''
LINES TERMINATED BY '\r\n'
IGNORE 1 LINES
( product_code
, product_name
, product_category )
;

/* SCD2 on product name and group                                  */

/* first, expire the existing product                               */

UPDATE
  product_dim a
, product_stg b
SET
  expiry_date = SUBDATE(CURRENT_DATE, 1)
WHERE
    a.product_code = b.product_code
AND (   a.product_name <> b.product_name
     OR a.product_category <> b.product_category )
AND expiry_date = '9999-12-31'
;

/* then, add a new row for the product                            */

INSERT INTO product_dim
SELECT
  NULL
, b.product_code
, b.product_name
, b.product_category
, CURRENT_DATE
, '9999-12-31'
FROM
  product_dim a
, product_stg b
WHERE
    a.product_code = b.product_code
AND (   a.product_name <> b.product_name
```

```
     OR a.product_category <> b.product_category )
AND EXISTS (
SELECT *
FROM product_dim x
WHERE     b.product_code = x.product_code
      AND a.expiry_date = SUBDATE(CURRENT_DATE, 1))
AND NOT EXISTS (
SELECT *
FROM product_dim y
WHERE     b.product_code = y.product_code
      AND y.expiry_date = '9999-12-31')
;

/* add new product                                                  */

INSERT INTO product_dim
SELECT
  NULL
, product_code
, product_name
, product_category
, CURRENT_DATE
, '9999-12-31'
FROM product_stg
WHERE product_code NOT IN(
SELECT y.product_code
FROM product_dim x, product_stg y
WHERE x.product_code = y.product_code )
;

/* end of product_dim loading                                       */

INSERT INTO order_dim (
  order_sk
, order_number
, effective_date
, expiry_date )
SELECT
  NULL
, order_number
, order_date
, '9999-12-31'
FROM source.sales_order
WHERE entry_date = CURRENT_DATE
;
```

```
INSERT INTO sales_order_fact
SELECT
  order_sk
, customer_sk
, product_sk
, date_sk
, order_amount
FROM
  source.sales_order a
, order_dim b
, customer_dim c
, product_dim d
, date_dim e
WHERE
    a.order_number = b.order_number
AND a.customer_number = c.customer_number
AND a.order_date >= c.effective_date
AND a.order_date <= c.expiry_date
AND a.product_code = d.product_code
AND a.order_date >= d.effective_date
AND a.order_date <= d.expiry_date
AND a.order_date = e.date
AND a.entry_date = CURRENT_DATE
;

/* end of script                                                    */
```

Testing Data

To test the regular population, you need to prepare the customer, product, and sales order test data. Each of the sources is discussed in the sections below.

The customer.csv File

The changes to the **customer.csv** file are as follows:

- The street number of customer number 6 is now 7777 Ritter Rd. (It was 7000 Ritter Rd.)
- The name of customer number 7 is now Distinguished Agencies. (It was Distinguished Partners).

- Add a new customer as the eighth customer.

Here is the content of the **customer.csv** file.

```
CUSTOMER NO,CUSTOMER NAME,STREET ADDRESS,ZIP CODE,CITY,STATE
1,Really Large Customers,7500 Louise Dr.,17050,Mechanicsburg,PA
2,Small Stores,2500 Woodland St.,17055,Pittsburgh,PA
3,Medium Retailers,1111 Ritter Rd.,17055,Pittsburgh,PA
4,Good Companies,9500 Scott St.,17050,Mechanicsburg,PA
5,Wonderful Shops,3333 Rossmoyne Rd.,17050,Mechanicsburg,PA
6,Extremely Loyal Clients,7777 Ritter Rd.,17055,Pittsburgh,PA
7,Distinguished Agencies,9999 Scott St.,17050,Mechanicsburg,PA
8,Subsidiaries,10000 Wetline Blvd.,17055,Pittsburgh,PA
```

The product.txt File

These are the changes to the product.txt file.

- The name of Product 3 is now Flat Panel. (It was LCD Panel).
- Add a new product as the fourth product.

Here is the modified **product.txt** file.

```
PRODUCT CODE,PRODUCT NAME,PRODUCT GROUP
1          Hard Disk Drive              Storage
2          Floppy Drive                 Storage
3          Flat Panel                   Monitor
4          Keyboard                     Peripheral
```

Sales Order Transactions

The last test data you need to prepare is the sales orders. Assuming you start the data warehouse operation on March 1, 2007 (the date the first time you run the regular population). The script in Listing 8.2 adds 16 sales orders with 2007-03-01 order dates.

Listing 8.2: Adding sales orders

```
/**************************************************************/
/*                                                            */
/* sales_order_regular.sql                                    */
/*                                                            */
/**************************************************************/
```

```
USE source;

INSERT INTO sales_order VALUES
  (22, 1, 1, '2007-03-01', '2007-03-01', 1000)
, (23, 2, 2, '2007-03-01', '2007-03-01', 2000)
, (24, 3, 3, '2007-03-01', '2007-03-01', 3000)
, (25, 4, 4, '2007-03-01', '2007-03-01', 4000)
, (26, 5, 2, '2007-03-01', '2007-03-01', 1000)
, (27, 6, 2, '2007-03-01', '2007-03-01', 3000)
, (28, 7, 3, '2007-03-01', '2007-03-01', 5000)
, (29, 8, 4, '2007-03-01', '2007-03-01', 7000)
, (30, 1, 1, '2007-03-01', '2007-03-01', 1000)
, (31, 2, 2, '2007-03-01', '2007-03-01', 2000)
, (32, 3, 3, '2007-03-01', '2007-03-01', 4000)
, (33, 4, 4, '2007-03-01', '2007-03-01', 6000)
, (34, 5, 1, '2007-03-01', '2007-03-01', 2500)
, (35, 6, 2, '2007-03-01', '2007-03-01', 5000)
, (36, 7, 3, '2007-03-01', '2007-03-01', 7500)
, (37, 8, 4, '2007-03-01', '2007-03-01', 1000)
;

/* end of script                                                  */
```

Run the **sales_order_regular.sql** the script using this command.

```
mysql> \. c:\mysql\scripts\sales_order_regular.sql
```

The response on your console should be similar to this.

```
Database changed
Query OK, 16 rows affected (0.08 sec)
Records: 16  Duplicates: 0  Warnings: 0
```

The **sales_order** table now has a total of 37 rows.

Running the Regular Population Script

Before you run the **dw_regular.sql** script in Listing 8.1, you need to set your MySQL date to March 1, 2007. Then, run the script by using this command.

```
mysql> \. c:\mysql\scripts\dw_regular.sql
```

You will see this on your console.

```
Database changed
Query OK, 7 rows affected (0.12 sec)

Query OK, 8 rows affected (0.05 sec)
Records: 8  Deleted: 0  Skipped: 0  Warnings: 0

Query OK, 1 row affected (0.06 sec)
Rows matched: 1  Changed: 1  Warnings: 0

Query OK, 1 row affected (0.07 sec)
Records: 1  Duplicates: 0  Warnings: 0

Query OK, 2 rows affected (0.06 sec)
Rows matched: 2  Changed: 2  Warnings: 0

Query OK, 1 row affected (0.06 sec)
Records: 1  Duplicates: 0  Warnings: 0

Query OK, 3 rows affected (0.05 sec)

Query OK, 4 rows affected (0.08 sec)
Records: 4  Deleted: 0  Skipped: 0  Warnings: 0

Query OK, 1 row affected (0.05 sec)
Rows matched: 1  Changed: 1  Warnings: 0

Query OK, 1 row affected (0.06 sec)
Records: 1  Duplicates: 0  Warnings: 0

Query OK, 1 row affected (0.06 sec)
Records: 1  Duplicates: 0  Warnings: 0

Query OK, 16 rows affected (0.07 sec)
Records: 16  Duplicates: 0  Warnings: 0

Query OK, 16 rows affected (0.11 sec)
Records: 16  Duplicates: 0  Warnings: 0
```

Confirming Successful Regular Population

To confirm your regular population was successful, you need to query the dimension and the fact tables.

To query the **customer_dim** table, use this SQL statement.

```
mysql> select * from customer_dim \G
```

The result is as follows.

```
************************** 1. row **************************
           customer_sk: 1
       customer_number: 1
         customer_name: Really Large Customers
customer_street_address: 7500 Louise Dr.
     customer_zip_code: 17050
         customer_city: Mechanicsburg
        customer_state: PA
        effective_date: 2005-03-01
           expiry_date: 9999-12-31
************************** 2. row **************************
           customer_sk: 2
       customer_number: 2
         customer_name: Small Stores
customer_street_address: 2500 Woodland St.
     customer_zip_code: 17055
         customer_city: Pittsburgh
        customer_state: PA
        effective_date: 2005-03-01
           expiry_date: 9999-12-31
************************** 3. row **************************
           customer_sk: 3
       customer_number: 3
         customer_name: Medium Retailers
customer_street_address: 1111 Ritter Rd.
     customer_zip_code: 17055
         customer_city: Pittsburgh
        customer_state: PA
        effective_date: 2005-03-01
           expiry_date: 9999-12-31
************************** 4. row **************************
           customer_sk: 4
       customer_number: 4
         customer_name: Good Companies
customer_street_address: 9500 Scott St.
     customer_zip_code: 17050
         customer_city: Mechanicsburg
        customer_state: PA
        effective_date: 2005-03-01
           expiry_date: 9999-12-31
************************** 5. row **************************
```

```
           customer_sk: 5
       customer_number: 5
         customer_name: Wonderful Shops
customer_street_address: 3333 Rossmoyne Rd.
       customer_zip_code: 17050
         customer_city: Mechanicsburg
        customer_state: PA
        effective_date: 2005-03-01
           expiry_date: 9999-12-31
************************** 6. row **************************
           customer_sk: 6
       customer_number: 6
         customer_name: Extremely Loyal Clients
customer_street_address: 7070 Ritter Rd.
       customer_zip_code: 17055
         customer_city: Pittsburgh
        customer_state: PA
        effective_date: 2005-03-01
           expiry_date: 2007-02-28
************************** 7. row **************************
           customer_sk: 7
       customer_number: 7
         customer_name: Distinguished Agencies
customer_street_address: 9999 Scott St.
       customer_zip_code: 17050
         customer_city: Mechanicsburg
        customer_state: PA
        effective_date: 2005-03-01
           expiry_date: 9999-12-31
************************** 8. row **************************
           customer_sk: 8
       customer_number: 6
         customer_name: Extremely Loyal Clients
customer_street_address: 7777 Ritter Rd.
       customer_zip_code: 17055
         customer_city: Pittsburgh
        customer_state: PA
        effective_date: 2007-03-01
           expiry_date: 9999-12-31
************************** 9. row **************************
           customer_sk: 9
       customer_number: 8
         customer_name: Subsidiaries
customer_street_address: 10000 Wetline Blvd.
       customer_zip_code: 17055
         customer_city: Pittsburgh
```

```
         customer_state: PA
         effective_date: 2007-03-01
            expiry_date: 9999-12-31
9 rows in set (0.00 sec)
```

The query result shows you that:

- SCD2 was applied on the street address of Customer 6
- SCD1 was applied to the name of both rows of Customer 6
- SCD1 was applied to the name of Customer 7
- A new customer 8 was added

To query the **product_dim** table, use this SQL statement.

```
mysql> select * from product_dim \G
```

The result is as follows.

```
*************************** 1. row **************************
      product_sk: 1
    product_code: 1
    product_name: Hard Disk Drive
product_category: Storage
  effective_date: 2005-03-01
     expiry_date: 9999-12-31
*************************** 2. row **************************
      product_sk: 2
    product_code: 2
    product_name: Floppy Drive
product_category: Storage
  effective_date: 2005-03-01
     expiry_date: 9999-12-31
*************************** 3. row **************************
      product_sk: 3
    product_code: 3
    product_name: LCD Panel
product_category: Monitor
  effective_date: 2005-03-01
     expiry_date: 2007-02-28
*************************** 4. row **************************
      product_sk: 4
    product_code: 3
    product_name: Flat Panel
product_category: Monitor
  effective_date: 2007-03-01
```

```
     expiry_date: 9999-12-31
************************** 5. row *************************
      product_sk: 5
    product_code: 4
    product_name: Keyboard
product_category: Peripheral
  effective_date: 2007-03-01
     expiry_date: 9999-12-31
5 rows in set (0.01 sec)
```

The result from querying the **product_dim** table shows you that

- SCD2 was applied to the name of Product 3
- The new product 4 was added

Now, query the **order_dim** table.

```
mysql> select * from order_dim;
```

Here is the result. You should now have 35 orders, 19 of which were loaded in Chapter 7, "Initial Population" and 16 of which were loaded in this chapter.

```
+----------+--------------+----------------+-------------+
| order_sk | order_number | effective_date | expiry_date |
+----------+--------------+----------------+-------------+
|        1 |            3 | 2005-03-01     | 9999-12-31  |
|        2 |            4 | 2005-04-15     | 9999-12-31  |
|        3 |            5 | 2005-05-20     | 9999-12-31  |
|        4 |            6 | 2005-07-30     | 9999-12-31  |
|        5 |            7 | 2005-09-01     | 9999-12-31  |
|        6 |            8 | 2005-11-10     | 9999-12-31  |
|        7 |            9 | 2006-01-05     | 9999-12-31  |
|        8 |           10 | 2006-02-10     | 9999-12-31  |
|        9 |           11 | 2006-03-15     | 9999-12-31  |
|       10 |           12 | 2006-04-20     | 9999-12-31  |
|       11 |           13 | 2006-05-30     | 9999-12-31  |
|       12 |           14 | 2006-06-01     | 9999-12-31  |
|       13 |           15 | 2006-07-15     | 9999-12-31  |
|       14 |           16 | 2006-08-30     | 9999-12-31  |
|       15 |           17 | 2006-09-05     | 9999-12-31  |
|       16 |           18 | 2006-10-05     | 9999-12-31  |
|       17 |           19 | 2007-01-10     | 9999-12-31  |
|       18 |           20 | 2007-02-20     | 9999-12-31  |
|       19 |           21 | 2007-02-28     | 9999-12-31  |
|       20 |           22 | 2007-03-01     | 9999-12-31  |
|       21 |           23 | 2007-03-01     | 9999-12-31  |
```

```
|       22 |           24 | 2007-03-01     | 9999-12-31   |
|       23 |           25 | 2007-03-01     | 9999-12-31   |
|       24 |           26 | 2007-03-01     | 9999-12-31   |
|       25 |           27 | 2007-03-01     | 9999-12-31   |
|       26 |           28 | 2007-03-01     | 9999-12-31   |
|       27 |           29 | 2007-03-01     | 9999-12-31   |
|       28 |           30 | 2007-03-01     | 9999-12-31   |
|       29 |           31 | 2007-03-01     | 9999-12-31   |
|       30 |           32 | 2007-03-01     | 9999-12-31   |
|       31 |           33 | 2007-03-01     | 9999-12-31   |
|       32 |           34 | 2007-03-01     | 9999-12-31   |
|       33 |           35 | 2007-03-01     | 9999-12-31   |
|       34 |           36 | 2007-03-01     | 9999-12-31   |
|       35 |           37 | 2007-03-01     | 9999-12-31   |
+----------+-------------+----------------+-------------+
35 rows in set (0.00 sec)
```

The Sales Order Fact

You can now query the **sales_order_fact** table.

```
mysql> select * from sales_order_fact;
```

Here is the output.

```
+--------+------------+-----------+---------------+-------------+
|order_sk| customer_sk | product_sk | order_date_sk | order_amount |
+--------+------------+-----------+---------------+-------------+
|      1 |          3 |         3 |             1 |     4000.00 |
|      2 |          4 |         1 |            46 |     4000.00 |
|      3 |          5 |         2 |            81 |     6000.00 |
|      4 |          6 |         3 |           152 |     6000.00 |
|      5 |          7 |         1 |           185 |     8000.00 |
|      6 |          1 |         2 |           255 |     8000.00 |
|      7 |          2 |         3 |           311 |     1000.00 |
|      8 |          3 |         1 |           347 |     1000.00 |
|      9 |          4 |         2 |           380 |     2000.00 |
|     10 |          5 |         3 |           416 |     2500.00 |
|     11 |          6 |         1 |           456 |     3000.00 |
|     12 |          7 |         2 |           458 |     3500.00 |
|     13 |          1 |         3 |           502 |     4000.00 |
|     14 |          2 |         1 |           548 |     4500.00 |
|     15 |          3 |         2 |           554 |     1000.00 |
|     16 |          4 |         3 |           584 |     1000.00 |
```

```
|      17 |           5 |          1 |          681 |      4000.00 |
|      18 |           6 |          2 |          722 |      4000.00 |
|      19 |           7 |          3 |          730 |      4000.00 |
|      20 |           1 |          1 |          731 |      1000.00 |
|      21 |           2 |          2 |          731 |      2000.00 |
|      22 |           3 |          4 |          731 |      3000.00 |
|      23 |           4 |          5 |          731 |      4000.00 |
|      24 |           5 |          2 |          731 |      1000.00 |
|      25 |           8 |          2 |          731 |      3000.00 |
|      26 |           7 |          4 |          731 |      5000.00 |
|      27 |           9 |          5 |          731 |      7000.00 |
|      28 |           1 |          1 |          731 |      1000.00 |
|      29 |           2 |          2 |          731 |      2000.00 |
|      30 |           3 |          4 |          731 |      4000.00 |
|      31 |           4 |          5 |          731 |      6000.00 |
|      32 |           5 |          1 |          731 |      2500.00 |
|      33 |           8 |          2 |          731 |      5000.00 |
|      34 |           7 |          4 |          731 |      7500.00 |
|      35 |           9 |          5 |          731 |      1000.00 |
+---------+-------------+------------+--------------+--------------+
35 rows in set (0.00 sec)
```

The query result shows that:

- The sixteen sales orders entered on March 1, 2007 were added
- The valid product and customer were picked up correctly based on the order dates:
  - Surrogate key 4 for Product 3, not the one with surrogate key 3
  - Surrogate key 8 for Customer 6, not the one with surrogate key 6

Summary

In this chapter you learned and tested a daily regular population in which the pull mode, whole source, and CDC extractions as well as SCD1 and 2 were applied. In the next chapter, you learn how to schedule this regular population to run daily on Windows.

Chapter 9
Regular Population Scheduling

Once a data warehouse begins its operation, you need to regularly feed new data from the source to your data warehouse, as discussed in Chapter 8, "Regular Population." To ensure a steady stream of data, you schedule regular population using the job scheduler available on your platform. This chapter, the last in Part II, shows you how to set up a regular population as a scheduled task in Windows. The scheduler will call a batch file that in turn invokes the script discussed in Chapter 8.

Preparing the Batch File

Chapter 8 discussed the **dw_regular.sql** script to load new data. This script needs to be run daily. Listing 9.1 presents a batch file that should be invoked to run the **dw_regular.sql** script.

Listing 9.1: DW regular population batch

```
mysql.exe -udwid uuserid -ppw -D dw <
      c:\mysql\scripts\dw_regular.sql
```

You must call the **mysql.exe** command with the correct user id and password and specify the database name and the full path to the **dw_regular.sql** script.

Scheduling the Batch Job

Now that you have a batch file that calls the **regular_dw.sql** script, you can proceed with scheduling it with Windows Scheduled Task. The following provides step-by-step instructions on how to do it.

1. Open your Control Panel and select **Scheduled Tasks**.

2. Click **Select Add Scheduled Task**. The first screen of the Scheduled Task Wizard will appear, as shown in Figure 9.1.

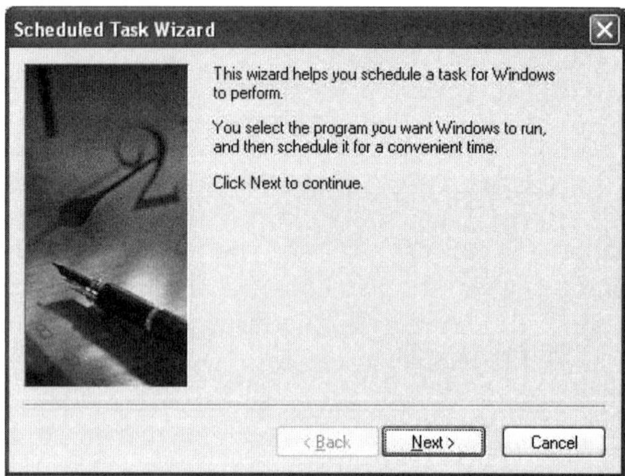

Figure 9.1: The first window of the Scheduled Task Wizard

3. Click **Next**. You will see the second window of the Scheduled Task Wizard. Locate **Command Prompt** from the Application list. Figure 9.2 shows the window after you select the application to be scheduled.

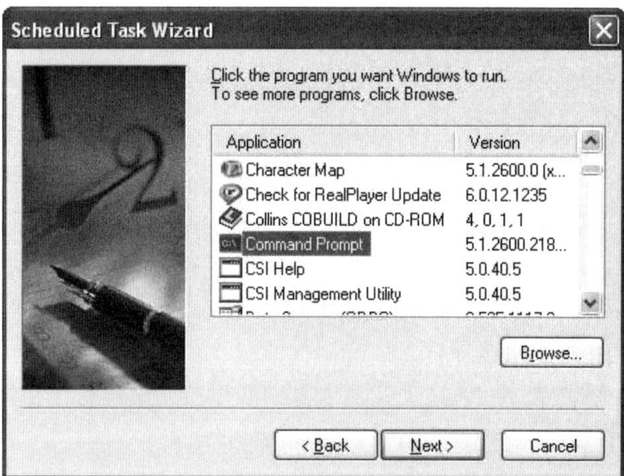

Figure 9.2: Selecting an application to schedule

4. Click **Next** again, you will see the third window of the Scheduled Task Wizard, as shown in Figure 9.3. Type in "DW Regular Load" as the

name of the scheduled task and select Daily from the "Perform this task:" option list.

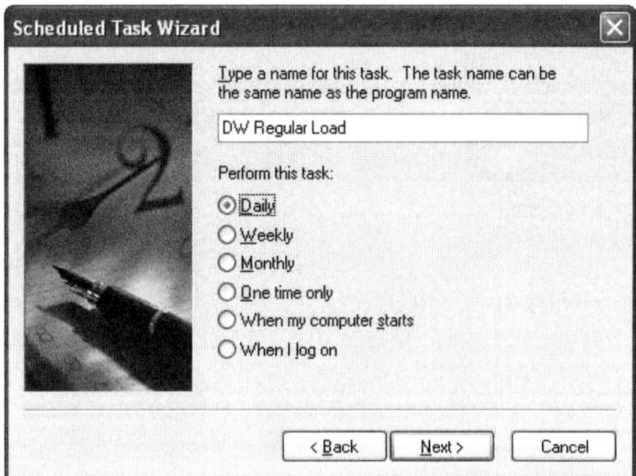

Figure 9.3: Entering a name and select a schedule

5. Click **Next** again and you will see the next screen that prompts you to select a time for invoking the scheduled task, as shown in Figure 9.4.

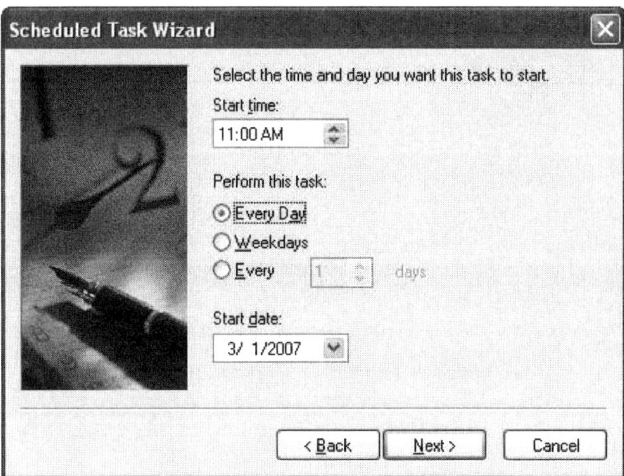

Figure 9.4: Setting the time

6. Click **Next** again. The next window appears, as shown in Figure 9.5. You will be asked to enter the name and password of the user whose credentials will be used to run the task.

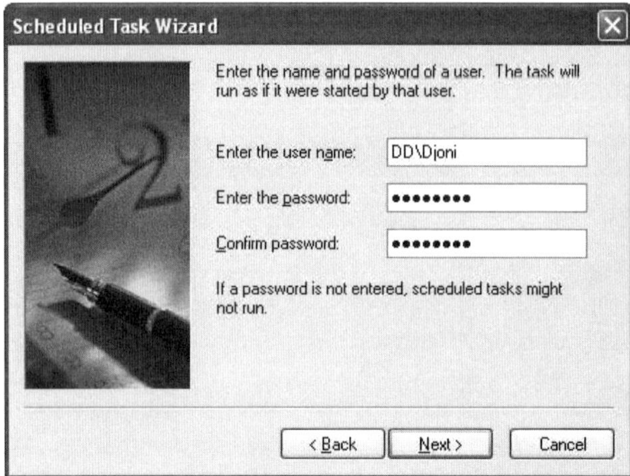

Figure 9.5: Entering Windows user name and password to run the task

7. Click **Next**. The next window in the Scheduled Task Wizard appears, as shown in Figure 9.6.

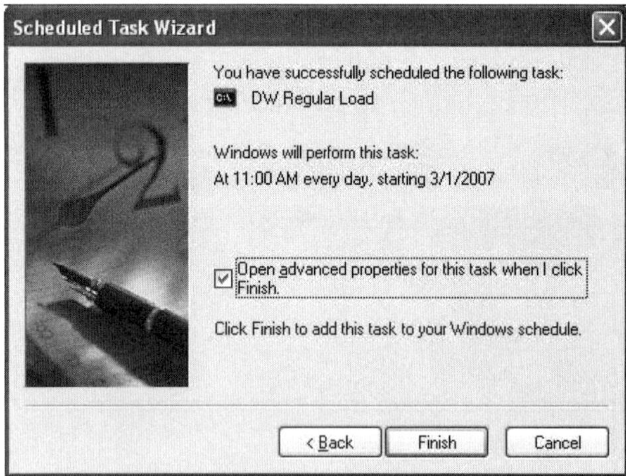

Figure 9.6: The next window

8. Enable the **Open advanced properties for this task when I click Finish** check box and click **Finish**.

9. The Advanced Properties window will appear, as shown in Figure 9.7.

Figure 9.7: The Advanced Properties window

10. Click the **Browse** button and browse the file system and select the **dw_regular_load.bat** file.
11. Click the **Set password** button and you will see the **Set Account Information** box similar to Figure 9.8. Type in your user name and password and click **OK**.

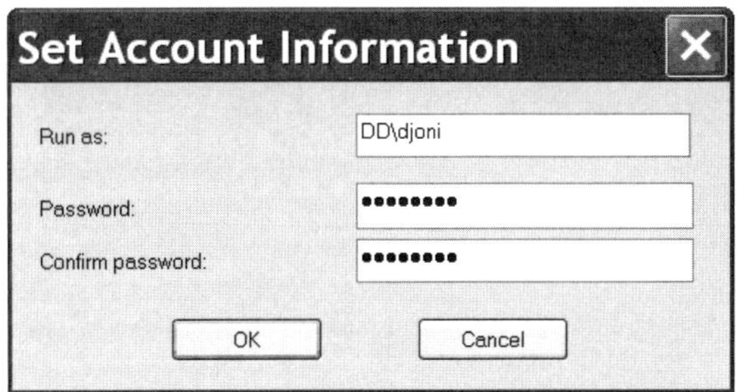

Figure 9.8: Setting account information

The daily scheduled task of your data warehouse regular load is now set up. It will start to run at the date and time you specified. You can see a new icon in the Scheduled Tasks window, as shown in Figure 9.9.

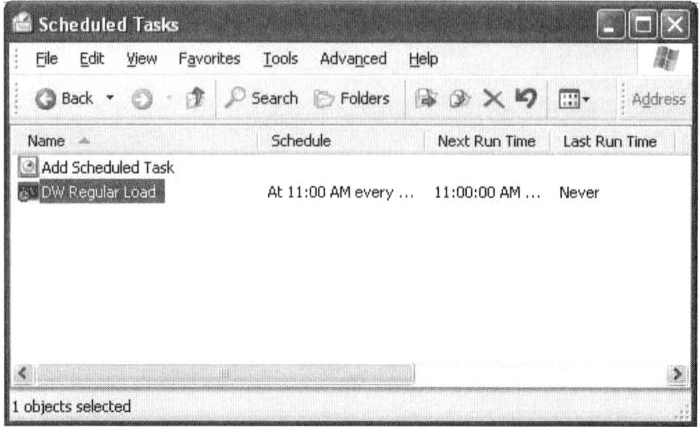

Figure 9.9: Your DW Regular Load task

Summary

In this chapter you learned to set up a regular population job as a Windows scheduled task. Having done the ETL process and the various types of population, including the regular population scheduling, you are now ready to get your starter data warehouse up and running.

Part III
Growth

If your starter data warehouse is successful, your users will want more. They may ask you to load more data to the data warehouse. By then, you should be prepared for growth.

Part III discusses how you can extend your data warehouse by

- adding columns and tables
- splitting dimensions
- using dimensions differently and for special purpose
- adding a derived star and a whole new star

Chapter 10
Adding Columns

This chapter teaches you the most commonly encountered extension of a starter data warehouse: adding columns to an existing dimension and the fact table. This chapter starts by discussing what should happen to the schema if you need to add a new column or two. It then proceeds by demonstrating how you can add a new column to the customer dimension and the sales order fact and apply SCD2 to the new column.

Enhancing the Schema

In this section I show you how to revise the data warehouse schema. Figure 10.1 shows the enhanced schema with new columns in the **customer_dim** table and the **sales_order_fact** table. The new columns in **customer_dim** are **shipping_address**, **shipping_zip_code**, **shipping_city**, and **shipping_state**. The **sales_order_fact** table has one new column: **order_quantity**.

The **shipping_address.sql** script in Listing 10.1 adds the new columns in the **customer_dim** and **customer_stg** tables. Before you run the script, set your MySQL date to March 1, 2007.

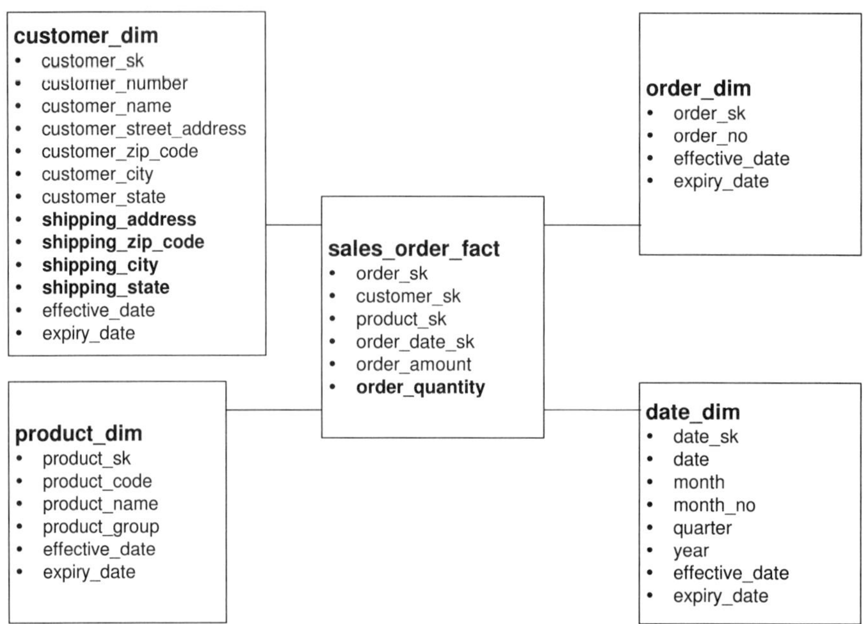

Figure 10.1: New columns in customer_dim and sales_order_fact

Listing 10.1: Adding new columns to the customer dimension

```
/******************************************************************/
/*                                                                */
/* shipping_address.sql                                           */
/*                                                                */
/******************************************************************/

USE dw;

ALTER TABLE customer_dim
  ADD shipping_address CHAR(50) AFTER customer_state
, ADD shipping_zip_code INT(5) AFTER shipping_address
, ADD shipping_city CHAR(30) AFTER shipping_zip_code
, ADD shipping_state CHAR(2) AFTER shipping_city
;

ALTER TABLE customer_stg
  ADD shipping_address CHAR(50) AFTER customer_state
, ADD shipping_zip_code INT(5) AFTER shipping_address
, ADD shipping_city CHAR(30) AFTER shipping_zip_code
, ADD shipping_state CHAR(2) AFTER shipping_city
;
```

```
/* end of script                                                   */
```

You run the above script by using this command.

```
mysql> \. c:\mysql\scripts\shipping_address.sql
```

This message will be printed on the MySQL console.

```
Database changed
Query OK, 9 rows affected (0.73 sec)
Records: 9  Duplicates: 0  Warnings: 0

Query OK, 8 rows affected (0.49 sec)
Records: 8  Duplicates: 0  Warnings: 0
```

To confirm that the new columns were added, query the **customer_dim** table.

```
mysql> select * from customer_dim \G
```

Here is the query result.

```
*************************** 1. row ***************************
            customer_sk: 1
        customer_number: 1
          customer_name: Really Large Customers
customer_street_address: 7500 Louise Dr.
      customer_zip_code: 17050
          customer_city: Mechanicsburg
         customer_state: PA
       shipping_address: NULL
      shipping_zip_code: NULL
          shipping_city: NULL
         shipping_state: NULL
         effective_date: 2005-03-01
            expiry_date: 9999-12-31
*************************** 2. row ***************************
            customer_sk: 2
        customer_number: 2
          customer_name: Small Stores
customer_street_address: 2500 Woodland St.
      customer_zip_code: 17055
          customer_city: Pittsburgh
         customer_state: PA
       shipping_address: NULL
      shipping_zip_code: NULL
```

```
           shipping_city: NULL
          shipping_state: NULL
          effective_date: 2005-03-01
             expiry_date: 9999-12-31
************************** 3. row ***************************
             customer_sk: 3
         customer_number: 3
           customer_name: Medium Retailers
customer_street_address: 1111 Ritter Rd.
       customer_zip_code: 17055
           customer_city: Pittsburgh
          customer_state: PA
        shipping_address: NULL
       shipping_zip_code: NULL
           shipping_city: NULL
          shipping_state: NULL
          effective_date: 2005-03-01
             expiry_date: 9999-12-31
************************** 4. row ***************************
             customer_sk: 4
         customer_number: 4
           customer_name: Good Companies
customer_street_address: 9500 Scott St.
       customer_zip_code: 17050
           customer_city: Mechanicsburg
          customer_state: PA
        shipping_address: NULL
       shipping_zip_code: NULL
           shipping_city: NULL
          shipping_state: NULL
          effective_date: 2005-03-01
             expiry_date: 9999-12-31
************************** 5. row ***************************
             customer_sk: 5
         customer_number: 5
           customer_name: Wonderful Shops
customer_street_address: 3333 Rossmoyne Rd.
       customer_zip_code: 17050
           customer_city: Mechanicsburg
          customer_state: PA
        shipping_address: NULL
       shipping_zip_code: NULL
           shipping_city: NULL
          shipping_state: NULL
          effective_date: 2005-03-01
             expiry_date: 9999-12-31
```

```
************************** 6. row **************************
            customer_sk: 6
        customer_number: 6
          customer_name: Extremely Loyal Clients
customer_street_address: 7070 Ritter Rd.
      customer_zip_code: 17055
          customer_city: Pittsburgh
         customer_state: PA
       shipping_address: NULL
      shipping_zip_code: NULL
          shipping_city: NULL
         shipping_state: NULL
         effective_date: 2005-03-01
            expiry_date: 2007-02-28
************************** 7. row **************************
            customer_sk: 7
        customer_number: 7
          customer_name: Distinguished Agencies
customer_street_address: 9999 Scott St.
      customer_zip_code: 17050
          customer_city: Mechanicsburg
         customer_state: PA
       shipping_address: NULL
      shipping_zip_code: NULL
          shipping_city: NULL
         shipping_state: NULL
         effective_date: 2005-03-01
            expiry_date: 9999-12-31
************************** 8. row **************************
            customer_sk: 8
        customer_number: 6
          customer_name: Extremely Loyal Clients
customer_street_address: 7777 Ritter Rd.
      customer_zip_code: 17055
          customer_city: Pittsburgh
         customer_state: PA
       shipping_address: NULL
      shipping_zip_code: NULL
          shipping_city: NULL
         shipping_state: NULL
         effective_date: 2007-03-01
            expiry_date: 9999-12-31
************************** 9. row **************************
            customer_sk: 9
        customer_number: 8
```

```
          customer_name: Subsidiaries
customer_street_address: 10000 Wetline Blvd.
      customer_zip_code: 17055
          customer_city: Pittsburgh
         customer_state: PA
       shipping_address: NULL
      shipping_zip_code: NULL
          shipping_city: NULL
         shipping_state: NULL
         effective_date: 2007-03-01
            expiry_date: 9999-12-31
9 rows in set (0.00 sec)
```

Note
The new columns are not populated yet, so their values are NULL.

The **order_quantity.sql** script in Listing 10.2 adds the **order_quantity** column to the **sales_order_fact** table.

Listing 10.2: Adding the order_quantity column

```
/******************************************************************/
/*                                                                */
/* order_quantity.sql                                             */
/*                                                                */
/******************************************************************/

USE dw;

ALTER TABLE sales_order_fact
  ADD order_quantity INT AFTER order_amount

;

/* end of script                                                  */
```

You run the above script by using this command.

```
mysql> \. c:\mysql\scripts\order_quantity.sql
```

Here is what you see on the console after you press Enter.

```
Database changed
Query OK, 35 rows affected (0.56 sec)
Records: 35  Duplicates: 0  Warnings: 0
```

To confirm that the new column was added, query the **sales_order_fact** table.

```
mysql> select order_sk osk, customer_sk csk, product_sk psk,
       order_date_sk odsk,
    -> order_amount amt, order_quantity qty
    -> from sales_order_fact;
```

The result should be as follows.

```
+------+------+------+------+---------+------+
| osk  | csk  | psk  | odsk | amt     | qty  |
+------+------+------+------+---------+------+
|    1 |    3 |    3 |    1 | 4000.00 | NULL |
|    2 |    4 |    1 |   46 | 4000.00 | NULL |
|    3 |    5 |    2 |   81 | 6000.00 | NULL |
|    4 |    6 |    3 |  152 | 6000.00 | NULL |
|    5 |    7 |    1 |  185 | 8000.00 | NULL |
|    6 |    1 |    2 |  255 | 8000.00 | NULL |
|    7 |    2 |    3 |  311 | 1000.00 | NULL |
|    8 |    3 |    1 |  347 | 1000.00 | NULL |
|    9 |    4 |    2 |  380 | 2000.00 | NULL |
|   10 |    5 |    3 |  416 | 2500.00 | NULL |
|   11 |    6 |    1 |  456 | 3000.00 | NULL |
|   12 |    7 |    2 |  458 | 3500.00 | NULL |
|   13 |    1 |    3 |  502 | 4000.00 | NULL |
|   14 |    2 |    1 |  548 | 4500.00 | NULL |
|   15 |    3 |    2 |  554 | 1000.00 | NULL |
|   16 |    4 |    3 |  584 | 1000.00 | NULL |
|   17 |    5 |    1 |  681 | 4000.00 | NULL |
|   18 |    6 |    2 |  722 | 4000.00 | NULL |
|   19 |    7 |    3 |  730 | 4000.00 | NULL |
|   20 |    1 |    1 |  731 | 1000.00 | NULL |
|   21 |    2 |    2 |  731 | 2000.00 | NULL |
|   22 |    3 |    4 |  731 | 3000.00 | NULL |
|   23 |    4 |    5 |  731 | 4000.00 | NULL |
|   24 |    5 |    2 |  731 | 1000.00 | NULL |
|   25 |    8 |    2 |  731 | 3000.00 | NULL |
|   26 |    7 |    4 |  731 | 5000.00 | NULL |
|   27 |    9 |    5 |  731 | 7000.00 | NULL |
|   28 |    1 |    1 |  731 | 1000.00 | NULL |
|   29 |    2 |    2 |  731 | 2000.00 | NULL |
|   30 |    3 |    4 |  731 | 4000.00 | NULL |
|   31 |    4 |    5 |  731 | 6000.00 | NULL |
|   32 |    5 |    1 |  731 | 2500.00 | NULL |
|   33 |    8 |    2 |  731 | 5000.00 | NULL |
|   34 |    7 |    4 |  731 | 7500.00 | NULL |
|   35 |    9 |    5 |  731 | 1000.00 | NULL |
```

```
+------+------+------+------+--------+------+
35 rows in set (0.00 sec)
```

Revising Regular Population Script

After you alter the database schema, you need to revise the script you've been using for regular population. Listing 10.3 presents the revised regular population script.

Let's assume that the source data provides the shipping address of active customers only; shipping addresses of non-active customers in the customer table will be empty. Therefore, you need to update the existing customers in the data warehouse when their shipping addresses become available in the data source. If the user wants you to maintain the history of the shipping address as well, you apply SCD2 to the shipping address column.

Let's also assume that the order quantity is made available in the sales orders source data and the user agrees sales orders already in the data warehouse will not be updated.

Listing 10.3: Revised daily DW regular population

```
/******************************************************************/
/*                                                                */
/* dw_regular_10.sql                                              */
/*                                                                */
/******************************************************************/

USE dw;

/* CUSTOMER_DIM POPULATION                                        */

TRUNCATE customer_stg;

LOAD DATA INFILE 'customer.csv'
INTO TABLE customer_stg
FIELDS TERMINATED BY ','
OPTIONALLY ENCLOSED BY '"'
LINES TERMINATED BY '\r\n'
IGNORE 1 LINES
( customer_number
, customer_name
, customer_street_address
```

```
, customer_zip_code
, customer_city
, customer_state
, shipping_address
, shipping_zip_code
, shipping_city
, shipping_state )
;

/* SCD 2 ON ADDRESSES                                          */

UPDATE
  customer_dim a
, customer_stg b
SET
  a.expiry_date = SUBDATE(CURRENT_DATE, 1)
WHERE
  a.customer_number = b.customer_number
AND (   a.customer_street_address <> b.customer_street_address
     OR a.customer_city <> b.customer_city
     OR a.customer_zip_code <> b.customer_zip_code
     OR a.customer_state <> b.customer_state
     OR a.shipping_address <> b.shipping_address
     OR a.shipping_city <> b.shipping_city
     OR a.shipping_zip_code <> b.shipping_zip_code
     OR a.shipping_state <> b.shipping_state
     OR a.shipping_address IS NULL
     OR a.shipping_city IS NULL
     OR a.shipping_zip_code IS NULL
     OR a.shipping_state IS NULL)
AND expiry_date = '9999-12-31'
;

INSERT INTO customer_dim
SELECT
  NULL
, b.customer_number
, b.customer_name
, b.customer_street_address
, b.customer_zip_code
, b.customer_city
, b.customer_state
, b.shipping_address
, b.shipping_zip_code
, b.shipping_city
```

```
, b.shipping_state
, CURRENT_DATE
, '9999-12-31'
FROM
  customer_dim a
, customer_stg b
WHERE
    a.customer_number = b.customer_number
AND (   a.customer_street_address <> b.customer_street_address
     OR a.customer_city <> b.customer_city
     OR a.customer_zip_code <> b.customer_zip_code
     OR a.customer_state <> b.customer_state
     OR a.shipping_address <> b.shipping_address
     OR a.shipping_city <> b.shipping_city
     OR a.shipping_zip_code <> b.shipping_zip_code
     OR a.shipping_state <> b.shipping_state
     OR a.shipping_address IS NULL
     OR a.shipping_city IS NULL
     OR a.shipping_zip_code IS NULL
     OR a.shipping_state IS NULL)
AND EXISTS (
SELECT *
FROM customer_dim x
WHERE b.customer_number = x.customer_number
AND a.expiry_date = SUBDATE(CURRENT_DATE, 1))
AND NOT EXISTS (
SELECT *
FROM customer_dim y
WHERE     b.customer_number = y.customer_number
      AND y.expiry_date = '9999-12-31')
;

/* END OF SCD 2                                                    */

/* SCD 1 ON NAME                                                   */

UPDATE customer_dim a, customer_stg b
SET a.customer_name = b.customer_name
WHERE     a.customer_number = b.customer_number
      AND a.expiry_date = '9999-12-31'
      AND a.customer_name <> b.customer_name
;

/* ADD NEW CUSTOMER                                                */

INSERT INTO customer_dim
```

```
SELECT
  NULL
, customer_number
, customer_name
, customer_street_address
, customer_zip_code
, customer_city
, customer_state
, shipping_address
, shipping_zip_code
, shipping_city
, shipping_state
, CURRENT_DATE
, '9999-12-31'
FROM customer_stg
WHERE customer_number NOT IN(
SELECT a.customer_number
FROM
  customer_dim a
, customer_stg b
WHERE b.customer_number = a.customer_number )
;

/* END OF CUSTOMER_DIM POPULATION                                  */

/* product dimension loading                                       */

TRUNCATE product_stg
;

LOAD DATA INFILE 'product.txt'
INTO TABLE product_stg
FIELDS TERMINATED BY ''
OPTIONALLY ENCLOSED BY ''
LINES TERMINATED BY '\r\n'
IGNORE 1 LINES
( product_code
, product_name
, product_category )
;

/* PRODUCT_DIM POPULATION                                          */

/* SCD2 ON PRODUCT NAME AND GROUP                                  */
```

```
UPDATE
  product_dim a
, product_stg b
SET
  expiry_date = SUBDATE(CURRENT_DATE, 1)
WHERE
    a.product_code = b.product_code
AND (   a.product_name <> b.product_name
     OR a.product_category <> b.product_category )
     AND expiry_date = '9999-12-31'
;

INSERT INTO product_dim
SELECT
  NULL
, b.product_code
, b.product_name
, b.product_category
, CURRENT_DATE
, '9999-12-31'
FROM
  product_dim a
, product_stg b
WHERE
    a.product_code = b.product_code
AND (   a.product_name <> b.product_name
     OR a.product_category <> b.product_category )
AND EXISTS (
SELECT *
FROM product_dim x
WHERE     b.product_code = x.product_code
             AND a.expiry_date = SUBDATE(CURRENT_DATE, 1))
AND NOT EXISTS (
SELECT *
FROM product_dim y
WHERE    b.product_code = y.product_code
             AND y.expiry_date = '9999-12-31')
;

/* END OF SCD 2                                                */

/* ADD NEW PRODUCT                                             */

INSERT INTO product_dim
SELECT
  NULL
```

```
, product_code
, product_name
, product_category
, CURRENT_DATE
, '9999-12-31'
FROM product_stg
WHERE product_code NOT IN(
SELECT y.product_code
FROM product_dim x, product_stg y
WHERE x.product_code = y.product_code )
;

/* END OF PRODUCT_DIM POPULATION                                  */

/* ORDER_DIM POPULATION                                           */

INSERT INTO order_dim (
  order_sk
, order_number
, effective_date
, expiry_date
)
SELECT
  NULL
, order_number
, order_date
, '9999-12-31'
FROM source.sales_order
WHERE entry_date = CURRENT_DATE
;

/* END OF ORDER_DIM POPULATION                                    */

/* SALES_ORDER_FACT POPULATION                                    */

INSERT INTO sales_order_fact
SELECT
  order_sk
, customer_sk
, product_sk
, date_sk
, order_amount
, order_quantity
FROM
  source.sales_order a
```

```
, order_dim b
, customer_dim c
, product_dim d
, date_dim e
WHERE
    a.order_number = b.order_number
AND a.customer_number = c.customer_number
AND a.order_date >= c.effective_date
AND a.order_date <= c.expiry_date
AND a.product_code = d.product_code
AND a.order_date >= d.effective_date
AND a.order_date <= d.expiry_date
AND a.order_date = e.date
AND a.entry_date = CURRENT_DATE
;

/* end of script                                                      */
```

The next section provides instructions on how to prepare the data required for the script in Listing 10.3 to run successfully.

Testing

Before you can run the script in Listing 10.3, there are a few things you need to do.

First, prepare the customer data as shown below and save it as **customer.csv**. The changes from the previous customer data are:

- The shipping address data of all existing eight customers are available
- Customer number 9 is a new customer, which has its shipping address data

```
CUSTOMER NO,CUSTOMER NAME,STREET ADDRESS,ZIP CODE,CITY,STATE,
SHIPPING ADDRESS,ZIP CODE,CITY,STATE
1,Really Large Customers,7500 Louise Dr.,17050,Mechanicsburg,PA,7500
      Louise Dr.,17050,Mechanicsburg,PA
2,Small Stores,2500 Woodland St.,17055,Pittsburgh,PA,2500 Woodland
      St.,17055,Pittsburgh,PA
3,Medium Retailers,1111 Ritter Rd.,17055,Pittsburgh,PA,1111 Ritter
      Rd.,17055,Pittsburgh,PA
4,Good Companies,9500 Scott St.,17050,Mechanicsburg,PA,9500 Scott
      St.,17050,Mechanicsburg,PA
```

```
5,Wonderful Shops,3333 Rossmoyne Rd.,17050,Mechanicsburg,PA,3333
      Rossmoyne Rd.,17050,Mechanicsburg,PA
6,Extremely Loyal Clients,7777 Ritter Rd.,17055,Pittsburgh,PA,7777
      Ritter Rd.,17055,Pittsburgh,PA
7,Distinguished Agencies,9999 Scott St.,17050,Mechanicsburg,PA,9999
      Scott St.,17050,Mechanicsburg,PA
8,Subsidiaries,10000 Wetline Blvd.,17055,Pittsburgh,PA,10000 Wetline
      Blvd.,17055,Pittsburgh,PA
9,Online Distributors,2323 Louise Dr.,17055,Pittsburgh,PA,2323
      Louise Dr.,17055,Pittsburgh,PA
```

Note

You will need the **product.txt** file used in the previous test even though there is no change to the file. This is because regular population must access all source data whenever it runs, and this includes the **product.txt** file.

The second thing you need to do is add the **order_quantity** column to the **sales_order** table in the **source** database using the **sales_order_quantity_data.sql** script in Listing 10.4. The data in this new column is the source for the new **order_quantity** column in the **sales_order_fact** table.

Listing 10.4: Adding the order_quantity column to the sales_order table

```
/******************************************************************/
/*                                                                */
/* add_sales_order_quantity.sql                                   */
/*                                                                */
/******************************************************************/

USE source;

ALTER TABLE sales_order
  ADD order_quantity INT AFTER order_amount

;

/* end of script                                                  */
```

Run the script using this command.

```
mysql> \. c:\mysql\scripts\add_sales_order_quantity.sql
```

You'll see this on your MySQL console.

```
Database changed
Query OK, 37 rows affected (0.39 sec)
Records: 37  Duplicates: 0  Warnings: 0
```

Now that the sales order source has the **order_quantity** column, you can add sales order test data. The script in Listing 10.5 adds nine sales orders into the **sales_order** table. Note that these sales orders have order quantities and their order dates are March 2, 2005.

Listing 10.5: Adding nine sales orders with order quantities

```
/**********************************************************************/
/*                                                                    */
/* sales_order_quantity_data.sql                                      */
/*                                                                    */
/**********************************************************************/

USE source;

INSERT INTO sales_order VALUES
  (38, 1, 1, '2007-03-02', '2007-03-02', 1000, 10)
, (39, 2, 2, '2007-03-02', '2007-03-02', 2000, 20)
, (40, 3, 3, '2007-03-02', '2007-03-02', 4000, 40)
, (41, 4, 4, '2007-03-02', '2007-03-02', 6000, 60)
, (42, 5, 1, '2007-03-02', '2007-03-02', 2500, 25)
, (43, 6, 2, '2007-03-02', '2007-03-02', 5000, 50)
, (44, 7, 3, '2007-03-02', '2007-03-02', 7500, 75)
, (45, 8, 4, '2007-03-02', '2007-03-02', 1000, 10)
, (46, 9, 1, '2007-03-02', '2007-03-02', 1000, 10)
;

/* end of script                                                      */
```

Next, you need to set your MySQL date to the order date of your test data, which is March 2, 2007.

Now, you are ready to run the **dw_regular_10.sql** script in Listing 10.3. You can invoke it using this command.

```
mysql> \. c:\mysql\scripts\dw_regular_10.sql
```

Here is what you'll see on the console.

```
Database changed
Query OK, 8 rows affected (0.05 sec)
```

```
Query OK, 9 rows affected (0.06 sec)
Records: 9  Deleted: 0  Skipped: 0  Warnings: 0

Query OK, 8 rows affected (0.06 sec)
Rows matched: 8  Changed: 8  Warnings: 0

Query OK, 8 rows affected (0.05 sec)
Records: 8  Duplicates: 0  Warnings: 0

Query OK, 0 rows affected (0.01 sec)
Rows matched: 0  Changed: 0  Warnings: 0

Query OK, 1 row affected (0.07 sec)
Records: 1  Duplicates: 0  Warnings: 0

Query OK, 4 rows affected (0.05 sec)

Query OK, 4 rows affected (0.06 sec)
Records: 4  Deleted: 0  Skipped: 0  Warnings: 0

Query OK, 0 rows affected (0.00 sec)
Rows matched: 0  Changed: 0  Warnings: 0

Query OK, 0 rows affected (0.00 sec)
Records: 0  Duplicates: 0  Warnings: 0

Query OK, 0 rows affected (0.00 sec)
Records: 0  Duplicates: 0  Warnings: 0

Query OK, 9 rows affected (0.07 sec)
Records: 9  Duplicates: 0  Warnings: 0

Query OK, 9 rows affected (0.10 sec)
Records: 9  Duplicates: 0  Warnings: 0
```

You can confirm if the revised regular population script was successfully executed by querying the customer dimension using this SQL statement.

```
mysql> select customer_number no, customer_name name,
    -> shipping_city, shipping_zip_code zip, shipping_state st,
    -> effective_date eff, expiry_date exp
    -> from customer_dim \G
```

A successful execution of the revised regular population script gives you the following result.

```
*************************** 1. row ***************************
           no: 1
         name: Really Large Customers
shipping_city: NULL
          zip: NULL
           st: NULL
          eff: 2005-03-01
          exp: 2007-03-01
*************************** 2. row ***************************
           no: 2
         name: Small Stores
shipping_city: NULL
          zip: NULL
           st: NULL
          eff: 2005-03-01
          exp: 2007-03-01
*************************** 3. row ***************************
           no: 3
         name: Medium Retailers
shipping_city: NULL
          zip: NULL
           st: NULL
          eff: 2005-03-01
          exp: 2007-03-01
*************************** 4. row ***************************
           no: 4
         name: Good Companies
shipping_city: NULL
          zip: NULL
           st: NULL
          eff: 2005-03-01
          exp: 2007-03-01
*************************** 5. row ***************************
           no: 5
         name: Wonderful Shops
shipping_city: NULL
          zip: NULL
           st: NULL
          eff: 2005-03-01
          exp: 2007-03-01
*************************** 6. row ***************************
           no: 6
         name: Extremely Loyal Clients
```

```
shipping_city: NULL
          zip: NULL
           st: NULL
          eff: 2005-03-01
          exp: 2007-02-28
*************************** 7. row ***************************
           no: 7
         name: Distinguished Agencies
shipping_city: NULL
          zip: NULL
           st: NULL
          eff: 2005-03-01
          exp: 2007-03-01
*************************** 8. row ***************************
           no: 6
         name: Extremely Loyal Clients
shipping_city: NULL
          zip: NULL
           st: NULL
          eff: 2007-03-01
          exp: 2007-03-01
*************************** 9. row ***************************
           no: 8
         name: Subsidiaries
shipping_city: NULL
          zip: NULL
           st: NULL
          eff: 2007-03-01
          exp: 2007-03-01
*************************** 10. row ***************************
           no: 1
         name: Really Large Customers
shipping_city: Mechanicsburg
          zip: 17050
           st: PA
          eff: 2007-03-02
          exp: 9999-12-31
*************************** 11. row ***************************
           no: 2
         name: Small Stores
shipping_city: Pittsburgh
          zip: 17055
           st: PA
          eff: 2007-03-02
          exp: 9999-12-31
```

```
*************************** 12. row ***************************
           no: 3
         name: Medium Retailers
shipping_city: Pittsburgh
          zip: 17055
           st: PA
          eff: 2007-03-02
          exp: 9999-12-31
*************************** 13. row ***************************
           no: 4
         name: Good Companies
shipping_city: Mechanicsburg
          zip: 17050
           st: PA
          eff: 2007-03-02
          exp: 9999-12-31
*************************** 14. row ***************************
           no: 5
         name: Wonderful Shops
shipping_city: Mechanicsburg
          zip: 17050
           st: PA
          eff: 2007-03-02
          exp: 9999-12-31
*************************** 15. row ***************************
           no: 6
         name: Extremely Loyal Clients
shipping_city: Pittsburgh
          zip: 17055
           st: PA
          eff: 2007-03-02
          exp: 9999-12-31
*************************** 16. row ***************************
           no: 7
         name: Distinguished Agencies
shipping_city: Mechanicsburg
          zip: 17050
           st: PA
          eff: 2007-03-02
          exp: 9999-12-31
*************************** 17. row ***************************
           no: 8
         name: Subsidiaries
shipping_city: Pittsburgh
          zip: 17055
           st: PA
```

```
           eff: 2007-03-02
           exp: 9999-12-31
************************** 18. row ***************************
            no: 9
          name: Online Distributors
shipping_city: Pittsburgh
           zip: 17055
            st: PA
           eff: 2007-03-02
           exp: 9999-12-31
18 rows in set (0.00 sec)
```

Note

The new records of all existing customers have shipping addresses. The older (expired) records do not. Customer number 9 is added and it has a shipping address.

To confirm that the sales data has been populated successfully, query the **sales_order_fact** table using this statement.

```
mysql> select order_sk o_sk, customer_sk c_sk, product_sk p_sk,
       order_date_sk od_sk,
    -> order_amount amt, order_quantity qty
    -> from sales_order_fact;
```

Here is the content of the fact table.

```
+------+------+------+-------+---------+------+
| o_sk | c_sk | p_sk | od_sk | amt     | qty  |
+------+------+------+-------+---------+------+
|    1 |    3 |    3 |     1 | 4000.00 | NULL |
|    2 |    4 |    1 |    46 | 4000.00 | NULL |
|    3 |    5 |    2 |    81 | 6000.00 | NULL |
|    4 |    6 |    3 |   152 | 6000.00 | NULL |
|    5 |    7 |    1 |   185 | 8000.00 | NULL |
|    6 |    1 |    2 |   255 | 8000.00 | NULL |
|    7 |    2 |    3 |   311 | 1000.00 | NULL |
|    8 |    3 |    1 |   347 | 1000.00 | NULL |
|    9 |    4 |    2 |   380 | 2000.00 | NULL |
|   10 |    5 |    3 |   416 | 2500.00 | NULL |
|   11 |    6 |    1 |   456 | 3000.00 | NULL |
|   12 |    7 |    2 |   458 | 3500.00 | NULL |
|   13 |    1 |    3 |   502 | 4000.00 | NULL |
|   14 |    2 |    1 |   548 | 4500.00 | NULL |
|   15 |    3 |    2 |   554 | 1000.00 | NULL |
```

```
|   16 |    4 |    3 |    584 | 1000.00 | NULL |
|   17 |    5 |    1 |    681 | 4000.00 | NULL |
|   18 |    6 |    2 |    722 | 4000.00 | NULL |
|   19 |    7 |    3 |    730 | 4000.00 | NULL |
|   20 |    1 |    1 |    731 | 1000.00 | NULL |
|   21 |    2 |    2 |    731 | 2000.00 | NULL |
|   22 |    3 |    4 |    731 | 3000.00 | NULL |
|   23 |    4 |    5 |    731 | 4000.00 | NULL |
|   24 |    5 |    2 |    731 | 1000.00 | NULL |
|   25 |    8 |    2 |    731 | 3000.00 | NULL |
|   26 |    7 |    4 |    731 | 5000.00 | NULL |
|   27 |    9 |    5 |    731 | 7000.00 | NULL |
|   28 |    1 |    1 |    731 | 1000.00 | NULL |
|   29 |    2 |    2 |    731 | 2000.00 | NULL |
|   30 |    3 |    4 |    731 | 4000.00 | NULL |
|   31 |    4 |    5 |    731 | 6000.00 | NULL |
|   32 |    5 |    1 |    731 | 2500.00 | NULL |
|   33 |    8 |    2 |    731 | 5000.00 | NULL |
|   34 |    7 |    4 |    731 | 7500.00 | NULL |
|   35 |    9 |    5 |    731 | 1000.00 | NULL |
|   36 |   10 |    1 |    732 | 1000.00 |   10 |
|   37 |   11 |    2 |    732 | 2000.00 |   20 |
|   38 |   12 |    4 |    732 | 4000.00 |   40 |
|   39 |   13 |    5 |    732 | 6000.00 |   60 |
|   40 |   14 |    1 |    732 | 2500.00 |   25 |
|   41 |   15 |    2 |    732 | 5000.00 |   50 |
|   42 |   16 |    4 |    732 | 7500.00 |   75 |
|   43 |   17 |    5 |    732 | 1000.00 |   10 |
|   44 |   18 |    1 |    732 | 1000.00 |   10 |
+------+------+------+-------+---------+------+
44 rows in set (0.00 sec)
```

Note

Only the nine new orders have an order quantity. Older sales data does not.

Summary

In this chapter you learned to extend a data warehouse by adding new columns to both dimension and fact tables. In the next chapter you will look into another type of population, on-demand population, which you likely need to implement in response to the growth of a data warehouse.

Chapter 11
On-Demand Population

You've learned initial population in Chapter 7 and regular population in Chapter 8. There is another type of population, on-demand population, that you need to familiarize yourself with. You apply on-demand population when you need to load source data outside the normal schedule, at the time the source data is available or as needed by the data warehouse. For example, sales promotion source data might be available only when a promotion is being scheduled and is not available otherwise.

The date pre-population discussed in Chapter 6, "Populating the Date Dimension" can be regarded as a type of on-demand population. You pre-populate your data warehouse with dates and when you almost run out of dates, you run the pre-population again.

On-demand population is the topic of this chapter. Here you learn how to enhance the schema and perform on-demand population for the **dw** database.

Enhancing the Schema

In this section I explain on-demand population using a sales promotion scenario. Regular population is not appropriate here as the data loading cannot be scheduled. The following is the content of a CSV flat file that needs to be loaded.

```
PROMOTION CODE,PROMOTION NAME,START DATE,LAST DATE
SO,Special Offer,2007-04-01,2007-04-10
DP,Disk Promotion,2007-05-05,2007-05-20
MS,Month Special,2007-06-01,2007-06-30
MS,Monitor Promotion,2007-07-10,2007-07-15
BS,Back to School,2007-08-10,2007-08-30
```

Note that the source data provides promotion periods, not individual promotion dates. Assuming your user wants to load only new promotions in the future, they don't need promotion history in the data warehouse.

The first thing you need to do is add a new column, **promo_ind** (for promotion indicator) to the **date_dim** table. The new schema after the addition is shown in Figure 11.1.

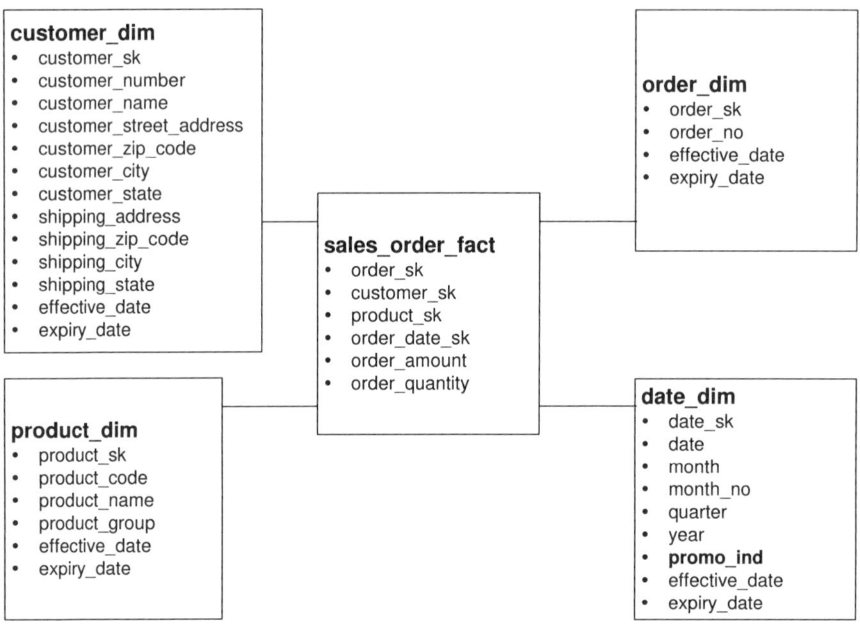

Figure 11.1: The new promo_ind column in date_dim

You use the **promotion_indicator.sql** script in Listing 11.1 to add the **promo_ind** column in the **date_dim** table.

Listing 11.1: Promotion indicator

```
/**********************************************************************/
/*                                                                    */
/* promotion_indicator.sql                                            */
/*                                                                    */
/**********************************************************************/

USE dw;

ALTER TABLE date_dim
```

```
ADD promo_ind CHAR(1) AFTER year
;

/* end of script                                                     */
```

You run the script using this command.

```
mysql> \. c:\mysql\scripts\promotion_indicator.sql
```

After you run the script, you'll see this on the console.

```
Database changed
Query OK, 2132 rows affected (0.45 sec)
Records: 2132  Duplicates: 0  Warnings: 0
```

Using the following SQL statement, query the date dimension to confirm there's no data in the new **promo_ind** column.

```
mysql> select * from date_dim where promo_ind IS NOT NULL;
```

All values of the column must be NULL, as shown here.

```
Empty set (0.01 sec)
```

Performing On-Demand Population

In this section, I show you how to perform on-demand population using a sales promotion as an example. Essentially, what the population does is set the **promo_ind** column in the **date_dim** table to 'Y' if there is a promotion scheduled on a date.

The on-demand population script to be used in this example is presented in Listing 11.2. You run the script after the dates are loaded. In other words, all the dates from the start date to the last date of all promotion schedules must be available in the date dimension.

Listing 11.2: Populating the promotion indicator

```
/**********************************************************************/
/*                                                                    */
/* on_demand.sql
/*                                                                    */
/**********************************************************************/
```

```
USE dw;

TRUNCATE promo_schedule_stg;

LOAD DATA INFILE 'promo_schedule.csv'
INTO TABLE promo_schedule_stg
FIELDS TERMINATED BY ','
OPTIONALLY ENCLOSED BY '"'
LINES TERMINATED BY '\r\n'
IGNORE 1 LINES
( promo_code
, promo_name
, promo_start_date
, promo_last_date )
;

UPDATE
  date_dim a
, promo_schedule_stg b
SET a.promo_ind = 'Y'
WHERE
    a.date >= b.promo_start_date
AND a.date <= b.promo_last_date
;

/* end of script                                                  */
```

The script in Listing 11.2 loads the content of the **promo_schedule.csv** file to a **promo_schedule_stg** table. Therefore, before you can run the script in Listing 11.2, you need to create the **promo_schedule_stg** table. The script in Listing 11.3 can be used to create the table.

> **Note**
> The **promo_schedule.csv** file is discussed in the next section.

Listing 11.3: Creating the promotion staging table

```
/******************************************************************/
/*                                                                */
/* create_promo_schedule_stg.sql                                  */
/*                                                                */
/******************************************************************/

USE dw;

CREATE TABLE promo_schedule_stg (
```

```
  promo_code CHAR(2)
, promo_name CHAR(30)
, promo_start_date DATE
, promo_last_date DATE
)
;

/* end of script                                                    */
```

Run the script in Listing 11.3 using this command.

```
mysql> \. c:\mysql\scripts\create_promo_schedule_stg.sql
```

You'll see the following as the response.

```
Database changed
Query OK, 0 rows affected (0.20 sec)
```

Testing

Before you run the script in Listing 11.2, you need to prepare the following promotion schedule CSV file and save it as **promo_schedule.csv**.

```
PROMOTION CODE,PROMOTION NAME,START DATE,LAST DATE
SO,Special Offer,2007-04-01,2007-04-10
DP,Disk Promotion,2007-05-05,2007-05-20
MS,Month Special,2007-06-01,2007-06-30
MS,Monitor Promotion,2007-07-10,2007-07-15
BS,Back to School,2007-08-10,2007-08-30
```

Note

There are 83 promotion dates in the five promotion periods. The first period has 10 dates (April 1, 2005; April 2, 2005; … April 10, 2005), the second 16 dates (May 5, 2005; May 6, 2005; …May 20, 2005), and so on.

You can then run the **on_demand.sql** script in Listing 11.2 using this command.

```
mysql> \. c:\mysql\scripts\on_demand.sql
```

Here is the response on the MySQL console.

```
Database changed
Query OK, 1 row affected (0.05 sec)

Query OK, 5 rows affected (0.06 sec)
Records: 5  Deleted: 0  Skipped: 0  Warnings: 0

Query OK, 83 rows affected (0.08 sec)
Rows matched: 83  Changed: 83  Warnings: 0
```

You can confirm the results (the promotion indicators are set to 'Y') by querying the promotion dates in the **date_dim** table. For example, a query on the first period should give you ten dates with the Y value on their **promo_ind** columns:

```
mysql> select * from date_dim where date >= '2007-04-01' and
    -> date <= '2007-04-10' \G
```

The result is as follows.

```
*************************** 1. row ***************************
       date_sk: 762
          date: 2007-04-01
    month_name: April
         month: 4
       quarter: 2
          year: 2007
     promo_ind: Y
effective_date: 0000-00-00
   expiry_date: 9999-12-31
*************************** 2. row ***************************
       date_sk: 763
          date: 2007-04-02
    month_name: April
         month: 4
       quarter: 2
          year: 2007
     promo_ind: Y
effective_date: 0000-00-00
   expiry_date: 9999-12-31
*************************** 3. row ***************************
       date_sk: 764
          date: 2007-04-03
    month_name: April
         month: 4
       quarter: 2
          year: 2007
```

```
     promo_ind: Y
effective_date: 0000-00-00
   expiry_date: 9999-12-31
*************************** 4. row ***************************
       date_sk: 765
          date: 2007-04-04
    month_name: April
         month: 4
       quarter: 2
          year: 2007
     promo_ind: Y
effective_date: 0000-00-00
   expiry_date: 9999-12-31
*************************** 5. row ***************************
       date_sk: 766
          date: 2007-04-05
    month_name: April
         month: 4
       quarter: 2
          year: 2007
     promo_ind: Y
effective_date: 0000-00-00
   expiry_date: 9999-12-31
*************************** 6. row ***************************
       date_sk: 767
          date: 2007-04-06
    month_name: April
         month: 4
       quarter: 2
          year: 2007
     promo_ind: Y
effective_date: 0000-00-00
   expiry_date: 9999-12-31
*************************** 7. row ***************************
       date_sk: 768
          date: 2007-04-07
    month_name: April
         month: 4
       quarter: 2
          year: 2007
     promo_ind: Y
effective_date: 0000-00-00
   expiry_date: 9999-12-31
*************************** 8. row ***************************
       date_sk: 769
```

```
          date: 2007-04-08
    month_name: April
         month: 4
       quarter: 2
          year: 2007
     promo_ind: Y
effective_date: 0000-00-00
   expiry_date: 9999-12-31
*************************** 9. row ***************************
       date_sk: 770
          date: 2007-04-09
    month_name: April
         month: 4
       quarter: 2
          year: 2007
     promo_ind: Y
effective_date: 0000-00-00
   expiry_date: 9999-12-31
*************************** 10. row ***************************
       date_sk: 771
          date: 2007-04-10
    month_name: April
         month: 4
       quarter: 2
          year: 2007
     promo_ind: Y
effective_date: 0000-00-00
   expiry_date: 9999-12-31
10 rows in set (0.01 sec)
```

Summary

In this chapter you learned the on-demand population technique that you can use to supplement regular population. Some extensions to an existing data warehouse that your user wants might not require adding anything new; you just need to re-use what is already implemented. In the next chapter, you will learn how to re-use a dimension.

Chapter 12
Subset Dimensions

Some users never need the most detailed data. For example, rather than requiring dates, it is more likely they want records for a certain month. Rather than the national sales data, they may be more interested in the data for a certain state. These special dimensions contain selected rows from the detailed dimensions, hence the name subset dimensions. Since subset dimensions are smaller than detailed dimensions, they are easier to use and provide faster query response.

In this chapter, you will prepare two special dimensions that you derive from existing dimensions: the month roll-up dimension (a subset of the date dimension) and the Pennsylvania state customer dimension (a subset of the customer dimension).

Month Roll-up Dimension

In this section I explain the month roll-up dimension population process, including its testing.

The script in Listing 12.1 creates the month roll-up dimension and initially populates the months from the date dimension. Note that the **promo_ind** column is not included. This column is not applicable to the month level, as you can have more than one promotion in a month. Rather, the promotion applies to the date level.

Listing 12.1: Implementing the month roll-up dimension

```
/**********************************************************************/
/*                                                                    */
/* month_rollup_dim.sql                                               */
/*                                                                    */
/**********************************************************************/
```

```
USE dw;

CREATE TABLE month_dim
( month_sk INT NOT NULL AUTO_INCREMENT PRIMARY KEY
, month_name CHAR(9)
, month INT(2)
, quarter INT(1)
, year INT(4)
, effective_date DATE
, expiry_date DATE )
;

INSERT INTO month_dim
SELECT DISTINCT
  NULL
, month_name
, month
, quarter
, year
, effective_date
, expiry_date
FROM date_dim
;

/* end of script                                                  */
```

The script in Listing 12.1 creates the **month_dim** table and inserts distinct months from the **date_dim** table, which contains dates from March 1, 2005 to December 31, 2010. Therefore, when you populate the **month_dim** table by running the script in Listing 12.1, the table gets 70 months (from March 2005 to December 2010).

Run the script as follows:

```
mysql> \. c:\mysql\scripts\month_rollup_dim.sql
```

You will see the following on your console.

```
Database changed
Query OK, 0 rows affected (0.14 sec)

Query OK, 70 rows affected (0.07 sec)
Records: 70  Duplicates: 0  Warnings: 0

mysql>
```

Now query the **month_dim** table to confirm correct population:

```
mysql> select month_sk msk, month_name, month, quarter q, year,
    -> effective_date efdate, expiry_date exdate
    -> from month_dim;
```

Here is the result of the query.

```
+-----+------------+-------+------+------+------------+------------+
| msk | month_name | month | q    | year | efdate     | exdate     |
+-----+------------+-------+------+------+------------+------------+
|   1 | March      |     3 |    1 | 2005 | 0000-00-00 | 9999-12-31 |
|   2 | April      |     4 |    2 | 2005 | 0000-00-00 | 9999-12-31 |
|   3 | May        |     5 |    2 | 2005 | 0000-00-00 | 9999-12-31 |
|   4 | June       |     6 |    2 | 2005 | 0000-00-00 | 9999-12-31 |
|   5 | July       |     7 |    3 | 2005 | 0000-00-00 | 9999-12-31 |
|   6 | August     |     8 |    3 | 2005 | 0000-00-00 | 9999-12-31 |
|   7 | September  |     9 |    3 | 2005 | 0000-00-00 | 9999-12-31 |
|   8 | October    |    10 |    4 | 2005 | 0000-00-00 | 9999-12-31 |
|   9 | November   |    11 |    4 | 2005 | 0000-00-00 | 9999-12-31 |
|  10 | December   |    12 |    4 | 2005 | 0000-00-00 | 9999-12-31 |
|  11 | January    |     1 |    1 | 2006 | 0000-00-00 | 9999-12-31 |
|  12 | February   |     2 |    1 | 2006 | 0000-00-00 | 9999-12-31 |
|  13 | March      |     3 |    1 | 2006 | 0000-00-00 | 9999-12-31 |
|  14 | April      |     4 |    2 | 2006 | 0000-00-00 | 9999-12-31 |
|  15 | May        |     5 |    2 | 2006 | 0000-00-00 | 9999-12-31 |
|  16 | June       |     6 |    2 | 2006 | 0000-00-00 | 9999-12-31 |
|  17 | July       |     7 |    3 | 2006 | 0000-00-00 | 9999-12-31 |
|  18 | August     |     8 |    3 | 2006 | 0000-00-00 | 9999-12-31 |
|  19 | September  |     9 |    3 | 2006 | 0000-00-00 | 9999-12-31 |
|  20 | October    |    10 |    4 | 2006 | 0000-00-00 | 9999-12-31 |
|  21 | November   |    11 |    4 | 2006 | 0000-00-00 | 9999-12-31 |
|  22 | December   |    12 |    4 | 2006 | 0000-00-00 | 9999-12-31 |
|  23 | January    |     1 |    1 | 2007 | 0000-00-00 | 9999-12-31 |
|  24 | February   |     2 |    1 | 2007 | 0000-00-00 | 9999-12-31 |
|  25 | March      |     3 |    1 | 2007 | 0000-00-00 | 9999-12-31 |
|  26 | April      |     4 |    2 | 2007 | 0000-00-00 | 9999-12-31 |
|  27 | May        |     5 |    2 | 2007 | 0000-00-00 | 9999-12-31 |
|  28 | June       |     6 |    2 | 2007 | 0000-00-00 | 9999-12-31 |
|  29 | July       |     7 |    3 | 2007 | 0000-00-00 | 9999-12-31 |
|  30 | August     |     8 |    3 | 2007 | 0000-00-00 | 9999-12-31 |
|  31 | September  |     9 |    3 | 2007 | 0000-00-00 | 9999-12-31 |
|  32 | October    |    10 |    4 | 2007 | 0000-00-00 | 9999-12-31 |
|  33 | November   |    11 |    4 | 2007 | 0000-00-00 | 9999-12-31 |
|  34 | December   |    12 |    4 | 2007 | 0000-00-00 | 9999-12-31 |
```

```
| 35 | January   |   1 |    1 | 2008 | 0000-00-00 | 9999-12-31 |
| 36 | February  |   2 |    1 | 2008 | 0000-00-00 | 9999-12-31 |
| 37 | March     |   3 |    1 | 2008 | 0000-00-00 | 9999-12-31 |
| 38 | April     |   4 |    2 | 2008 | 0000-00-00 | 9999-12-31 |
| 39 | May       |   5 |    2 | 2008 | 0000-00-00 | 9999-12-31 |
| 40 | June      |   6 |    2 | 2008 | 0000-00-00 | 9999-12-31 |
| 41 | July      |   7 |    3 | 2008 | 0000-00-00 | 9999-12-31 |
| 42 | August    |   8 |    3 | 2008 | 0000-00-00 | 9999-12-31 |
| 43 | September |   9 |    3 | 2008 | 0000-00-00 | 9999-12-31 |
| 44 | October   |  10 |    4 | 2008 | 0000-00-00 | 9999-12-31 |
| 45 | November  |  11 |    4 | 2008 | 0000-00-00 | 9999-12-31 |
| 46 | December  |  12 |    4 | 2008 | 0000-00-00 | 9999-12-31 |
| 47 | January   |   1 |    1 | 2009 | 0000-00-00 | 9999-12-31 |
| 48 | February  |   2 |    1 | 2009 | 0000-00-00 | 9999-12-31 |
| 49 | March     |   3 |    1 | 2009 | 0000-00-00 | 9999-12-31 |
| 50 | April     |   4 |    2 | 2009 | 0000-00-00 | 9999-12-31 |
| 51 | May       |   5 |    2 | 2009 | 0000-00-00 | 9999-12-31 |
| 52 | June      |   6 |    2 | 2009 | 0000-00-00 | 9999-12-31 |
| 53 | July      |   7 |    3 | 2009 | 0000-00-00 | 9999-12-31 |
| 54 | August    |   8 |    3 | 2009 | 0000-00-00 | 9999-12-31 |
| 55 | September |   9 |    3 | 2009 | 0000-00-00 | 9999-12-31 |
| 56 | October   |  10 |    4 | 2009 | 0000-00-00 | 9999-12-31 |
| 57 | November  |  11 |    4 | 2009 | 0000-00-00 | 9999-12-31 |
| 58 | December  |  12 |    4 | 2009 | 0000-00-00 | 9999-12-31 |
| 59 | January   |   1 |    1 | 2010 | 0000-00-00 | 9999-12-31 |
| 60 | February  |   2 |    1 | 2010 | 0000-00-00 | 9999-12-31 |
| 61 | March     |   3 |    1 | 2010 | 0000-00-00 | 9999-12-31 |
| 62 | April     |   4 |    2 | 2010 | 0000-00-00 | 9999-12-31 |
| 63 | May       |   5 |    2 | 2010 | 0000-00-00 | 9999-12-31 |
| 64 | June      |   6 |    2 | 2010 | 0000-00-00 | 9999-12-31 |
| 65 | July      |   7 |    3 | 2010 | 0000-00-00 | 9999-12-31 |
| 66 | August    |   8 |    3 | 2010 | 0000-00-00 | 9999-12-31 |
| 67 | September |   9 |    3 | 2010 | 0000-00-00 | 9999-12-31 |
| 68 | October   |  10 |    4 | 2010 | 0000-00-00 | 9999-12-31 |
| 69 | November  |  11 |    4 | 2010 | 0000-00-00 | 9999-12-31 |
| 70 | December  |  12 |    4 | 2010 | 0000-00-00 | 9999-12-31 |
+----+-----------+-----+------+------+------------+------------+
70 rows in set (0.00 sec)
```

To have the month dimension populated regularly from the date dimension, you embed its population in the date dimension population script. You need to update the date pre-population stored procedure discussed in Chapter 6. The revised stored procedure is shown in Listing 12.2. The change is printed in bold. The revised script now populates the month roll-up dimension whenever it adds a date entry and its month is not in the month dimension.

Listing 12.2: The revised date pre-population script

```
/*******************************************************************/
/*                                                                 */
/* pre_populate_date_12.sql                                        */
/*                                                                 */
/*******************************************************************/

USE dw;

DELIMITER // ;

DROP PROCEDURE IF EXISTS pre_populate_date //

CREATE PROCEDURE pre_populate_date (IN start_dt DATE, IN end_dt
       DATE)
BEGIN
       WHILE start_dt <= end_dt DO
              INSERT INTO date_dim(
                date_sk
              , date
              , month_name
              , month
              , quarter
              , year
              , effective_date
              , expiry_date
              )
              VALUES(
                NULL
              , start_dt
              , MONTHNAME(start_dt)
              , MONTH(start_dt)
              , QUARTER(start_dt)
              , YEAR(start_dt)
              , '0000-00-00'
              , '9999-12-31'
       )
              ;
              SET start_dt = ADDDATE(start_dt, 1);
       END WHILE;

INSERT INTO month_dim
SELECT DISTINCT
  NULL
```

```
, month_name
, month
, quarter
, year
, effective_date
, expiry_date
FROM date_dim
WHERE CONCAT(month, year) NOT IN
(SELECT CONCAT(month, year) FROM month_dim)
;

END
//

DELIMITER ; //

/* end of script                                                   */
```

Recompile the stored procedure by invoking the script in Listing 12.2 using this command.

```
mysql> \. c:\mysql\scripts\pre_populate_date_12.sql
```

Here is the response you'll see on your console.

```
Database changed
Query OK, 0 rows affected (0.22 sec)

Query OK, 0 rows affected (0.04 sec)
```

To test the revised date pre-population, run the stored procedure to add the dates from January 1, 2011 to December 31, 2011 using this command.

```
mysql> call pre_populate_date('2011-01-01', '2011-12-31');
```

MySQL will indicate that there are twelve records affected.

```
Query OK, 12 rows affected (23.07 sec)
```

To confirm the 12 months were loaded correctly, query the **month_dim** table using this statement.

```
mysql> select * from month_dim where year = 2011 \G
```

Here is the query result.

```
*************************** 1. row ***************************
      month_sk: 71
```

```
     month_name: January
          month: 1
        quarter: 1
           year: 2011
 effective_date: 0000-00-00
    expiry_date: 9999-12-31
*************************** 2. row ***************************
       month_sk: 72
     month_name: February
          month: 2
        quarter: 1
           year: 2011
 effective_date: 0000-00-00
    expiry_date: 9999-12-31
*************************** 3. row ***************************
       month_sk: 73
     month_name: March
          month: 3
        quarter: 1
           year: 2011
 effective_date: 0000-00-00
    expiry_date: 9999-12-31
*************************** 4. row ***************************
       month_sk: 74
     month_name: April
          month: 4
        quarter: 2
           year: 2011
 effective_date: 0000-00-00
    expiry_date: 9999-12-31
*************************** 5. row ***************************
       month_sk: 75
     month_name: May
          month: 5
        quarter: 2
           year: 2011
 effective_date: 0000-00-00
    expiry_date: 9999-12-31
*************************** 6. row ***************************
       month_sk: 76
     month_name: June
          month: 6
        quarter: 2
           year: 2011
 effective_date: 0000-00-00
```

```
   expiry_date: 9999-12-31
************************** 7. row **************************
      month_sk: 77
    month_name: July
         month: 7
       quarter: 3
          year: 2011
effective_date: 0000-00-00
   expiry_date: 9999-12-31
************************** 8. row **************************
      month_sk: 78
    month_name: August
         month: 8
       quarter: 3
          year: 2011
effective_date: 0000-00-00
   expiry_date: 9999-12-31
************************** 9. row **************************
      month_sk: 79
    month_name: September
         month: 9
       quarter: 3
          year: 2011
effective_date: 0000-00-00
   expiry_date: 9999-12-31
************************** 10. row **************************
      month_sk: 80
    month_name: October
         month: 10
       quarter: 4
          year: 2011
effective_date: 0000-00-00
   expiry_date: 9999-12-31
************************** 11. row **************************
      month_sk: 81
    month_name: November
         month: 11
       quarter: 4
          year: 2011
effective_date: 0000-00-00
   expiry_date: 9999-12-31
************************** 12. row **************************
      month_sk: 82
    month_name: December
         month: 12
       quarter: 4
```

```
         year: 2011
effective_date: 0000-00-00
   expiry_date: 9999-12-31
12 rows in set (0.00 sec)
```

Pennsylvania Customer Dimension

In this section I use the Pennsylvania customer subset dimension to explain the second type of subset dimension. I also show you how to test the subset dimension.

While a roll-up dimension contains all higher level data of its base dimension, a specific subset dimension selects a specific set of its base dimension. The script in listing 12.3 creates the table and populates the Pennsylvania (PA) customer subset dimension.

Note that there are two things that differentiates the PA customer subset dimension from the month subset dimension:

- The **pa_customer_dim** table has exactly the same columns as the **customer_dim**. The **month_dim** does not have dates columns in the **date_dim** table.
- The **pa_customer_dim** table's surrogate keys are the surrogate keys of the customer dimension. The surrogate keys of the month dimension belong to the **month_dim** table and do not come from the date dimension.

Listing 12.3: PA customers

```
/******************************************************************/
/*                                                                */
/* pa_customer.sql                                                */
/*                                                                */
/******************************************************************/

USE dw;

CREATE TABLE pa_customer_dim
( customer_sk INT NOT NULL AUTO_INCREMENT PRIMARY KEY
, customer_number INT
, customer_name CHAR(50)
```

```
, customer_street_address CHAR(50)
, customer_zip_code INT(5)
, customer_city CHAR(30)
, customer_state CHAR(2)
, shipping_address CHAR(50)
, shipping_zip_code INT(5)
, shipping_city CHAR(30)
, shipping_state CHAR(2)
, effective_date DATE
, expiry_date DATE )
;

INSERT INTO pa_customer_dim
SELECT
  customer_sk
, customer_number
, customer_name
, customer_street_address
, customer_zip_code
, customer_city
, customer_state
, shipping_address
, shipping_zip_code
, shipping_city
, shipping_state
, effective_date
, expiry_date
FROM customer_dim
WHERE customer_state = 'PA'
;

/* end of script                                                 */
```

To test the PA subset dimension script, you first need to add three customers who reside in Ohio using the script in Listing 12.4.

Listing 12.4: Non-PA customers

```
/******************************************************************/
/*                                                                */
/* non_pa_customer.sql                                            */
/*                                                                */
/******************************************************************/

/* default to dw                                                  */
```

```
USE dw;

INSERT INTO customer_dim
( customer_sk
, customer_number
, customer_name
, customer_street_address
, customer_zip_code
, customer_city
, customer_state
, shipping_address
, shipping_zip_code
, shipping_city
, shipping_state
, effective_date
, expiry_date )
VALUES
  (NULL, 10, 'Bigger Customers', '7777 Ridge Rd.', '44102',
       'Cleveland', 'OH', '7777 Ridge Rd.', '44102', 'Cleveland',
       'OH', CURRENT_DATE, '9999-12-31')
, (NULL, 11, 'Smaller Stores', '8888 Jennings Fwy.', '44102',
       'Cleveland', 'OH', '8888 Jennings Fwy.', '44102',
       'Cleveland', 'OH', CURRENT_DATE, '9999-12-31')
, (NULL, 12, 'Small-Medium Retailers', '9999 Memphis Ave.', '44102',
       'Cleveland', 'OH', '9999 Memphis Ave.', '44102', 'Cleveland',
       'OH', CURRENT_DATE, '9999-12-31')
;

/* end of script                                                   */
```

Run the script in Listing 12.4 using this command.

```
mysql> \. c:\mysql\scripts\non_pa_customer.sql
```

The response on your MySQL console should be

```
Database changed
Query OK, 3 rows affected (0.86 sec)
Records: 3  Duplicates: 0  Warnings: 0
```

Now, you're ready to run the **pa_customer.sql** script in Listing 12.3. Before you do that, make sure your MySQL date is still March 2, 2007.

You run the **pa_customer.sql** script by using this command.

```
mysql> \. c:\mysql\scripts\pa_customer.sql
```

Here is what you should see on your console.

```
Database changed
Query OK, 0 rows affected (0.20 sec)

Query OK, 18 rows affected (0.08 sec)
Records: 18  Duplicates: 0  Warnings: 0
```

To confirm the three OH customers are loaded correctly, query the **customer_dim** table:

```
mysql> select customer_name, customer_state, effective_date
    -> from customer_dim;
```

You should see the following on your console.

```
+-------------------------+----------------+----------------+
| customer_name           | customer_state | effective_date |
+-------------------------+----------------+----------------+
| Really Large Customers  | PA             | 2005-03-01     |
| Small Stores            | PA             | 2005-03-01     |
| Medium Retailers        | PA             | 2005-03-01     |
| Good Companies          | PA             | 2005-03-01     |
| Wonderful Shops         | PA             | 2005-03-01     |
| Extremely Loyal Clients | PA             | 2005-03-01     |
| Distinguished Agencies  | PA             | 2005-03-01     |
| Extremely Loyal Clients | PA             | 2007-03-01     |
| Subsidiaries            | PA             | 2007-03-01     |
| Really Large Customers  | PA             | 2007-03-02     |
| Small Stores            | PA             | 2007-03-02     |
| Medium Retailers        | PA             | 2007-03-02     |
| Good Companies          | PA             | 2007-03-02     |
| Wonderful Shops         | PA             | 2007-03-02     |
| Extremely Loyal Clients | PA             | 2007-03-02     |
| Distinguished Agencies  | PA             | 2007-03-02     |
| Subsidiaries            | PA             | 2007-03-02     |
| Online Distributors     | PA             | 2007-03-02     |
| Bigger Customers        | OH             | 2007-03-02     |
| Smaller Stores          | OH             | 2007-03-02     |
| Small-Medium Retailers  | OH             | 2007-03-02     |
+-------------------------+----------------+----------------+
21 rows in set (0.00 sec)
```

Now, query the **pa_customer_dim** table to confirm only PA customers are in the PA customer dimension table.

```
mysql> select customer_name, customer_state, effective_date
```

```
    -> from pa_customer_dim;
```

The result should be as follows.

```
+-------------------------+----------------+----------------+
| customer_name           | customer_state | effective_date |
+-------------------------+----------------+----------------+
| Really Large Customers  | PA             | 2004-01-01     |
| Small Stores            | PA             | 2004-01-01     |
| Medium Retailers        | PA             | 2004-01-01     |
| Good Companies          | PA             | 2004-01-01     |
| Wonderful Shops         | PA             | 2004-01-01     |
| Extremely Loyal Clients | PA             | 2004-01-01     |
| Distinguished Agencies  | PA             | 2004-01-01     |
| Extremely Loyal Clients | PA             | 2005-11-01     |
| Subsidiaries            | PA             | 2005-11-01     |
| Really Large Customers  | PA             | 2005-11-03     |
| Small Stores            | PA             | 2005-11-03     |
| Medium Retailers        | PA             | 2005-11-03     |
| Good Companies          | PA             | 2005-11-03     |
| Wonderful Shops         | PA             | 2005-11-03     |
| Extremely Loyal Clients | PA             | 2005-11-03     |
| Distinguished Agencies  | PA             | 2005-11-03     |
| Subsidiaries            | PA             | 2005-11-03     |
| Online Distributors     | PA             | 2005-11-03     |
+-------------------------+----------------+----------------+
18 rows in set (0.00 sec)
```

As you can see, only PA customers got into the table. The recently added OH customers are not there.

Revising the Regular Population

To populate the PA customer dimension whenever a new PA customer is inserted into the customer dimension, you need to merge the PA customer subset dimension population into the data warehouse regular population. The revised regular population script is presented in Listing 12.5. The change (addition) is printed in bold. Note that the script rebuilds (truncates, then adds all PA customers) the PA customer subset dimension every time you run the daily regular population script.

Listing 12.5: The revised daily DW regular population

```
/*****************************************************************/
/*                                                               */
/* dw_regular_12.sql                                             */
/*                                                               */
/*****************************************************************/

USE dw;

/* CUSTOMER_DIM POPULATION                                       */

TRUNCATE customer_stg;

LOAD DATA INFILE 'customer.csv'
INTO TABLE customer_stg
FIELDS TERMINATED BY ','
OPTIONALLY ENCLOSED BY '"'
LINES TERMINATED BY '\r\n'
IGNORE 1 LINES
( customer_number
, customer_name
, customer_street_address
, customer_zip_code
, customer_city
, customer_state
, shipping_address
, shipping_zip_code
, shipping_city
, shipping_state )
;

/* SCD 2 ON ADDRESSES                                            */

UPDATE
  customer_dim a
, customer_stg b
SET
  a.expiry_date = SUBDATE(CURRENT_DATE, 1)
WHERE
  a.customer_number = b.customer_number
AND (   a.customer_street_address <> b.customer_street_address
     OR a.customer_city <> b.customer_city
     OR a.customer_zip_code <> b.customer_zip_code
     OR a.customer_state <> b.customer_state
     OR a.shipping_address <> b.shipping_address
```

```
     OR a.shipping_city <> b.shipping_city
     OR a.shipping_zip_code <> b.shipping_zip_code
     OR a.shipping_state <> b.shipping_state
     OR a.shipping_address IS NULL
     OR a.shipping_city IS NULL
     OR a.shipping_zip_code IS NULL
     OR a.shipping_state IS NULL)
AND expiry_date = '9999-12-31'
;

INSERT INTO customer_dim
SELECT
  NULL
, b.customer_number
, b.customer_name
, b.customer_street_address
, b.customer_zip_code
, b.customer_city
, b.customer_state
, b.shipping_address
, b.shipping_zip_code
, b.shipping_city
, b.shipping_state
, CURRENT_DATE
, '9999-12-31'
FROM
  customer_dim a
, customer_stg b
WHERE
    a.customer_number = b.customer_number
AND (   a.customer_street_address <> b.customer_street_address
     OR a.customer_city <> b.customer_city
     OR a.customer_zip_code <> b.customer_zip_code
     OR a.customer_state <> b.customer_state
     OR a.shipping_address <> b.shipping_address
     OR a.shipping_city <> b.shipping_city
     OR a.shipping_zip_code <> b.shipping_zip_code
     OR a.shipping_state <> b.shipping_state
     OR a.shipping_address IS NULL
     OR a.shipping_city IS NULL
     OR a.shipping_zip_code IS NULL
     OR a.shipping_state IS NULL)
AND EXISTS (
SELECT *
FROM customer_dim x
```

```
WHERE b.customer_number = x.customer_number
AND a.expiry_date = SUBDATE(CURRENT_DATE, 1))
AND NOT EXISTS (
SELECT *
FROM customer_dim y
WHERE     b.customer_number = y.customer_number
      AND y.expiry_date = '9999-12-31')
;

/* END OF SCD 2                                                    */

/* SCD 1 ON NAME                                                   */

UPDATE customer_dim a, customer_stg b
SET a.customer_name = b.customer_name
WHERE     a.customer_number = b.customer_number
      AND a.expiry_date = '9999-12-31'
      AND a.customer_name <> b.customer_name
;

/* ADD NEW CUSTOMER                                                */

INSERT INTO customer_dim
SELECT
  NULL
, customer_number
, customer_name
, customer_street_address
, customer_zip_code
, customer_city
, customer_state
, shipping_address
, shipping_zip_code
, shipping_city
, shipping_state
, CURRENT_DATE
, '9999-12-31'
FROM customer_stg
WHERE customer_number NOT IN(
SELECT a.customer_number
FROM
  customer_dim a
, customer_stg b
WHERE b.customer_number = a.customer_number )
;
```

```
/* RE-BUILD PA CUSTOMER DIMENSION                                  */

TRUNCATE pa_customer_dim;

INSERT INTO pa_customer_dim
SELECT
  customer_sk
, customer_number
, customer_name
, customer_street_address
, customer_zip_code
, customer_city
, customer_state
, shipping_address
, shipping_zip_code
, shipping_city
, shipping_state
, effective_date
, expiry_date
FROM customer_dim
WHERE customer_state = 'PA'
;
/* END OF CUSTOMER_DIM POPULATION                                  */

/* product dimension loading                                       */

TRUNCATE product_stg
;

LOAD DATA INFILE 'product.txt'
INTO TABLE product_stg
FIELDS TERMINATED BY ''
OPTIONALLY ENCLOSED BY ''
LINES TERMINATED BY '\r\n'
IGNORE 1 LINES
( product_code
, product_name
, product_category )
;

/* PRODUCT_DIM POPULATION                                          */

/* SCD2 ON PRODUCT NAME AND GROUP                                  */

UPDATE
```

```
  product_dim a
, product_stg b
SET
  expiry_date = SUBDATE(CURRENT_DATE, 1)
WHERE
    a.product_code = b.product_code
AND (   a.product_name <> b.product_name
     OR a.product_category <> b.product_category )
     AND expiry_date = '9999-12-31'
;

INSERT INTO product_dim
SELECT
  NULL
, b.product_code
, b.product_name
, b.product_category
, CURRENT_DATE
, '9999-12-31'
FROM
  product_dim a
, product_stg b
WHERE
    a.product_code = b.product_code
AND (   a.product_name <> b.product_name
     OR a.product_category <> b.product_category )
AND EXISTS (
SELECT *
FROM product_dim x
WHERE     b.product_code = x.product_code
      AND a.expiry_date = SUBDATE(CURRENT_DATE, 1))
AND NOT EXISTS (
SELECT *
FROM product_dim y
WHERE    b.product_code = y.product_code
     AND y.expiry_date = '9999-12-31')
;

/* END OF SCD 2                                                  */

/* ADD NEW PRODUCT                                               */

INSERT INTO product_dim
SELECT
  NULL
, product_code
```

```
, product_name
, product_category
, CURRENT_DATE
, '9999-12-31'
FROM product_stg
WHERE product_code NOT IN(
SELECT y.product_code
FROM product_dim x, product_stg y
WHERE x.product_code = y.product_code )
;

/* END OF PRODUCT_DIM POPULATION                                    */

/* ORDER_DIM POPULATION                                             */

INSERT INTO order_dim (
  order_sk
, order_number
, effective_date
, expiry_date
)
SELECT
  NULL
, order_number
, order_date
, '9999-12-31'
FROM source.sales_order
WHERE entry_date = CURRENT_DATE
;

/* END OF ORDER_DIM POPULATION                                      */

/* SALES_ORDER_FACT POPULATION                                      */

INSERT INTO sales_order_fact
SELECT
  order_sk
, customer_sk
, product_sk
, date_sk
, order_amount
, order_quantity
FROM
  source.sales_order a
, order_dim b
```

```
, customer_dim c
, product_dim d
, date_dim e
WHERE
    a.order_number = b.order_number
AND a.customer_number = c.customer_number
AND a.order_date >= c.effective_date
AND a.order_date <= c.expiry_date
AND a.product_code = d.product_code
AND a.order_date >= d.effective_date
AND a.order_date <= d.expiry_date
AND a.order_date = e.date
AND a.entry_date = CURRENT_DATE
;

/* end of script                                                  */
```

Testing the Revised Regular Population

Now you can test the script in Listing 12.5. Before you do this, add some customer data by running the script in Listing 12.6 to add one PA customer and one OH customer into the customer dimension.

Listing 12.6: Adding two customers

```
/******************************************************************/
/*                                                                */
/* two_more_customers.sql                                         */
/*                                                                */
/******************************************************************/

/* default to dw                                                  */

USE dw;

INSERT INTO customer_dim
( customer_sk
, customer_number
, customer_name
, customer_street_address
, customer_zip_code
, customer_city
, customer_state
, shipping_address
```

```
, shipping_zip_code
, shipping_city
, shipping_state
, effective_date
, expiry_date )
VALUES
  (NULL, 13, 'PA Customer', '1111 Louise Dr.', '17050',
       'Mechanicsburg', 'PA', '1111 Louise Dr.', '17050',
       'Mechanicsburg', 'PA', CURRENT_DATE, '9999-12-31')
, (NULL, 14, 'OH Customer', '6666 Ridge Rd.', '44102',
       'Cleveland', 'OH', '6666 Ridge Rd.', '44102',
       'Cleveland', 'OH', CURRENT_DATE, '9999-12-31')
;

/* end of script                                                  */
```

Now run the script in Listing 12.6.

```
mysql> \. c:\mysql\scripts\two_more_customers.sql
```

MySQL should indicate that there are two rows affected.

```
Database changed
Query OK, 2 rows affected (0.06 sec)
Records: 2  Duplicates: 0  Warnings: 0
```

Now change your MySQL date to March 3, 2007 so that old data will not get re-loaded and run the **dw_regular_12.sql** script by issuing this command.

```
mysql> \. c:\mysql\scripts\dw_regular_12.sql
```

You should see the following response on your console.

```
Database changed
Query OK, 9 rows affected (0.15 sec)

Query OK, 9 rows affected (0.14 sec)
Records: 9  Deleted: 0  Skipped: 0  Warnings: 0

Query OK, 0 rows affected (0.05 sec)
Rows matched: 0  Changed: 0  Warnings: 0

Query OK, 0 rows affected (0.01 sec)
Records: 0  Duplicates: 0  Warnings: 0

Query OK, 0 rows affected (0.00 sec)
```

```
Rows matched: 0  Changed: 0  Warnings: 0

Query OK, 0 rows affected (0.00 sec)
Records: 0  Duplicates: 0  Warnings: 0

Query OK, 18 rows affected (0.04 sec)

Query OK, 19 rows affected (0.06 sec)
Records: 19  Duplicates: 0  Warnings: 0

Query OK, 4 rows affected (0.09 sec)

Query OK, 4 rows affected (0.07 sec)
Records: 4  Deleted: 0  Skipped: 0  Warnings: 0

Query OK, 0 rows affected (0.06 sec)
Rows matched: 0  Changed: 0  Warnings: 0

Query OK, 0 rows affected (0.00 sec)
Records: 0  Duplicates: 0  Warnings: 0

Query OK, 0 rows affected (0.00 sec)
Records: 0  Duplicates: 0  Warnings: 0

Query OK, 0 rows affected (0.15 sec)
Records: 0  Duplicates: 0  Warnings: 0

Query OK, 0 rows affected (0.17 sec)
Records: 0  Duplicates: 0  Warnings: 0
```

Now query the **pa_customer_dim** table using this statement. You will see that only the new PA customer was inserted into the table.

```
mysql> select customer_name, customer_state, effective_date
    -> from pa_customer_dim;
```

Here is the query result.

```
+-------------------------+----------------+----------------+
| customer_name           | customer_state | effective_date |
+-------------------------+----------------+----------------+
| Really Large Customers  | PA             | 2005-03-01     |
| Small Stores            | PA             | 2005-03-01     |
| Medium Retailers        | PA             | 2005-03-01     |
```

```
| Good Companies          | PA              | 2005-03-01      |
| Wonderful Shops         | PA              | 2005-03-01      |
| Extremely Loyal Clients | PA              | 2005-03-01      |
| Distinguished Agencies  | PA              | 2005-03-01      |
| Extremely Loyal Clients | PA              | 2007-03-01      |
| Subsidiaries            | PA              | 2007-03-01      |
| Really Large Customers  | PA              | 2007-03-02      |
| Small Stores            | PA              | 2007-03-02      |
| Medium Retailers        | PA              | 2007-03-02      |
| Good Companies          | PA              | 2007-03-02      |
| Wonderful Shops         | PA              | 2007-03-02      |
| Extremely Loyal Clients | PA              | 2007-03-02      |
| Distinguished Agencies  | PA              | 2007-03-02      |
| Subsidiaries            | PA              | 2007-03-02      |
| Online Distributors     | PA              | 2007-03-02      |
| PA Customer             | PA              | 2007-03-03      |
+-------------------------+-----------------+-----------------+
19 rows in set (0.00 sec)
```

Summary

In this chapter you learned two types of subset dimensions. The month subset dimension is an example of a roll-up dimension, which is a higher level dimension populated from its more detailed base dimension. The PA customer is a specific subset dimension; populated from its base dimension by selecting PA customers only.

In the next chapter, you learn another technique of reusing an existing dimension, called role-playing dimension

Chapter 13
Dimension Role Playing

This chapter teaches you dimension role-playing, a technique you use when a fact needs a dimension more than once. For example, if the sales order fact has more than one date, say an order date and a request delivery date, you need to use the date dimension more than once.

In this chapter you also learn two types of dimension role playing implementations, table alias and database view. Both types use MySQL functions. The table alias type uses the dimension more than once in an SQL statement by assigning an alias for each use. As for the database view type, you create as many views as the number of roles you need the dimension on the fact.

Adding Request Delivery Dates

In this section I show you how to add a request delivery date, revise the data warehouse regular population, and test the revised regular population script. This preparation is for showing the implementation of date dimension role-playing in the next section.

The first thing you need to do is add a **request_delivery_date** column to the **sales_order_fact** table. The schema now looks like that in Figure 13.1.

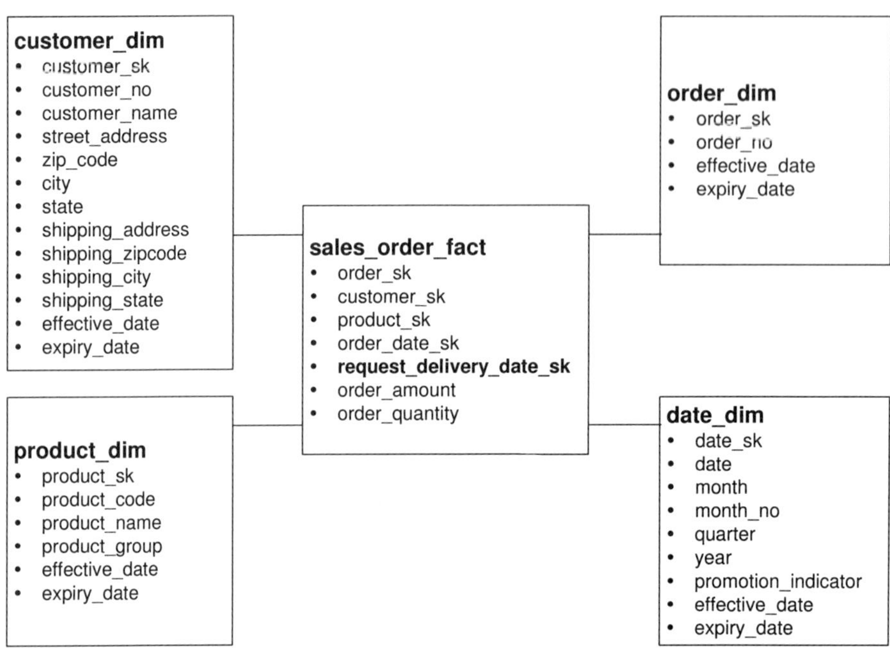

Figure 13.1: Adding request_delivery_date to sales_order_fact

You can use the script in Listing 13.1 to add the **request_delivery_date** column.

Listing 13.1: Adding the request_delivery_date_sk column

```
/**********************************************************************/
/*                                                                    */
/* request_delivery_date_sk.sql                                       */
/*                                                                    */
/**********************************************************************/

USE dw;

ALTER TABLE sales_order_fact
ADD request_delivery_date_sk INT AFTER order_date_sk
;

/* end of script                                                      */
```

You run the script in Listing 13.1 using this command.

```
mysql> \. c:\mysql\scripts\request_delivery_date_sk.sql
```

MySQL will indicate that there are 44 rows affected by the command.

```
Database changed
Query OK, 44 rows affected (0.39 sec)
Records: 44  Duplicates: 0  Warnings: 0
```

Since the structure of the **sales_order_fact** table has changed, you also need to update the script for regularly populating this table. The new script is shown in Listing 13.2.

Listing 13.2: The revised daily DW regular population

```
/*****************************************************************/
/*                                                               */
/* dw_regular_13.sql                                             */
/*                                                               */
/*****************************************************************/

USE dw;

/* CUSTOMER_DIM POPULATION                                       */

TRUNCATE customer_stg;

LOAD DATA INFILE 'customer.csv'
INTO TABLE customer_stg
FIELDS TERMINATED BY ','
OPTIONALLY ENCLOSED BY '"'
LINES TERMINATED BY '\r\n'
IGNORE 1 LINES
( customer_number
, customer_name
, customer_street_address
, customer_zip_code
, customer_city
, customer_state
, shipping_address
, shipping_zip_code
, shipping_city
, shipping_state )
;

/* SCD 2 ON ADDRESSES                                            */

UPDATE
```

```
  customer_dim a
, customer_stg b
SET
  a.expiry_date = SUBDATE(CURRENT_DATE, 1)
WHERE
  a.customer_number = b.customer_number
AND (   a.customer_street_address <> b.customer_street_address
     OR a.customer_city <> b.customer_city
     OR a.customer_zip_code <> b.customer_zip_code
     OR a.customer_state <> b.customer_state
     OR a.shipping_address <> b.shipping_address
     OR a.shipping_city <> b.shipping_city
     OR a.shipping_zip_code <> b.shipping_zip_code
     OR a.shipping_state <> b.shipping_state
     OR a.shipping_address IS NULL
     OR a.shipping_city IS NULL
     OR a.shipping_zip_code IS NULL
     OR a.shipping_state IS NULL)
AND expiry_date = '9999-12-31'
;

INSERT INTO customer_dim
SELECT
  NULL
, b.customer_number
, b.customer_name
, b.customer_street_address
, b.customer_zip_code
, b.customer_city
, b.customer_state
, b.shipping_address
, b.shipping_zip_code
, b.shipping_city
, b.shipping_state
, CURRENT_DATE
, '9999-12-31'
FROM
  customer_dim a
, customer_stg b
WHERE
    a.customer_number = b.customer_number
AND (   a.customer_street_address <> b.customer_street_address
     OR a.customer_city <> b.customer_city
     OR a.customer_zip_code <> b.customer_zip_code
     OR a.customer_state <> b.customer_state
     OR a.shipping_address <> b.shipping_address
```

```
     OR a.shipping_city <> b.shipping_city
     OR a.shipping_zip_code <> b.shipping_zip_code
     OR a.shipping_state <> b.shipping_state
     OR a.shipping_address IS NULL
     OR a.shipping_city IS NULL
     OR a.shipping_zip_code IS NULL
     OR a.shipping_state IS NULL)
AND EXISTS (
SELECT *
FROM customer_dim x
WHERE b.customer_number = x.customer_number
AND a.expiry_date = SUBDATE(CURRENT_DATE, 1))
AND NOT EXISTS (
SELECT *
FROM customer_dim y
WHERE     b.customer_number = y.customer_number
      AND y.expiry_date = '9999-12-31')
;

/* END OF SCD 2                                                    */

/* SCD 1 ON NAME                                                   */

UPDATE customer_dim a, customer_stg b
SET a.customer_name = b.customer_name
WHERE     a.customer_number = b.customer_number
      AND a.expiry_date = '9999-12-31'
      AND a.customer_name <> b.customer_name
;

/* ADD NEW CUSTOMER                                                */

INSERT INTO customer_dim
SELECT
  NULL
, customer_number
, customer_name
, customer_street_address
, customer_zip_code
, customer_city
, customer_state
, shipping_address
, shipping_zip_code
, shipping_city
, shipping_state
```

```
, CURRENT_DATE
, '9999-12-31'
FROM customer_stg
WHERE customer_number NOT IN(
SELECT a.customer_number
FROM
  customer_dim a
, customer_stg b
WHERE b.customer_number = a.customer_number )
;

/* RE-BUILD PA CUSTOMER DIMENSION                                    */

TRUNCATE pa_customer_dim;

INSERT INTO pa_customer_dim
SELECT
  customer_sk
, customer_number
, customer_name
, customer_street_address
, customer_zip_code
, customer_city
, customer_state
, shipping_address
, shipping_zip_code
, shipping_city
, shipping_state
, effective_date
, expiry_date
FROM customer_dim
WHERE customer_state = 'PA'
;

/* END OF CUSTOMER_DIM POPULATION                                    */

/* PRODUCT_DIM POPULATION                                            */

TRUNCATE product_stg
;

LOAD DATA INFILE 'product.txt'
INTO TABLE product_stg
FIELDS TERMINATED BY ''
OPTIONALLY ENCLOSED BY ''
LINES TERMINATED BY '\r\n'
```

```
IGNORE 1 LINES
( product_code
, product_name
, product_category )
;

/* SCD2 ON PRODUCT NAME AND GROUP                                  */

UPDATE
  product_dim a
, product_stg b
SET
  expiry_date = SUBDATE(CURRENT_DATE, 1)
WHERE
    a.product_code = b.product_code
AND (   a.product_name <> b.product_name
     OR a.product_category <> b.product_category )
     AND expiry_date = '9999-12-31'
;

INSERT INTO product_dim
SELECT
  NULL
, b.product_code
, b.product_name
, b.product_category
, CURRENT_DATE
, '9999-12-31'
FROM
  product_dim a
, product_stg b
WHERE
    a.product_code = b.product_code
AND (   a.product_name <> b.product_name
     OR a.product_category <> b.product_category )
AND EXISTS (
SELECT *
FROM product_dim x
WHERE     b.product_code = x.product_code
            AND a.expiry_date = SUBDATE(CURRENT_DATE, 1))
AND NOT EXISTS (
SELECT *
FROM product_dim y
WHERE    b.product_code = y.product_code
            AND y.expiry_date = '9999-12-31')
```

```
;

/* END OF SCD 2                                                  */

/* ADD NEW PRODUCT                                               */

INSERT INTO product_dim
SELECT
  NULL
, product_code
, product_name
, product_category
, CURRENT_DATE
, '9999-12-31'
FROM product_stg
WHERE product_code NOT IN(
SELECT y.product_code
FROM product_dim x, product_stg y
WHERE x.product_code = y.product_code )
;

/* END OF PRODUCT_DIM POPULATION                                 */

/* ORDER_DIM POPULATION                                          */

INSERT INTO order_dim (
  order_sk
, order_number
, effective_date
, expiry_date
)
SELECT
  NULL
, order_number
, order_date
, '9999-12-31'
FROM source.sales_order
WHERE entry_date = CURRENT_DATE
;

/* END OF ORDER_DIM POPULATION                                   */

/* SALES_ORDER_FACT POPULATION                                   */

INSERT INTO sales_order_fact
SELECT
```

```
  order_sk
, customer_sk
, product_sk
, e.date_sk
, f.date_sk
, order_amount
, order_quantity
FROM
  source.sales_order a
, order_dim b
, customer_dim c
, product_dim d
, date_dim e
, date_dim f
WHERE
    a.order_number = b.order_number
AND a.customer_number = c.customer_number
AND a.order_date >= c.effective_date
AND a.order_date <= c.expiry_date
AND a.product_code = d.product_code
AND a.order_date >= d.effective_date
AND a.order_date <= d.expiry_date
AND a.order_date = e.date
AND a.request_delivery_date = f.date
AND a.entry_date = CURRENT_DATE
;

/* end of script                                                  */
```

Before you can test the revised regular population for the **sales_order_fact** table, you need to modify the **sales_order** table in the **source** database. To be precise, you need to add a **request_delivery_date** column to this table. The script in Listing 13.3 can help you achieve this.

Listing 13.3: Adding the request_delivery_date column to the sales_order table

```
/******************************************************************/
/*                                                                */
/* request_delivery_date.sql                                      */
/*                                                                */
/******************************************************************/

USE source;
```

```
ALTER TABLE sales_order
  ADD request_delivery_date DATE AFTER order_date

;

/* end of script                                                  */
```

Run the script in Listing 13.3 using this command.

```
mysql> \. c:\mysql\scripts\request_delivery_date.sql
```

MySQL will indicate that there are 46 rows affected.

```
Database changed
Query OK, 46 rows affected (0.41 sec)
Records: 46  Duplicates: 0  Warnings: 0
```

In addition to changing the **sales_order** table structure, you also need to add more sales orders to the **sales_order** table using the script in Listing 13.4.

Listing 13.4: Adding three sales orders with request delivery dates

```
/******************************************************************/
/*                                                                */
/* request_delivery_date_source.sql                               */
/*                                                                */
/******************************************************************/

USE source;

INSERT INTO sales_order VALUES
  (47, 1, 1, '2007-03-04', '2007-03-30', '2007-03-04', 7500, 75)
, (48, 2, 2, '2007-03-04', '2007-03-30', '2007-03-04', 1000, 10)
, (49, 3, 3, '2007-03-04', '2007-03-30', '2007-03-04', 1000, 10)
;

/* end of script                                                  */
```

Now run the script in Listing 13.4.

```
mysql> \. c:\mysql\scripts\request_delivery_date_source.sql
```

Finally, set your MySQL date to March 4, 2007 (the order date of the three recently added sales orders), and run the **dw_regular_13.sql** script in Listing 13.2.

```
mysql> \. c:\mysql\scripts\dw_regular_13.sql
```

Here is how the response should look like.

```
Database changed
Query OK, 9 rows affected (0.07 sec)

Query OK, 9 rows affected (0.05 sec)
Records: 9  Deleted: 0  Skipped: 0  Warnings: 0

Query OK, 0 rows affected (0.00 sec)
Rows matched: 0  Changed: 0  Warnings: 0

Query OK, 0 rows affected (0.00 sec)
Records: 0  Duplicates: 0  Warnings: 0

Query OK, 0 rows affected (0.00 sec)
Rows matched: 0  Changed: 0  Warnings: 0

Query OK, 0 rows affected (0.00 sec)
Records: 0  Duplicates: 0  Warnings: 0

Query OK, 19 rows affected (0.08 sec)

Query OK, 19 rows affected (0.06 sec)
Records: 19  Duplicates: 0  Warnings: 0

Query OK, 4 rows affected (0.05 sec)

Query OK, 4 rows affected (0.06 sec)
Records: 4  Deleted: 0  Skipped: 0  Warnings: 0

Query OK, 0 rows affected (0.00 sec)
Rows matched: 0  Changed: 0  Warnings: 0

Query OK, 0 rows affected (0.00 sec)
Records: 0  Duplicates: 0  Warnings: 0

Query OK, 0 rows affected (0.00 sec)
Records: 0  Duplicates: 0  Warnings: 0

Query OK, 3 rows affected (0.07 sec)
Records: 3  Duplicates: 0  Warnings: 0

Query OK, 3 rows affected (0.12 sec)
Records: 3  Duplicates: 0  Warnings: 0
```

If you query the **sales_order_fact** table, you will learn that the three new sales orders have values for the **request_ delivery_date_sk** column, whereas the older records don't.

Here is a command for querying the **sales_order_face** table.

```
mysql> select a.order_sk, request_delivery_date_sk
    -> from sales_order_fact a, date_dim b
    -> where a.order_date_sk = b.date_sk;
```

Here is the result of the query.

```
+----------+--------------------------+
| order_sk | request_delivery_date_sk |
+----------+--------------------------+
|        1 |                     NULL |
|        2 |                     NULL |
|        3 |                     NULL |
|        4 |                     NULL |
|        5 |                     NULL |
|        6 |                     NULL |
|        7 |                     NULL |
|        8 |                     NULL |
|        9 |                     NULL |
|       10 |                     NULL |
|       11 |                     NULL |
|       12 |                     NULL |
|       13 |                     NULL |
|       14 |                     NULL |
|       15 |                     NULL |
|       16 |                     NULL |
|       17 |                     NULL |
|       18 |                     NULL |
|       19 |                     NULL |
|       20 |                     NULL |
|       21 |                     NULL |
|       22 |                     NULL |
|       23 |                     NULL |
|       24 |                     NULL |
|       25 |                     NULL |
|       26 |                     NULL |
|       27 |                     NULL |
|       28 |                     NULL |
|       29 |                     NULL |
|       30 |                     NULL |
|       31 |                     NULL |
```

```
|       32 |                        NULL |
|       33 |                        NULL |
|       34 |                        NULL |
|       35 |                        NULL |
|       36 |                        NULL |
|       37 |                        NULL |
|       38 |                        NULL |
|       39 |                        NULL |
|       40 |                        NULL |
|       41 |                        NULL |
|       42 |                        NULL |
|       43 |                        NULL |
|       44 |                        NULL |
|       45 |                         760 |
|       46 |                         760 |
|       47 |                         760 |
+----------+-----------------------------+
47 rows in set (0.01 sec)
```

You can verify that the date for the **request_delivery_date_sk** 760 is March 30, 2007; using this query.

```
mysql> select date_sk, date from date_dim where date_sk = 760;
```

The response shows that 760 has a value of 2007-03-30.

```
+---------+------------+
| date_sk | date       |
+---------+------------+
|     760 | 2007-03-30 |
+---------+------------+
1 row in set (0.00 sec)
```

Now that you have revised the schema and the regular population script, you're ready to implement the date dimension role-playing. The next two sections show how you can use each type of dimension role playing implementation types, table alias and database view.

Table Alias Implementation

The query in Listing 13.5 is an example of the table alias type. The query in the script essentially uses the date dimension table twice, once for the order date (whose alias is **order_date_dim**) and once for the request delivery date (whose alias is **request_delivery_date_dim**).

Listing 13.5: Daily sales summary

```
/**********************************************************************/
/*                                                                    */
/* table_alias.sql                                                    */
/*                                                                    */
/**********************************************************************/

SELECT
  order_date_dim.date order_date
, request_delivery_date_dim.date request_delivery_date
, SUM(order_amount)
, COUNT(*)
FROM
  sales_order_fact a
, date_dim order_date_dim
, date_dim request_delivery_date_dim
WHERE
    a.order_date_sk = order_date_dim.date_sk
AND a.request_delivery_date_sk = request_delivery_date_dim.date_sk
GROUP BY
  order_date_dim.date
, request_delivery_date_dim.date
ORDER BY
  order_date_dim.date
, request_delivery_date_dim.date
;

/* end of script                                                      */
```

You run the query using this command.

```
mysql> \. c:\mysql\scripts\table_alias.sql
```

The result of the query is as follows.

```
+-----------+-----------------------+-------------------+----------+
| order_date| request_delivery_date | SUM(order_amount) | COUNT(*) |
+-----------+-----------------------+-------------------+----------+
| 2007-03-04| 2007-03-30            |           9500.00 |        3 |
+-----------+-----------------------+-------------------+----------+
1 row in set (0.00 sec)
```

The output shows the total of the three new orders whose request delivery dates are selected.

Database View

You implement the second type of date dimension role-playing by creating two database views, one for each of the two dates. You or your user can then use these views as dimension tables in the queries.

The script in Listing 13.6 can be used to create the views.

Listing 13.6: Creating date views

```
/**********************************************************************/
/*                                                                    */
/* date_views.sql                                                     */
/*                                                                    */
/**********************************************************************/

USE dw;

CREATE VIEW order_date_dim (
  order_date_sk
, order_date
, month_name
, month
, quarter
, year
, promo_ind
, effective_date
, expiry_date
)
AS SELECT
  date_sk
, date
, month_name
, month
, quarter
, year
, promo_ind
, effective_date
, expiry_date
FROM date_dim
```

```
;

CREATE VIEW request_delivery_date_dim (
  request_delivery_date_sk
, request_delivery_date
, month_name
, month
, quarter
, year
, promo_ind
, effective_date
, expiry_date
)
AS SELECT
  date_sk
, date
, month_name
, month
, quarter
, year
, promo_ind
, effective_date
, expiry_date
FROM date_dim
;

/* end of script                                                  */
```

Use this command to execute the script in Listing 13.6 to create the views.

```
mysql> \. c:\mysql\scripts\date_views.sql
```

The query in Listing 13.7 uses the two date views to accomplish the same objective as the previous query that uses table alias.

Listing 13.7: Database view role playing

```
/******************************************************************/
/*                                                                */
/* database_view.sql                                              */
/*                                                                */
/******************************************************************/

SELECT
  order_date
, request_delivery_date
, SUM(order_amount)
```

```
, COUNT(*)
FROM
  sales_order_fact a
, order_date_dim b
, request_delivery_date_dim c
WHERE
    a.order_date_sk = b.order_date_sk
AND a.request_delivery_date_sk = c.request_delivery_date_sk
GROUP BY order_date, request_delivery_date
ORDER BY order_date, request_delivery_date
;

/* end of script                                                  */
```

Run the **database_view.sql** script using this command.

```
mysql> \. c:\mysql\scripts\database_view.sql
```

The result should be the same as the result from the previous query.

```
+-----------+-----------------------+-------------------+----------+
|order_date | request_delivery_date | SUM(order_amount) | COUNT(*) |
+-----------+-----------------------+-------------------+----------+
|2007-03-04 | 2007-03-30            |           9500.00 |        3 |
+-----------+-----------------------+-------------------+----------+
1 row in set (0.00 sec)
```

Summary

In this chapter you learned dimension role-playing for the date dimension and applied the two types of the technique: table alias and database view.

In the next chapter, you will learn to re-use facts.

Chapter 14 Snapshots

The first three chapters in Part III dealt with dimension extensions. This chapter, on the other hand, discusses two techniques for extending the fact.

Some users, especially managers, may require data for a particular time. In other words, they need snapshots of data. The two fact extension techniques that deals with snapshots are periodic and accumulating.

A periodic snapshot is a periodic summary of the fact at a certain time. For example, a monthly sales order periodic snapshot is the total sales order amount at the end of every month.

An accumulating snapshot tracks the changes of a fact. For example, the data warehouse may need to accumulate (store) the data of a sales order as it progresses through the order life cycle, starting from the time the order was placed to the time products are allocated to fulfill the order to packing, shipping, and receiving. The user can take a snapshot on the accumulated sales order progress status at certain times.

The following sections discuss periodic snapshots and accumulated snapshots in detail.

Periodic Snapshots

This section shows how you can implement a periodic snapshot using the month end sales order summary as an example.

The first thing you need to do is add a new fact table. The schema in Figure 14.1 shows a new fact table called **month_end_sales_order_fact**. You need the new table because you need two new measures, **month_order_amount** and **month_order_quantity**, and you cannot add these measures to the **sales_order_fact** table. The reason you cannot do this is because the **sales_order_fact** table and the new measures have different time aspects. The **sales_order_fact** table includes a date in each record. The new measures require monthly data.

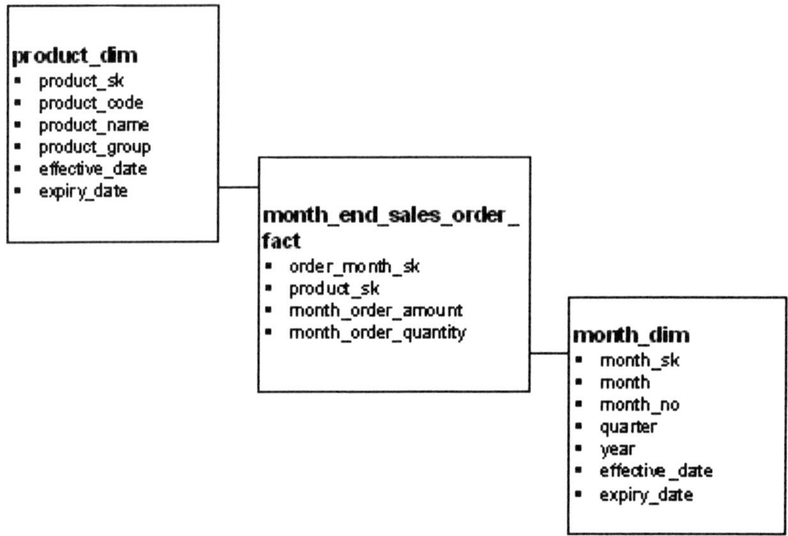

Figure 14.1: The schema for the sales order monthly snapshot

The script in Listing 14.1 is used to create the **monthly_sales_order_fact** table.

Listing 14.1: Creating monthly_sales_order_fact

```
/**********************************************************************/
/*                                                                    */
/* create_month_end_sales_order_fact.sql                              */
/*                                                                    */
/**********************************************************************/

USE dw;

CREATE TABLE month_end_sales_order_fact
( month_order_sk INT
, product_sk INT
, month_order_amount DEC(10,2)
, month_order_quantity INT )
;

/* end of script                                                      */
```

Now run the script in Listing 14.1 using this command.

```
mysql> \. c:\mysql\scripts\create_month_end_sales_order_fact.sql
```

The response from MySQL should look like this.

```
Database changed
Query OK, 0 rows affected (0.17 sec)
```

Having created the **month_end_sales_order_fact** table, you now need to populate the table.

The source for the month end sales order fact is the existing sales order fact. The script in Listing 14.2 populates the month end sales order fact. You run it at every month end after the daily sales order population.

Listing 14.2: Populating month_end_sales_order_fact

```
/******************************************************************/
/*                                                                */
/* month_end_sales_order.sql                                      */
/*                                                                */
/******************************************************************/

USE dw;

INSERT INTO month_end_sales_order_fact
SELECT
  b.month_sk
, a.product_sk
, SUM(order_amount)
, SUM(order_quantity)
FROM
  sales_order_fact a
, month_dim b
, order_date_dim d
WHERE
    a.order_date_sk = d.order_date_sk
AND b.month = d.month
ND b.year = d.year
AND b.month = MONTH(CURRENT_DATE)
AND b.year = YEAR(CURRENT_DATE)
GROUP BY b.month, b.year, a.product_sk
;

/* end of script                                                  */
```

Before you run the script in Listing 14.2, set your MySQL date to February 28, 2007 (the month end of February 2007). This step is required because the script may only be executed at month end.

Once you change your MySQL date, run the script using this command.

```
mysql> \. c:\mysql\scripts\month_end_sales_order.sql
```

Once you press Enter, you should see this on your command prompt.

```
Database changed
Query OK, 2 rows affected (0.10 sec)
Records: 2  Duplicates: 0  Warnings: 0
```

Now, you can query the **month_end_sales_order_fact** table using this command.

```
mysql> select * from month_end_sales_order_fact \G
```

The output is as follows.

```
*************************** 1. row ***************************
      month_order_sk: 24
          product_sk: 2
  month_order_amount: 4000.00
month_order_quantity: NULL
*************************** 2. row ***************************
      month_order_sk: 24
          product_sk: 3
  month_order_amount: 4000.00
month_order_quantity: NULL
2 rows in set (0.00 sec)
```

Note

The **month_sk** 24 is February 2007.

The **month_sales_order_fact** table contains only two rows, both from sales orders placed in February 2007.

Accumulating Snapshots

In this section I demonstrate how to implement an accumulating snapshot on sales orders. This accumulating snapshot tracks five sales order milestones: Order, Allocate, Pack, Ship, and Receive.

The five dates and their quantities come from the **sales_order** table in the **source** database. An order with a completed life cycle is described by five rows: one for the time the order is placed, one for the time the ordered products are allocated, one for the time the products are packed, one for the time the order is shipped, and one for the time the order is received by the customer. Each milestone also contains a status, whose value can be one of these: **N** for New, **A** for Allocate, **P** for Pack, **S** for Ship, and **R** for Receive.

For the **sales_order** table to handle the five different statuses, its structure must be changed. The script in Listing 14.3 changes the **order_date** column to **status_date**, adds a new column called **order_status**, and changes the **order_quantity** column to **quantity**. As the name implies, the **order_status** column is used to store one of N, A, P, S, or R. The status describes the value of the **status_date** column. If a record has a status of N, the value in the **status_date** column contains the order date. If the status is R, the **status_date** column contains the received date.

Listing 14.3: Modifying the sales order table

```
/******************************************************************/
/*                                                                */
/* order_status.sql                                               */
/*                                                                */
/******************************************************************/
USE source;

ALTER TABLE sales_order
  CHANGE order_date status_date DATE
, ADD order_status CHAR(1) AFTER status_date
, CHANGE order_quantity quantity INT
;
/* end of script                                                  */
```

Run the **order_status.sql** script in Listing 14.3 by using this command.

```
mysql> \. c:\mysql\scripts\order_status.sql
```

Here is how the response on your console should look like.

```
Database changed
Query OK, 49 rows affected (0.40 sec)
Records: 49  Duplicates: 0  Warnings: 0
```

Having changed the source database, you now need to add four new quantities and four date surrogate keys to the existing **sales_order_fact** table. Here are the new columns:

- **allocate_date_sk**
- **allocate_quantity**
- **packing_date_sk**
- **packing_quantity**
- **ship_date_sk**
- **ship_quantity**
- **receive_date_sk**
- **receive_quantity**

Figure 14.2 shows the schema with the eight new columns.

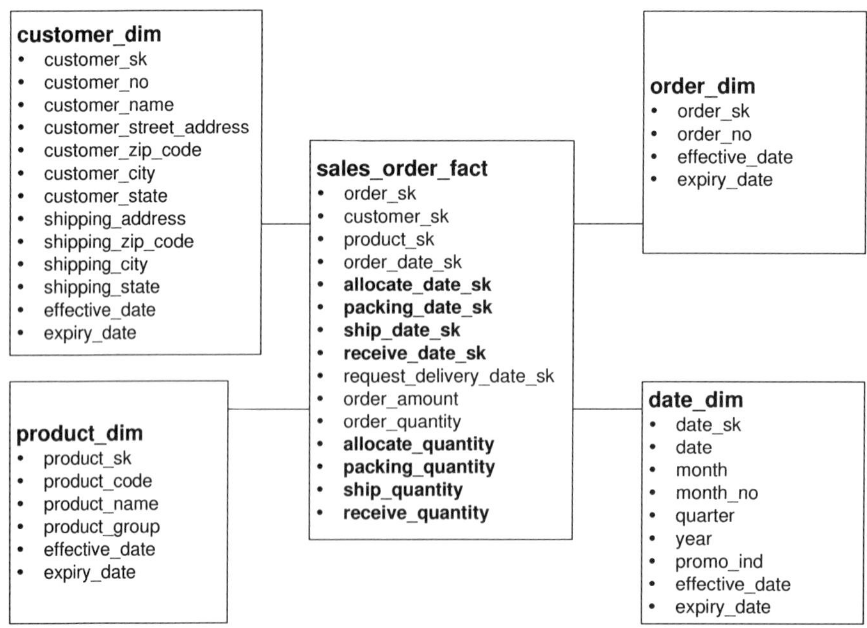

Figure 14.2: The schema for accumulating snapshots

One sales order row in the fact table can now take the five milestones. In other words, the five milestone dates and quantities are accumulated in one sales order fact, hence the term accumulating snapshot.

You use the script in Listing 14.4 to add the four quantities and four date surrogate keys to the **sales_order_fact** table.

Listing 14.4: Adding four date surrogate keys

```
/**********************************************************************/
/*                                                                    */
/* add_four_milestones.sql                                            */
/*                                                                    */
/**********************************************************************/

USE dw;

ALTER TABLE sales_order_fact
  ADD allocate_date_sk INT AFTER order_date_sk
, ADD allocate_quantity INT
, ADD packing_date_sk INT AFTER allocate_date_sk
, ADD packing_quantity INT
, ADD ship_date_sk INT AFTER packing_date_sk
, ADD ship_quantity INT
, ADD receive_date_sk INT AFTER ship_date_sk
, ADD receive_quantity INT
;

/* end of script                                                      */
```

Run the **add_four_milestones.sql** script to add the new fact columns using this command.

```
mysql> \. c:\mysql\scripts\add_four_milestones.sql
```

The following should be printed on the console as the response.

```
Database changed
Query OK, 47 rows affected (0.36 sec)
Records: 47  Duplicates: 0  Warnings: 0
```

You must now apply the database view role-playing technique on the date dimension for the new four dates. The script in Listing 14.5 creates the four date views you need.

Note

You created the **order_date_dim** view in Chapter 13.

Listing 14.5: Creating four date views

```
/**********************************************************************/
/*                                                                    */
/* create_four_date_views.sql                                         */
/*                                                                    */
/**********************************************************************/

USE dw;

CREATE VIEW allocate_date_dim (
  allocate_date_sk
, allocate_date
, month_name
, month
, quarter
, year
, promo_ind
, effective_date
, expiry_date
)
AS SELECT
  date_sk
, date
, month_name
, month
, quarter
, year
, promo_ind
, effective_date
, expiry_date
FROM date_dim
;

CREATE VIEW packing_date_dim (
  packing_date_sk
, packing_date
, month_name
, month
, quarter
, year
, promo_ind
, effective_date
```

```
, expiry_date
)
AS SELECT
  date_sk
, date
, month_name
, month
, quarter
, year
, promo_ind
, effective_date
, expiry_date
FROM date_dim
;

CREATE VIEW ship_date_dim (
  ship_date_sk
, ship_date
, month_name
, month
, quarter
, year
, promo_ind
, effective_date
, expiry_date
)
AS SELECT
  date_sk
, date
, month_name
, month
, quarter
, year
, promo_ind
, effective_date
, expiry_date
FROM date_dim
;

CREATE VIEW receive_date_dim (
  receive_date_sk
, receive_date
, month_name
, month
, quarter
```

```
, year
, promo_ind
, effective_date
, expiry_date
)
AS SELECT
  date_sk
, date
, month_name
, month
, quarter
, year
, promo_ind
, effective_date
, expiry_date
FROM date_dim
;

/* end of script                                                  */
```

Run the script in Listing 14.5 using this command.

```
mysql> \. c:\mysql\scripts\create_four_date_views.sql
```

Now, you need to revise your regular population script as well since the structure of the fact table has changed. The script in Listing 14.6 is the new regular population script. The five statements that handle the five milestone statuses and dates are commented. More than one transaction for a sales order can be recorded on the same date, in which case the relevant milestone dates are updated at the same time.

Listing 14.6: The revised daily DW regular population

```
/*****************************************************************/
/*                                                               */
/* dw_regular_14.sql                                             */
/*                                                               */
/*****************************************************************/

USE dw;

/* CUSTOMER_DIM POPULATION                                       */

TRUNCATE customer_stg;

LOAD DATA INFILE 'customer.csv'
```

```
INTO TABLE customer_stg
FIELDS TERMINATED BY ','
OPTIONALLY ENCLOSED BY '"'
LINES TERMINATED BY '\r\n'
IGNORE 1 LINES
( customer_number
, customer_name
, customer_street_address
, customer_zip_code
, customer_city
, customer_state
, shipping_address
, shipping_zip_code
, shipping_city
, shipping_state )
;

/* SCD 2 ON ADDRESSES                                              */

UPDATE
  customer_dim a
, customer_stg b
SET
  a.expiry_date = SUBDATE(CURRENT_DATE, 1)
WHERE
  a.customer_number = b.customer_number
AND (   a.customer_street_address <> b.customer_street_address
     OR a.customer_city <> b.customer_city
     OR a.customer_zip_code <> b.customer_zip_code
     OR a.customer_state <> b.customer_state
     OR a.shipping_address <> b.shipping_address
     OR a.shipping_city <> b.shipping_city
     OR a.shipping_zip_code <> b.shipping_zip_code
     OR a.shipping_state <> b.shipping_state
     OR a.shipping_address IS NULL
     OR a.shipping_city IS NULL
     OR a.shipping_zip_code IS NULL
     OR a.shipping_state IS NULL)
AND expiry_date = '9999-12-31'
;

INSERT INTO customer_dim
SELECT
  NULL
, b.customer_number
```

```
, b.customer_name
, b.customer_street_address
, b.customer_zip_code
, b.customer_city
, b.customer_state
, b.shipping_address
, b.shipping_zip_code
, b.shipping_city
, b.shipping_state
, CURRENT_DATE
, '9999-12-31'
FROM
  customer_dim a
, customer_stg b
WHERE
    a.customer_number = b.customer_number
AND (   a.customer_street_address <> b.customer_street_address
     OR a.customer_city <> b.customer_city
     OR a.customer_zip_code <> b.customer_zip_code
     OR a.customer_state <> b.customer_state
     OR a.shipping_address <> b.shipping_address
     OR a.shipping_city <> b.shipping_city
     OR a.shipping_zip_code <> b.shipping_zip_code
     OR a.shipping_state <> b.shipping_state
     OR a.shipping_address IS NULL
     OR a.shipping_city IS NULL
     OR a.shipping_zip_code IS NULL
     OR a.shipping_state IS NULL)
AND EXISTS (
SELECT *
FROM customer_dim x
WHERE b.customer_number = x.customer_number
AND a.expiry_date = SUBDATE(CURRENT_DATE, 1))
AND NOT EXISTS (
SELECT *
FROM customer_dim y
WHERE     b.customer_number = y.customer_number
      AND y.expiry_date = '9999-12-31')
;

/* END OF SCD 2                                                      */

/* SCD 1 ON NAME                                                     */

UPDATE customer_dim a, customer_stg b
SET a.customer_name = b.customer_name
```

```
WHERE     a.customer_number = b.customer_number
      AND a.expiry_date = '9999-12-31'
      AND a.customer_name <> b.customer_name
;

/* ADD NEW CUSTOMER                                                  */

INSERT INTO customer_dim
SELECT
  NULL
, customer_number
, customer_name
, customer_street_address
, customer_zip_code
, customer_city
, customer_state
, shipping_address
, shipping_zip_code
, shipping_city
, shipping_state
, CURRENT_DATE
, '9999-12-31'
FROM customer_stg
WHERE customer_number NOT IN(
SELECT a.customer_number
FROM
  customer_dim a
, customer_stg b
WHERE b.customer_number = a.customer_number )
;

/* RE-BUILD PA CUSTOMER DIMENSION                                    */

TRUNCATE pa_customer_dim;

INSERT INTO pa_customer_dim
SELECT
  customer_sk
, customer_number
, customer_name
, customer_street_address
, customer_zip_code
, customer_city
, customer_state
, shipping_address
```

```
, shipping_zip_code
, shipping_city
, shipping_state
, effective_date
, expiry_date
FROM customer_dim
WHERE customer_state = 'PA'
;

/* END OF CUSTOMER_DIM POPULATION                                */

/* PRODUCT_DIM POPULATION                                        */

TRUNCATE product_stg
;

LOAD DATA INFILE 'product.txt'
INTO TABLE product_stg
FIELDS TERMINATED BY ''
OPTIONALLY ENCLOSED BY ''
LINES TERMINATED BY '\r\n'
IGNORE 1 LINES
( product_code
, product_name
, product_category )
;

/* SCD2 ON PRODUCT NAME AND GROUP                                */

UPDATE
  product_dim a
, product_stg b
SET
  expiry_date = SUBDATE(CURRENT_DATE, 1)
WHERE
    a.product_code = b.product_code
AND (   a.product_name <> b.product_name
     OR a.product_category <> b.product_category )
     AND expiry_date = '9999-12-31'
;

INSERT INTO product_dim
SELECT
  NULL
, b.product_code
, b.product_name
```

```
, b.product_category
, CURRENT_DATE
, '9999-12-31'
FROM
  product_dim a
, product_stg b
WHERE
    a.product_code = b.product_code
AND (   a.product_name <> b.product_name
     OR a.product_category <> b.product_category )
AND EXISTS (
SELECT *
FROM product_dim x
WHERE     b.product_code = x.product_code
             AND a.expiry_date = SUBDATE(CURRENT_DATE, 1))
AND NOT EXISTS (
SELECT *
FROM product_dim y
WHERE    b.product_code = y.product_code
             AND y.expiry_date = '9999-12-31')
;

/* END OF SCD 2                                                */

/* ADD NEW PRODUCT                                             */

INSERT INTO product_dim
SELECT
  NULL
, product_code
, product_name
, product_category
, CURRENT_DATE
, '9999-12-31'
FROM product_stg
WHERE product_code NOT IN(
SELECT y.product_code
FROM product_dim x, product_stg y
WHERE x.product_code = y.product_code )
;

/* END OF PRODUCT_DIM POPULATION                             */

/* ORDER_DIM POPULATION                                      */
```

```
INSERT INTO order_dim (
  order_sk
, order_number
, effective_date
, expiry_date
)
SELECT
  NULL
, order_number
, status_date
, '9999-12-31'
FROM source.sales_order
WHERE
    order_status = 'N'
AND entry_date = CURRENT_DATE
;

/* INSERTING New ORDER                                                    */

INSERT INTO sales_order_fact
SELECT
  order_sk
, customer_sk
, product_sk
, e.order_date_sk
, NULL
, NULL
, NULL
, NULL
, f.request_delivery_date_sk
, order_amount
, quantity
, NULL
, NULL
, NULL
, NULL
FROM
  source.sales_order a
, order_dim b
, customer_dim c
, product_dim d
, order_date_dim e
, request_delivery_date_dim f
WHERE
    a.order_status = 'N'
AND a.order_number = b.order_number
```

```
AND a.customer_number = c.customer_number
AND a.status_date >= c.effective_date
AND a.status_date <= c.expiry_date
AND a.product_code = d.product_code
AND a.status_date >= d.effective_date
AND a.status_date <= d.expiry_date
AND a.status_date = e.order_date
AND a.request_delivery_date = f.request_delivery_date
AND a.entry_date = CURRENT_DATE
;

/* UPDATING the new sales order to Allocated status                */

UPDATE
  sales_order_fact a
, source.sales_order b
, allocate_date_dim c
, order_dim g
SET
  a.allocate_date_sk = c.allocate_date_sk
, a.allocate_quantity = b.quantity
WHERE
    order_status = 'A'
AND b.entry_date = CURRENT_DATE
AND b.order_number = g.order_number
AND a.order_sk = g.order_sk
AND c.allocate_date = b.status_date
;

/* UPDATING the allocated order to Packed status                   */

UPDATE
  sales_order_fact a
, source.sales_order b
, packing_date_dim d
, order_dim g
SET
  a.packing_date_sk = d.packing_date_sk
, a.packing_quantity = b.quantity
WHERE
    order_status = 'P'
AND b.entry_date = CURRENT_DATE
AND b.order_number = g.order_number
AND a.order_sk = g.order_sk
AND d.packing_date = b.status_date
```

```
;

/* UPDATING the packed order to Shipped status                          */

UPDATE
  sales_order_fact a
, source.sales_order b
, ship_date_dim e
, order_dim g
SET
  a.ship_date_sk = e.ship_date_sk
, a.ship_quantity = b.quantity
WHERE
    order_status = 'S'
AND b.entry_date = CURRENT_DATE
AND b.order_number = g.order_number
AND a.order_sk = g.order_sk
AND e.ship_date = b.status_date
;

/* UPDATING the shipped order to Received status                        */

UPDATE
  sales_order_fact a
, source.sales_order b
, receive_date_dim f
, order_dim g
SET
  a.receive_date_sk = f.receive_date_sk
, a.receive_quantity = b.quantity
WHERE
    order_status = 'R'
AND b.entry_date = CURRENT_DATE
AND b.order_number = g.order_number
AND a.order_sk = g.order_sk
AND f.receive_date = b.status_date
;
/* end of script                                                        */
```

Preparing Data for Regular Population

Before you can run the new regular population script (**dw_regular_14.sql**) in Listing 14.6, you need to prepare some data. In fact, there are six steps you need to do to track the life cycles of two sales orders:

1. Adding two new sales orders
2. Running the **dw_regular_14.sql** script and confirming correct population
3. Adding sales orders for the two orders with Allocate and/or Pack milestones
4. Running the dw_regular_14.sql script and confirming correct population
5. Adding sales orders for the two orders with their next milestones: Allocate, Ship, and/or Receive. Note that the four dates can be the same
6. Running the **dw_regular_14.sql** script and confirming correct population.

The following sub-sections guide you to perform these six steps.

Step 1: Adding Two New Sales Orders

The script in Listing 14.7 adds two new orders placed on March 5, 2007.

Listing 14.7: Adding two sales orders

```
/**********************************************************************/
/*                                                                    */
/* add_two_sales_orders.sql                                           */
/*                                                                    */
/**********************************************************************/

USE source;

INSERT INTO sales_order VALUES
  (50, 1, 1, '2007-03-05', 'N', '2007-03-10', '2007-03-05', 7500,
       75)
, (51, 2, 2, '2007-03-05', 'N', '2007-03-10', '2007-03-05', 1000,
       10)
;

/* end of script                                                      */
```

Run the preceding script using this command.

```
mysql> \. c:\mysql\scripts\add_two_sales_orders.sql
```

Step 2: Running the DW Regular Population Script

You must now set your MySQL date to March 5, 2007, the entry date of the two new sales orders that you have just added. Run the **dw_regular_14.sql** script using this command.

```
mysql> \. c:\mysql\scripts\dw_regular_14.sql
```

You can confirm its success by querying the two sales orders in the **sales_order_fact** table using this statement.

```
mysql> select order_number, a.order_date_sk, allocate_date_sk,
    -> packing_date_sk, ship_date_sk, receive_date_sk
    -> from sales_order_fact a, order_dim b, order_date_dim c
    -> where order_number IN(50, 51)
    -> and a.order_sk = b.order_sk
    -> and a.order_date_sk = c.order_date_sk \G
```

Here are the correct records.

```
*************************** 1. row ***************************
    order_number: 50
   order_date_sk: 735
allocate_date_sk: NULL
 packing_date_sk: NULL
    ship_date_sk: NULL
 receive_date_sk: NULL
*************************** 2. row ***************************
    order_number: 51
   order_date_sk: 735
allocate_date_sk: NULL
 packing_date_sk: NULL
    ship_date_sk: NULL
 receive_date_sk: NULL
2 rows in set (0.01 sec)
```

Note

Only the **order_date_sk** column has values, the other dates are NULL because these two orders are new and have not been allocated, packed, shipped, or received.

Step 3: Adding Three Sales Orders with Allocate and Packing Dates

You can run the script in Listing 14.8 to add two sales order transaction records with allocate dates and packing dates as well as one transaction record with an allocate date. These transactions are for the same two orders (order no 50 and 51) you added in the preceding step.

Listing 14.8: Adding three sales orders with Allocate and/or Packing dates

```
/*****************************************************************/
/*                                                               */
/* sales_orders_step3.sql                                        */
/*                                                               */
/*****************************************************************/

USE source;

INSERT INTO sales_order VALUES
  (50, 1, 1, '2007-03-06', 'A', '2007-03-10', '2007-03-06', 7500,
      75)
, (50, 1, 1, '2007-03-06', 'P', '2007-03-10', '2007-03-06', 7500,
      75)
, (51, 2, 2, '2007-03-06', 'A', '2007-03-10', '2007-03-06', 1000,
      10)
;

/* end of script                                                 */
```

Run the script by issuing this command.

```
mysql> \. c:\mysql\scripts\sales_orders_step3.sql
```

Step 4: Running the DW Regular Population Script

Set your MySQL date to March 6, 2007, then run the **dw_regular_14.sql** script using this command.

```
mysql> \. c:\mysql\scripts\dw_regular_14.sql
```

Query the two sales orders in the **sales_order_fact** table to confirm correct population using this SQL statement.

```
mysql> select order_number, a.order_date_sk, allocate_date_sk,
    -> packing_date_sk, ship_date_sk, receive_date_sk
    -> from sales_order_fact a, order_dim b, order_date_dim c
    -> where order_number IN(50, 51)
    -> and a.order_sk = b.order_sk
    -> and a.order_date_sk = c.order_date_sk \G
```

Here are the result of the query.

```
*************************** 1. row ***************************
    order_number: 50
   order_date_sk: 735
allocate_date_sk: 736
 packing_date_sk: 736
    ship_date_sk: NULL
 receive_date_sk: NULL
*************************** 2. row ***************************
    order_number: 51
   order_date_sk: 735
allocate_date_sk: 736
 packing_date_sk: NULL
    ship_date_sk: NULL
 receive_date_sk: NULL
2 rows in set (0.00 sec)

mysql>
```

Note

The first order gets the **allocate_date_sk** and **packing_date_sk**, the second two gets the **allocate_date_sk** only.

Step 5: Addding Three Sales Orders with Ship, Receive, and Packing Dates

The script in Listing 14.9 can be used to add three sales order transaction records with ship and receive dates, which complete the cycle of this order. The script also adds a record with allocate and packing dates. Again, these transactions are for the same two orders (orders 50 and 51).

Listing 14.9: Sales orders with Allocate and/or Packing dates

```
/******************************************************************/
/*                                                                */
/* sales_orders_step5.sql                                         */
```

```
/*                                                                  */
/********************************************************************/

USE source;

INSERT INTO sales_order VALUES
  (50, 1, 1, '2007-03-07', 'S', '2007-03-10', '2007-03-07', 7500,
      75)
, (50, 1, 1, '2007-03-07', 'R', '2007-03-10', '2007-03-07', 7500,
      75)
, (51, 2, 2, '2007-03-07', 'P', '2007-03-10', '2007-03-07', 1000,
      10)
;

/* end of script                                                    */
```

Run the script using this command.

```
mysql> \. c:\mysql\scripts\sales_orders_step5.sql
```

Step 6: Running the DW Regular Population Script

Set your MySQL date to March 7, 2007, then run the **dw_regular_14.sql** script again.

```
mysql> \. c:\mysql\scripts\dw_regular_14.sql
```

Now query the two sales order in the **sales_order_fact** table using this statement.

```
mysql> select order_number, a.order_date_sk, allocate_date_sk,
    -> packing_date_sk, ship_date_sk, receive_date_sk
    -> from sales_order_fact a, order_dim b, order_date_dim c
    -> where order_number IN(50, 51)
    -> and a.order_sk = b.order_sk
    -> and a.order_date_sk = c.order_date_sk \G
```

Here is the result of the query.

```
*************************** 1. row ***************************
    order_number: 50
   order_date_sk: 735
allocate_date_sk: 736
 packing_date_sk: 736
    ship_date_sk: 737
```

```
 receive_date_sk: 737
*************************** 2. row ***************************
    order_number: 51
   order_date_sk: 735
allocate_date_sk: 736
 packing_date_sk: 737
    ship_date_sk: NULL
 receive_date_sk: NULL
2 rows in set (0.00 sec)
```

Note

The first order, order number 50, gets all the **date_sk**'s, meaning this order is completed (already received by the customer). The second order is packed, but not shipped yet.

Summary

In this chapter you learned two type of snapshots: periodic and accumulating. You applied and tested them on two sales order by tracking their status milestones.

In the next chapter, you'll learn the dimension hierarchy

Chapter 15
Dimension Hierarchies

Most dimensions have one or more hierarchies. For instance, the date dimension has one hierarchy with four levels: the year level, the quarter level, the month level, and the date level. These levels are represented by columns in the **date_dim** table. The date dimension has one-path hierarchy as it does not have any other hierarchy than the year-quarter-month-date path. In this chapter you learn about single-path hierarchies. In addition, this chapter talks about grouping and drilling queries on dimensions with hierarchies.

Note

Multi-path hierarchies are discussed in Chapter 16, "Multi-Path and Ragged Hicrarchies.".

Hierarchies in A Data Warehouse

I'll start discussing dimension hierarchies by showing you how to identify hierarchies in the dimensions of a data warehouse.

To identify a hierarchy in a dimension, you must first understand the meaning of dimension columns. You can then identify two or more columns that are of the same subject. For example, the date, the month, the quarter, and the year have the same subject because they all have something to do with the calendar. Columns of the same subject form a group. A column in a group must contain at least another member of the group. As an example, in the group mentioned earlier, the month contains the date. The chain of these columns form a hierarchy. For example, the date-month-quarter-year chain is a hierarchy in the date dimension.

In addition to the date dimension, the product and customer dimensions also have hierarchies. Figure 15.1 shows the columns of the hierarchies in bold.

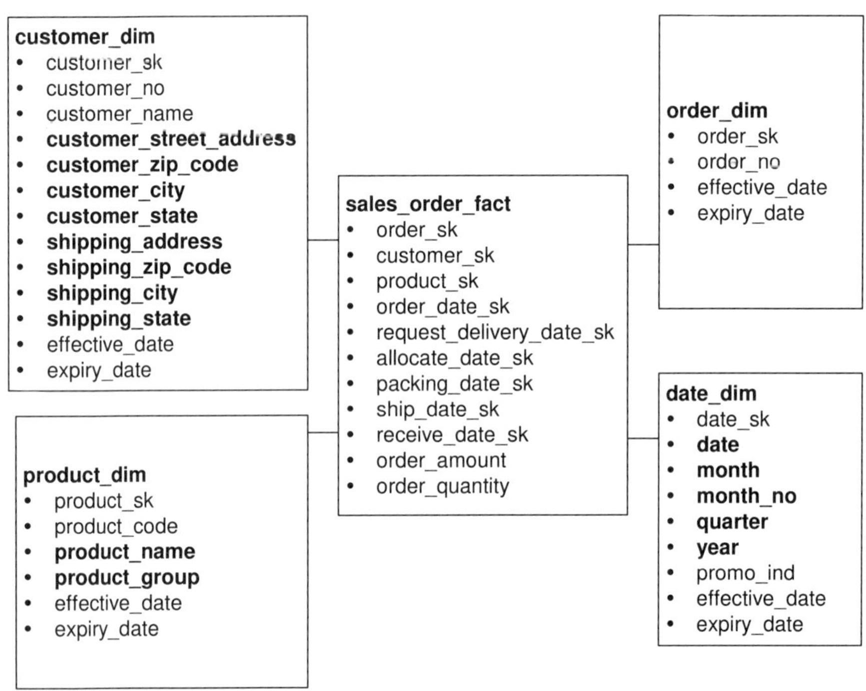

Figure 15.1: Schema Showing Hierarchies

Table 15.1 shows the hierarchies of the three dimensions. Note that the customer dimension has two-path hierarchies.

customer_dim		product_dim	date_dim
customer_street_address	shipping_address	product_name	date
customer_zip_code	shipping_zip_code	product_category	month_name
customer_city	shipping_city		quarter
customer_state	shipping_state		year

Table 15.1: Hierarchies in customer_dim, product_dim, and date_dim

Grouping and Drilling Queries

You can do grouping and drilling queries on hierarchies. A grouping query groups the facts on one or more levels of a dimension. The script in Listing

15.1 is an example of a grouping query. It is a query that retrieves the sales amount grouped by products (**product_category**) and the three hierarchy levels (columns) of the date dimension (**year**, **quarter**, and **month_name**).

Listing 15.1: A grouping query

```
/**********************************************************************/
/*                                                                    */
/* grouping.sql                                                       */
/*                                                                    */
/**********************************************************************/

USE dw;

SELECT
  product_category
, year
, quarter
, month_name
, SUM(order_amount)
FROM
  sales_order_fact a
, product_dim b
, date_dim c
WHERE
a.product_sk = b.product_sk
AND a.order_date_sk = c.date_sk
GROUP BY
  product_category
, year
, quarter
, month
ORDER BY
  product_category
, year
, quarter
, month
;

/* end of script                                                      */
```

You can run the **grouping.sql** script in Listing 15.1 by using this command.

```
mysql> \. c:\mysql\scripts\grouping.sql
```

If you've been following the instructions in Chapter 1 to Chapter 14, you'll get the following output.

```
Database changed
+----------------+------+---------+-----------+-------------------+
|product_category| year | quarter | month_name | SUM(order_amount) |
+----------------+------+---------+-----------+-------------------+
| Monitor        | 2005 |       1 | March      |           4000.00 |
| Monitor        | 2005 |       3 | July       |           6000.00 |
| Monitor        | 2006 |       1 | January    |           1000.00 |
| Monitor        | 2006 |       2 | April      |           2500.00 |
| Monitor        | 2006 |       3 | July       |           4000.00 |
| Monitor        | 2006 |       4 | October    |           1000.00 |
| Monitor        | 2007 |       1 | February   |           4000.00 |
| Monitor        | 2007 |       1 | March      |          32000.00 |
| Peripheral     | 2007 |       1 | March      |          25000.00 |
| Storage        | 2005 |       2 | April      |           4000.00 |
| Storage        | 2005 |       2 | May        |           6000.00 |
| Storage        | 2005 |       3 | September  |           8000.00 |
| Storage        | 2005 |       4 | November   |           8000.00 |
| Storage        | 2006 |       1 | February   |           1000.00 |
| Storage        | 2006 |       1 | March      |           2000.00 |
| Storage        | 2006 |       2 | May        |           3000.00 |
| Storage        | 2006 |       2 | June       |           3500.00 |
| Storage        | 2006 |       3 | August     |           4500.00 |
| Storage        | 2006 |       3 | September  |           1000.00 |
| Storage        | 2007 |       1 | January    |           4000.00 |
| Storage        | 2007 |       1 | February   |           4000.00 |
| Storage        | 2007 |       1 | March      |          46000.00 |
+----------------+------+---------+-----------+-------------------+
22 rows in set (0.42 sec)
```

The grouping query output shows the measure (sales order amount) grouped along the year-quarter-month hierarchy on each row.

Like a grouping query, a drilling query also groups its facts on one or more levels of a dimension. However, unlike a grouping query that shows the grouped facts (e.g. the sum of order amounts) of only the dimension's lowest level (e.g. the month level), a drilling query shows the grouped facts of each level of the dimension. The drilling query in Listing 15.2 shows the sum of order amounts at each of the date dimension levels (year, quarter, and month levels).

Listing 15.2: A drilling query

```
/******************************************************************/
```

```
/*                                                               */
/* drilling.sql                                                  */
/*                                                               */
/*****************************************************************/

USE dw;

SELECT
  product_category
, time
, order_amount
FROM (

( SELECT
  product_category
, date
, year time
, 1 sequence
, SUM(order_amount) order_amount
FROM
  sales_order_fact a
, product_dim b
, date_dim c
WHERE
    a.product_sk = b.product_sk
AND a.order_date_sk = c.date_sk
GROUP BY
  product_category
,  year
ORDER BY date
)

UNION ALL

( SELECT
  product_category
, date
, quarter time
, 2 sequence
, SUM(order_amount)
FROM
  sales_order_fact a
, product_dim b
, date_dim c
WHERE
```

```
    a.product_sk = b.product_sk
AND a.order_date_sk = c.date_sk
GROUP BY product_category, year, quarter
ORDER BY date
)

UNION ALL

( SELECT
  product_category
, date
, month_name time
, 3 sequence
, SUM(order_amount)
FROM
  sales_order_fact a
, product_dim b
, date_dim c
WHERE
    a.product_sk = b.product_sk
AND a.order_date_sk = c.date_sk
GROUP BY
  product_category
, year
, quarter
, month_name
ORDER BY date
)

) x

ORDER BY
  product_category
, date
, sequence
, time
;

/* end of script                                                   */
```

You can run the **drilling.sql** script by using this command.

```
mysql> \. c:\mysql\scripts\drilling.sql
```

Here is the output of the drilling query.

```
Database changed
```

```
+------------------+-----------+--------------+
| product_category | time      | order_amount |
+------------------+-----------+--------------+
| Monitor          | 2005      |     10000.00 |
| Monitor          | 1         |      4000.00 |
| Monitor          | March     |      4000.00 |
| Monitor          | 3         |      6000.00 |
| Monitor          | July      |      6000.00 |
| Monitor          | 2006      |      8500.00 |
| Monitor          | 1         |      1000.00 |
| Monitor          | January   |      1000.00 |
| Monitor          | 2         |      2500.00 |
| Monitor          | April     |      2500.00 |
| Monitor          | 3         |      4000.00 |
| Monitor          | July      |      4000.00 |
| Monitor          | 4         |      1000.00 |
| Monitor          | October   |      1000.00 |
| Monitor          | 2007      |     36000.00 |
| Monitor          | 1         |     36000.00 |
| Monitor          | February  |      4000.00 |
| Monitor          | March     |     32000.00 |
| Peripheral       | 2007      |     25000.00 |
| Peripheral       | 1         |     25000.00 |
| Peripheral       | March     |     25000.00 |
| Storage          | 2005      |     26000.00 |
| Storage          | 2         |     10000.00 |
| Storage          | April     |      4000.00 |
| Storage          | May       |      6000.00 |
| Storage          | 3         |      8000.00 |
| Storage          | September |      8000.00 |
| Storage          | 4         |      8000.00 |
| Storage          | November  |      8000.00 |
| Storage          | 2006      |     15000.00 |
| Storage          | 1         |      3000.00 |
| Storage          | February  |      1000.00 |
| Storage          | March     |      2000.00 |
| Storage          | 2         |      6500.00 |
| Storage          | May       |      3000.00 |
| Storage          | June      |      3500.00 |
| Storage          | 3         |      5500.00 |
| Storage          | August    |      4500.00 |
| Storage          | September |      1000.00 |
| Storage          | 2007      |     54000.00 |
| Storage          | 1         |     54000.00 |
| Storage          | January   |      4000.00 |
```

```
| Storage          | February  |      4000.00 |
| Storage          | March     |     46000.00 |
+------------------+-----------+--------------+
44 rows in set (0.03 sec)
```

Note

Drilling queries use the **UNION** set operator. Each of the three unions in the drilling query in Listing 15.2 gives you the rows of each of the three levels. The sequence column helps order the monthly sales orders from the year to the quarter to the month.

Summary

In this chapter you learn grouping and drilling queries on a single-path hierarchy and their differences. In the next chapter you learn multi-path hierarchy and their queries.

Chapter 16
Multi-Path and Ragged Hierarchies

This chapter discusses the multi-path hierarchy, expanding on the single-path hierarchy you learned in Chapter 15, "Dimension Hierarchies." You might recall from Chapter 15, the month dimension in our data warehouse has one hierarchy path, the year-quarter-month path. In this chapter we will add a new level, campaign session, and add a new hierarchy path of year-campaign-month. The month dimension will then have two hierarchy paths and therefore has a multi-path hierarchy.

Another topic of discussion in this chapter is the ragged hierarchy, which is a hierarchy that does not have data in one or more of its levels.

Adding A Hierarchy

I explain in this section how to add a hierarchy in a dimension that already has a hierarchy, thus forming a multi-path hierarchy. I also show how to populate the new hierarchy and verify that the population is successful.

First of all, you need to add a new column called **campaign_session** to the **month_dim** table. Figure 16.1 shows the schema after the addition.

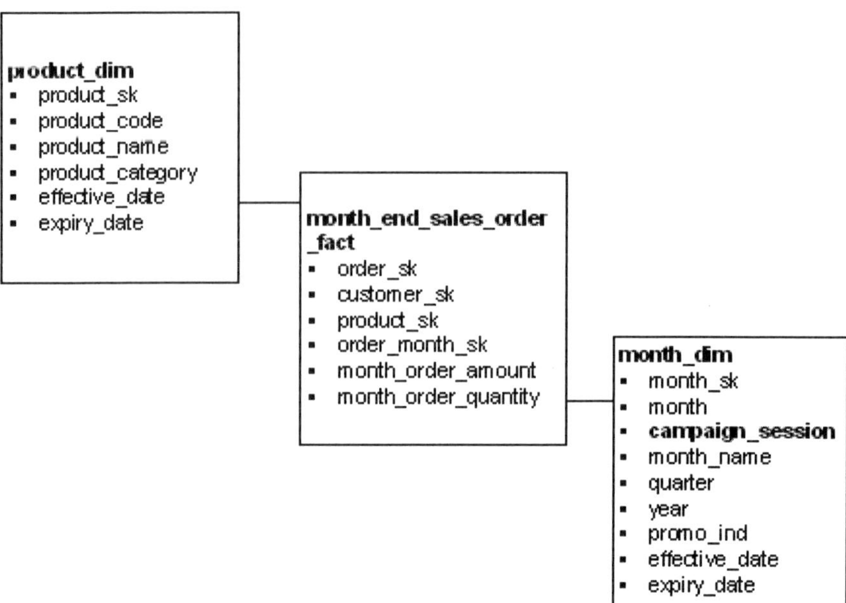

Figure 16.1: The schema after adding campaign_session

You can use the script in Listing 16.1 to add the new column.

Listing 16.1: Adding the campaign_session column

```
/**********************************************************************/
/*                                                                    */
/* add_campaign_session.sql                                           */
/*                                                                    */
/**********************************************************************/

USE dw;

ALTER TABLE month_dim
ADD campaign_session CHAR(30) AFTER month
;

/* end of script                                                      */
```

Run the script in Listing 16.1 now.

```
mysql> \. c:\mysql\scripts\add_campaign_session.sql
```

You should see this on your console upon running the script.

```
Database changed
Query OK, 82 rows affected (0.63 sec)
Records: 82  Duplicates: 0  Warnings: 0
```

To understand how the campaign session works, look at the sample campaign sessions in Table 16.1.

Campaign Session	Month
2005 First Campaign	January – April
2005 Second Campaign	May – July
2005 Third Campaign	August – August
2005 Last Campaign	September – December

Table 16.1: 2005 Campaign Sessions

Each campaign session lasts one or more months. A campaign session might not run exactly in one quarter. This means, campaign session levels do not roll up to the quarter (the campaign session's next higher level). Rather, the campaign sessions roll up to the year level.

Now you need to populate the **campaign_session** column. I've provided the following campaign session data for 2006 in the **campaign_session.csv** file.

```
CAMPAIGN SESSION,MONTH,YEAR
2006 First Campaign,1,2006
2006 First Campaign,2,2006
2006 First Campaign,3,2006
2006 First Campaign,4,2006
2006 Second Campaign,5,2006
2006 Second Campaign,6,2006
2006 Second Campaign,7,2006
2006 Third Campaign,8,2006
2006 Last Campaign,9,2006
2006 Last Campaign,10,2006
2006 Last Campaign,11,2006
2006 Last Campaign,12,2006
```

As usual, you don't load data from a text file directly to a data warehouse table. Instead, you use a staging table. Listing 16.2 shows a script that creates a **campaign_session_stg** table.

Listing 16.2: Creating the campaign_session_stg table

```
/**********************************************************************/
/*                                                                    */
/* create_campaign_stg.sql                                            */
/*                                                                    */
/**********************************************************************/

USE dw;

CREATE TABLE campaign_session_stg
( campaign_session CHAR(30)
, month CHAR(9)
, year INT(4)
)
;

/* end of script                                                      */
```

Run the script by calling the script name this way.

```
mysql> \. c:\mysql\scripts\create_campaign_stg.sql
```

Now you can load the 2006 campaign sessions into the month dimension. Listing 16.3 shows the script to do that.

Listing 16.3: Campaign session population

```
/**********************************************************************/
/*                                                                    */
/* campaign_session.sql                                               */
/*                                                                    */
/**********************************************************************/

USE dw;

TRUNCATE campaign_session_stg;

LOAD DATA INFILE 'campaign_session.csv'
INTO TABLE campaign_session_stg
FIELDS TERMINATED BY ','
OPTIONALLY ENCLOSED BY '"'
LINES TERMINATED BY '\r\n'
IGNORE 1 LINES
(
  campaign_session
, month
```

```
, year
)
;

UPDATE month_dim a, campaign_session_stg b
SET a.campaign_session = b.campaign_session
WHERE
    a.month = b.month
AND a.year = b.year
;

/* end of script                                                    */
```

Run the script using this command.

```
mysql> \. c:\mysql\scripts\campaign_session.sql
```

Here is what you should see on the console.

```
Database changed
Query OK, 1 row affected (0.05 sec)

Query OK, 12 rows affected (0.09 sec)
Records: 12  Deleted: 0  Skipped: 0  Warnings: 0

Query OK, 12 rows affected (0.05 sec)
Rows matched: 12  Changed: 12  Warnings: 0
```

Now query the **month_dim** table to confirm the table has been correctly populated.

```
mysql> select month_sk, month_name, year, campaign_session
    -> from month_dim
    -> where year = 2006;
```

Here is the result.

```
+----------+------------+------+----------------------+
| month_sk | month_name | year | campaign_session     |
+----------+------------+------+----------------------+
|       11 | January    | 2006 | 2006 First Campaign  |
|       12 | February   | 2006 | 2006 First Campaign  |
|       13 | March      | 2006 | 2006 First Campaign  |
|       14 | April      | 2006 | 2006 First Campaign  |
|       15 | May        | 2006 | 2006 Second Campaign |
|       16 | June       | 2006 | 2006 Second Campaign |
```

```
|        17 | July       | 2006 | 2006 Second Campaign |
|        18 | August     | 2006 | 2006 Third Campaign  |
|        19 | September  | 2006 | 2006 Last Campaign   |
|        20 | October    | 2006 | 2006 Last Campaign   |
|        21 | November   | 2006 | 2006 Last Campaign   |
|        22 | December   | 2006 | 2006 Last Campaign   |
+----------+------------+------+---------------------+
12 rows in set (0.00 sec)
```

Note

You load the campaign session CSV file in January every year when you get the data from the user and must do so before the population of the **month_end_sales_order_fact** table.

Adding 2006 Data

In Chapter 14, "Snapshots" you populated the **month_end_sales_order_fact** table with February 2006 data. You now need to add more data (January 2006 data and March 2006 through December 2006 data) by running the **month_end_sales_order.sql** script from Chapter 14. You must run the script once a month. Don't forget to set your MySQL date to the month end date right before each run. All runs look exactly the same on the MySQL monitor. Here's an example.

```
mysql> \. c:\mysql\scripts\month_end_sales_order.sql

Database changed
Query OK, 1 row affected (0.09 sec)
Records: 1  Duplicates: 0  Warnings: 0
```

When you finish loading additional data (eleven times altogether), use the following SQL statement to query the **month_end_sales_order_fact** table to make sure it has been populated correctly.

```
mysql> select month, year, product_name,
    -> month_order_amount mo_amt, month_order_quantity mo_qty
    -> from  month_end_sales_order_fact a, month_dim b, product_dim
       c
    -> where a.month_order_sk = b.month_sk
    -> and a.product_sk = c.product_sk
    -> and year = 2006
    -> order BY month, year, product_name;
```

Here is the query result.

```
+-------+------+-------------------------+----------+--------+
| month | year | product_name            | mo_amt   | mo_qty |
+-------+------+-------------------------+----------+--------+
|     1 | 2006 | LCD Panel               |  1000.00 |   NULL |
|     2 | 2006 | Hard Disk Drive         |  1000.00 |   NULL |
|     4 | 2006 | LCD Panel               |  2500.00 |   NULL |
|     5 | 2006 | Hard Disk Drive         |  3000.00 |   NULL |
|     6 | 2006 | Floppy Drive            |  3500.00 |   NULL |
|     7 | 2006 | LCD Panel               |  4000.00 |   NULL |
|     8 | 2006 | Hard Disk Drive         |  4500.00 |   NULL |
|     9 | 2006 | Floppy Drive            |  1000.00 |   NULL |
|    10 | 2006 | LCD Panel               |  1000.00 |   NULL |
+-------+------+-------------------------+----------+--------+
10 rows in set (0.09 sec)
```

Note that there is no data for November and December.

Hierarchical Queries

In this section I present two example queries that use the two hierarchical paths of the month dimension. The first query, shown in Listing 16.4, drills on the year-quarter-month path. This query is similar to the drilling query in Chapter 15, "Dimension Hierarchies" except that this one queries the **month_end_sales_order_fact** table, whereas the one in Chapter 15 queried the **sales_order_fact** table.

Listing 16.4: Quarter path drilling query

```
/**********************************************************************/
/*                                                                    */
/* quarter_path.sql                                                   */
/*                                                                    */
/**********************************************************************/

USE dw;

SELECT
  product_category
, time
, order_amount
```

```
, order_quantity
FROM (

( SELECT
  product_category
, year
, 1 month
, year time
, 1 sequence
, SUM(month_order_amount) order_amount
, SUM(month_order_quantity) order_quantity
FROM
  month_end_sales_order_fact a
, product_dim b
, month_dim c
WHERE
    a.product_sk = b.product_sk
AND a.month_order_sk = c.month_sk
AND year = 2006
GROUP BY
  product_category
, year
)

UNION ALL

( SELECT
  product_category
, year
, month
, quarter time
, 2 sequence
, SUM(month_order_amount) order_amount
, SUM(month_order_quantity) order_quantity
FROM
  month_end_sales_order_fact a
, product_dim b
, month_dim c
WHERE
    a.product_sk = b.product_sk
AND a.month_order_sk = c.month_sk
AND year = 2006
GROUP BY product_category, year, quarter
)

UNION ALL
```

```
( SELECT
  product_category
, year
, month
, month_name time
, 3 sequence
, SUM(month_order_amount) order_amount
, SUM(month_order_quantity) order_quantity
FROM
  month_end_sales_order_fact a
, product_dim b
, month_dim c
WHERE
    a.product_sk = b.product_sk
AND a.month_order_sk = c.month_sk
AND year = 2006
GROUP BY
  product_category
, year
, quarter
, month
)

) x

ORDER BY
  product_category
, year
, month
, sequence
;

/* end of script                                                    */
```

Run the script in Listing 16.4 using this command.

```
mysql> \. c:\mysql\scripts\quarter_path.sql
```

Here is the query result.

```
Database changed
+------------------+-----------+--------------+----------------+
| product_category | time      | order_amount | order_quantity |
+------------------+-----------+--------------+----------------+
| Monitor          | 2006      |      8500.00 |           NULL |
```

```
| Monitor          | 1         |     1000.00 |            NULL |
| Monitor          | January   |     1000.00 |            NULL |
| Monitor          | 2         |     2500.00 |            NULL |
| Monitor          | April     |     2500.00 |            NULL |
| Monitor          | 3         |     4000.00 |            NULL |
| Monitor          | July      |     4000.00 |            NULL |
| Monitor          | 4         |     1000.00 |            NULL |
| Monitor          | October   |     1000.00 |            NULL |
| Storage          | 2006      |    15000.00 |            NULL |
| Storage          | 1         |     3000.00 |            NULL |
| Storage          | February  |     1000.00 |            NULL |
| Storage          | March     |     2000.00 |            NULL |
| Storage          | 2         |     6500.00 |            NULL |
| Storage          | May       |     3000.00 |            NULL |
| Storage          | June      |     3500.00 |            NULL |
| Storage          | 3         |     5500.00 |            NULL |
| Storage          | August    |     4500.00 |            NULL |
| Storage          | September |     1000.00 |            NULL |
+------------------+-----------+-------------+-----------------+
19 rows in set (0.02 sec)
```

The second query, presented in Listing 16.5, drills the campaign session year-campaign-month hierarchy. This query has the same structure as the first one, except that it groups by campaign and not by quarter.

Listing 16.5: Drilling the campaign session path

```
/********************************************************************/
/*                                                                  */
/* campaign_session_path.sql                                        */
/*                                                                  */
/********************************************************************/

SELECT
  product_category pc
, time
, order_amount amt
, order_quantity qty
FROM (

( SELECT
  product_category
, year
, 1 month
, year time
, 1 sequence
```

```
, SUM(month_order_amount) order_amount
, SUM(month_order_quantity) order_quantity
FROM
  month_end_sales_order_fact a
, product_dim b
, month_dim c
WHERE
    a.product_sk = b.product_sk
AND a.month_order_sk = c.month_sk
AND year = 2006
GROUP BY
  product_category
, year
)

UNION ALL

( SELECT
  product_category
, year
, month
, campaign_session time
, 2 sequence
, SUM(month_order_amount) order_amount
, SUM(month_order_quantity) order_quantity
FROM
  month_end_sales_order_fact a
, product_dim b
, month_dim c
WHERE
    a.product_sk = b.product_sk
AND a.month_order_sk = c.month_sk
AND year = 2006
GROUP BY
  product_category
, year
, campaign_session
)

UNION ALL

( SELECT
  product_category
, year
, month
```

```
, month_name time
, 3 sequence
, SUM(month_order_amount) order_amount
, SUM(month_order_quantity) order_quantity
FROM
  month_end_sales_order_fact a
, product_dim b
, month_dim c
WHERE
    a.product_sk = b.product_sk
AND a.month_order_sk = c.month_sk
AND year = 2006
GROUP BY
  product_category
, year
, campaign_session
, month_name
)

) x

ORDER BY
  product_category
, year
, month
, sequence
;

/* end of script                                                    */
```

Run the query in Listing 16.5 using this command.

```
mysql> \. c:\mysql\scripts\campaign_session_path.sql
```

Here is the query result.

```
+------------+----------------------+----------+------+
| pc         | time                 | amt      | qty  |
+------------+----------------------+----------+------+
| Monitor    | 2006                 |  8500.00 | NULL |
| Monitor    | 2006 First Campaign  |  3500.00 | NULL |
| Monitor    | January              |  1000.00 | NULL |
| Monitor    | April                |  2500.00 | NULL |
| Monitor    | 2006 Second Campaign |  4000.00 | NULL |
| Monitor    | July                 |  4000.00 | NULL |
| Monitor    | 2006 Last Campaign   |  1000.00 | NULL |
| Monitor    | October              |  1000.00 | NULL |
```

```
| Storage     | 2006                   | 15000.00 | NULL |
| Storage     | 2006 First Campaign    |  3000.00 | NULL |
| Storage     | February               |  1000.00 | NULL |
| Storage     | March                  |  2000.00 | NULL |
| Storage     | 2006 Second Campaign   |  6500.00 | NULL |
| Storage     | May                    |  3000.00 | NULL |
| Storage     | June                   |  3500.00 | NULL |
| Storage     | 2006 Third Campaign    |  4500.00 | NULL |
| Storage     | August                 |  4500.00 | NULL |
| Storage     | 2006 Last Campaign     |  1000.00 | NULL |
| Storage     | September              |  1000.00 | NULL |
+-------------+------------------------+----------+------+
19 rows in set (0.00 sec)
```

Ragged Hierarchies

A hierarchy that does not have data in one or more level is called a ragged hierarchy. For example, if your users don't have any campaign session for certain months, then the month dimension is said to have a ragged campaign hierarchy. In this section I explain the ragged hierarchy and how to apply it on campaign sessions.

Here's a sample ragged campaign (in the **ragged_campaign.csv** file) that does not have January, April, September, October, November, and December 2006 campaign sessions.

```
CAMPAIGN SESSION,MONTH,YEAR
NULL,1,2006
2006 Early Spring Campaign,2,2006
2006 Early Spring Campaign,3,2006
NULL,4,2006
2006 Spring Campaign,5,2006
2006 Spring Campaign,6,2006
2006 Last Campaign,7,2006
2006 Last Campaign,8,2006
NULL,9,2006
NULL,10,2006
NULL,11,2006
NULL,12,2006
```

The script in Listing 16.6 loads the campaign session into the **month_dim** table.

Listing 16.6: Ragged campaign session

```
/******************************************************************/
/*                                                                */
/* ragged_campaign.sql                                            */
/*                                                                */
/******************************************************************/

USE dw;

TRUNCATE campaign_session_stg;

LOAD DATA INFILE 'ragged_campaign.csv'
INTO TABLE campaign_session_stg
FIELDS TERMINATED BY ','
OPTIONALLY ENCLOSED BY '"'
LINES TERMINATED BY '\r\n'
IGNORE 1 LINES
(
  campaign_session
, month
, year
)
;

UPDATE
  month_dim a
, campaign_session_stg b
SET a.campaign_session = b.campaign_session
WHERE
    a.month = b.month
AND a.year = b.year
AND b.campaign_session IS NOT NULL
;

UPDATE
  month_dim a
, campaign_session_stg b
SET a.campaign_session = a.month_name
WHERE
    a.month = b.month
AND a.year = b.year
AND b.campaign_session IS NULL
;

/* end of script                                                  */
```

To see how it works, clean up the existing campaign session column (set its value to NULL) by running the script in Listing 16.7.

Listing 16.7: Nullifying the campaign_session column

```
/*****************************************************************/
/*                                                               */
/* nullify_campaign_session.sql                                  */
/*                                                               */
/*****************************************************************/

USE dw;

UPDATE month_dim
SET campaign_session = NULL
;

/* end of script                                                 */
```

Run the script by using this command:

```
mysql> \. c:\mysql\scripts\nullify_campaign_session.sql
```

You should see a message similar to this on your console.

```
Database changed
Query OK, 12 rows affected (0.05 sec)
Rows matched: 96  Changed: 12  Warnings: 0
```

Now, run the **ragged_campaign.sql** script in Listing 16.7 to load the campaign session CSV file by calling the script file name.

```
mysql> \. c:\mysql\scripts\ragged_campaign.sql
```

Here is what should be printed on the console.

```
Database changed
Query OK, 12 rows affected (0.05 sec)

Query OK, 12 rows affected (0.05 sec)
Records: 12  Deleted: 0  Skipped: 0  Warnings: 0

Query OK, 6 rows affected (0.07 sec)
Rows matched: 6  Changed: 6  Warnings: 0

Query OK, 6 rows affected (0.06 sec)
Rows matched: 6  Changed: 6  Warnings: 0
```

To verify that the **month_dim** table was populated, query the table using this SQL statement.

```
mysql> select month_sk, month_name, year, campaign_session
    -> from month_dim
    -> where year = 2006;
```

The correct result is as follows.

```
+----------+------------+------+----------------------------+
| month_sk | month_name | year | campaign_session           |
+----------+------------+------+----------------------------+
|       11 | January    | 2006 | January                    |
|       12 | February   | 2006 | 2006 Early Spring Campaign |
|       13 | March      | 2006 | 2006 Early Spring Campaign |
|       14 | April      | 2006 | April                      |
|       15 | May        | 2006 | 2006 Spring Campaign       |
|       16 | June       | 2006 | 2006 Spring Campaign       |
|       17 | July       | 2006 | 2006 Last Campaign         |
|       18 | August     | 2006 | 2006 Last Campaign         |
|       19 | September  | 2006 | September                  |
|       20 | October    | 2006 | October                    |
|       21 | November   | 2006 | November                   |
|       22 | December   | 2006 | December                   |
+----------+------------+------+----------------------------+
12 rows in set (0.00 sec)
```

You can then run the **campaign_session_path.sql** script using this command.

```
mysql> \. c:\mysql\scripts\campaign_session_path.sql
```

Here is the query result.

```
+------------+----------------------------+----------+------+
| pc         | time                       | amt      | qty  |
+------------+----------------------------+----------+------+
| Monitor    | 2005                       | 44500.00 |  125 |
| Monitor    | January                    |  1000.00 | NULL |
| Monitor    | January                    |  1000.00 | NULL |
| Monitor    | April                      |  2500.00 | NULL |
| Monitor    | April                      |  2500.00 | NULL |
| Monitor    | 2005 Last Campaign         |  4000.00 | NULL |
| Monitor    | July                       |  4000.00 | NULL |
| Monitor    | October                    |  5000.00 | NULL |
```

```
| Monitor    | October                    |  5000.00 | NULL |
| Monitor    | November                   | 32000.00 |  125 |
| Monitor    | November                   | 32000.00 |  125 |
| Peripheral | 2005                       | 25000.00 |   70 |
| Peripheral | November                   | 25000.00 |   70 |
| Peripheral | November                   | 25000.00 |   70 |
| Storage    | 2005                       | 69000.00 |  285 |
| Storage    | 2005 Early Spring Campaign |  3000.00 | NULL |
| Storage    | February                   |  1000.00 | NULL |
| Storage    | March                      |  2000.00 | NULL |
| Storage    | 2005 Spring Campaign       |  6500.00 | NULL |
| Storage    | May                        |  3000.00 | NULL |
| Storage    | June                       |  3500.00 | NULL |
| Storage    | 2005 Last Campaign         |  4500.00 | NULL |
| Storage    | August                     |  4500.00 | NULL |
| Storage    | September                  |  1000.00 | NULL |
| Storage    | September                  |  1000.00 | NULL |
| Storage    | October                    |  8000.00 | NULL |
| Storage    | October                    |  8000.00 | NULL |
| Storage    | November                   | 37500.00 |  200 |
| Storage    | November                   | 37500.00 |  200 |
| Storage    | December                   |  8500.00 |   85 |
| Storage    | December                   |  8500.00 |   85 |
+------------+----------------------------+----------+------+
31 rows in set (0.00 sec)
```

The query output shows that the rows of year and month levels are the same as the output of the non-ragged hierarchy's campaign path. However, the months with no campaign are listed right above the months themselves. This is to say, the months roll themselves up to their non-existing campaign levels. For example, January does not have a campaign, so you see two January rows for Monitor (2nd and 3rd rows). The third row is for the month, the second represents the non-existing campaign row. The sales order amount (the **amt** column in the query output) for the non-existing campaign is the same as the month amount.

February and March for Storage belong to the same campaign, namely '2005 Early Spring Campaign'. Therefore, both months have one row each that roll up to their campaign; the sum of their sales order amounts is the amount for the campaign.

Summary

In this chapter you learned the multi-path hierarchy and ragged hierarchy. You also applied drilling queries to test the multi-path hierarchy in the month dimension.

In Chapter 17, "Degenerate Dimensions" you will learn a technique called degenerate dimension, which you can use to simplify a dimensional schema.

Chapter 17
Degenerate Dimensions

This chapter teaches you a technique for consolidating dimensions called the degenerate dimension. The technique reduces the number of dimensions and simplifies a dimensional data warehouse schema. A simpler schema is easier to understand than a complex one and delivers faster query performance.

You degenerate a dimension when the dimension does not have any data needed by the data warehouse user. You relocate the data from the degenerated dimension into the fact table and remove the degenerated dimension.

Degenerating the Order Dimension

In this section I explain how to degenerate the order dimension, including revising the schema and the regular population script. The first thing you do with the degenerate dimension technique is identify any column that is never used for data analysis.

For example, the **order_number** column in the order dimension is potentially such a column. However, your users might still need the order number if they want to see the details of a transaction. Therefore, before you degenerate the order dimension, you have to relocate order numbers to the **sales_order_fact** table. Figure 17.1 shows the schema after the relocation.

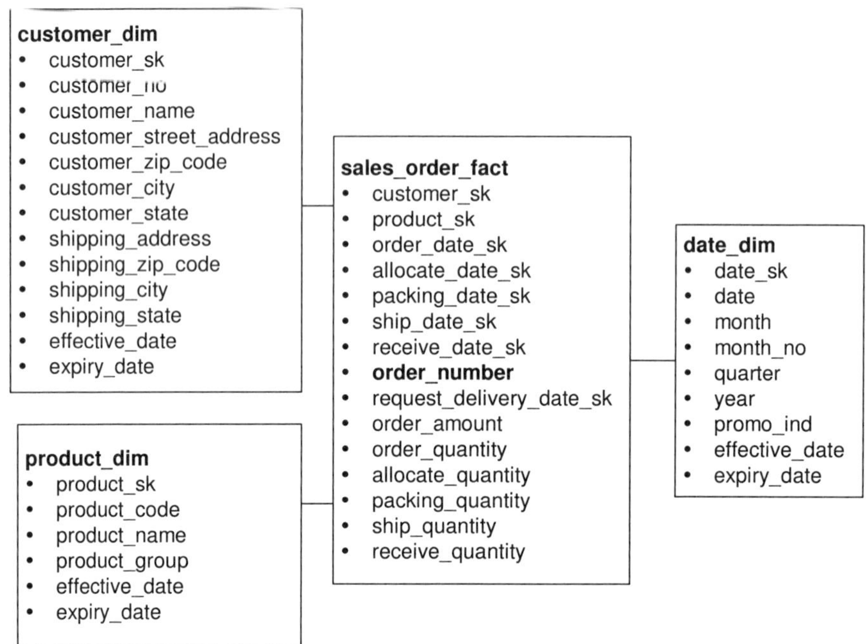

Figure 17.1: The schema with the order dimension degenerated

To degenerate the **order_dim** table, do the following four steps in sequence:

1. Add the **order_number** column to the **sales_order_fact** table.
2. Move the existing order numbers from the **order_dim** table to **sales_order_fact** table.
3. Remove the **order_sk** column in the **sales_order_fact** table.
4. Remove the **order_dim** table.

The script in Listing 17.1 does all of the necessary steps.

Listing 17.1: Degenerating order dimension

```
/**********************************************************************/
/*                                                                    */
/* degenerate.sql                                                     */
/*                                                                    */
/**********************************************************************/

/* default to dw database                                             */
```

```
USE dw;

/* adding order_number column                                    */

ALTER TABLE sales_order_fact
ADD order_number INT AFTER receive_date_sk
;

/* loading existing order_number                                 */

UPDATE sales_order_fact a, order_dim b
SET a.order_number = b.order_number
WHERE a.order_sk = b.order_sk
;

/* removing order_sk column                                      */

ALTER TABLE sales_order_fact
  DROP order_sk
;

/* removing the order_dim table                                  */

DROP TABLE order_dim
;

/* end of script                                                 */
```

Run the script in Listing 17.1 by calling the script file name.

```
mysql> \. c:\mysql\scripts\degenerate.sql
```

You should see the following on the console.

```
Database changed
Query OK, 49 rows affected (0.34 sec)
Records: 49  Duplicates: 0  Warnings: 0

Query OK, 49 rows affected (0.06 sec)
Rows matched: 49  Changed: 49  Warnings: 0

Query OK, 49 rows affected (0.32 sec)
Records: 49  Duplicates: 0  Warnings: 0

Query OK, 0 rows affected (0.04 sec)
```

The message indicates that you had 49 orders in the order dimensions truncated. This is the number of order numbers that moved to the fact table.

Confirm that the **order_number** column was added to the **sales_fact_table** by typing the following statement.

```
mysql> desc sales_order_fact;
```

The result is given below.

```
+------------------------+-------------+----+---+---------+-------+
| Field                  |Type         |Null|Key| Default | Extra |
+------------------------+-------------+----+---+---------+-------+
|customer_sk             |int(11)      | YES|   | NULL    |       |
|product_sk              |int(11)      | YES|   | NULL    |       |
|order_date_sk           |int(11)      | YES|   | NULL    |       |
|allocate_date_sk        |int(11)      | YES|   | NULL    |       |
|packing_date_sk         |int(11)      | YES|   | NULL    |       |
|ship_date_sk            |int(11)      | YES|   | NULL    |       |
|receive_date_sk         |int(11)      | YES|   | NULL    |       |
|order_number            |int(11)      | YES|   | NULL    |       |
|request_delivery_date_sk|int(11)      | YES|   | NULL    |       |
|order_amount            |decimal(10,2)| YES|   | NULL    |       |
|order_quantity          |int(11)      | YES|   | NULL    |       |
|allocate_quantity       |int(11)      | YES|   | NULL    |       |
|packing_quantity        |int(11)      | YES|   | NULL    |       |
|ship_quantity           |int(11)      | YES|   | NULL    |       |
|receive_quantity        |int(11)      | YES|   | NULL    |       |
+------------------------+-------------+----+---+---------+-------+
15 rows in set (0.00 sec)
```

You can confirm that the 49 order numbers from **order_dim** have been relocated to the **sales_order_fact** table by using this statement.

```
mysql> select count(0) from sales_order_fact where order_number IS
       NOT NULL;
```

The result of the query is given below.

```
+----------+
| count(0) |
+----------+
|       49 |
+----------+
1 row in set (0.00 sec)
```

You should also confirm that the **order_sk** column was removed from the **sales_order_fact** table using this statement.

```
mysql> desc sales_order_fact;
```

You will see the following on your console.

```
+------------------------+-------------+------+---+-------+-------+
|Field                   |Type         | Null |Key|Default| Extra |
+------------------------+-------------+------+---+-------+-------+
|customer_sk             |int(11)      | YES  |   | NULL  |       |
|product_sk              |int(11)      | YES  |   | NULL  |       |
|order_date_sk           |int(11)      | YES  |   | NULL  |       |
|allocate_date_sk        |int(11)      | YES  |   | NULL  |       |
|packing_date_sk         |int(11)      | YES  |   | NULL  |       |
|ship_date_sk            |int(11)      | YES  |   | NULL  |       |
|receive_date_sk         |int(11)      | YES  |   | NULL  |       |
|order_number            |int(11)      | YES  |   | NULL  |       |
|request_delivery_date_sk|int(11)      | YES  |   | NULL  |       |
|order_amount            |decimal(10,2)| YES  |   | NULL  |       |
|order_quantity          |int(11)      | YES  |   | NULL  |       |
|allocate_quantity       |int(11)      | YES  |   | NULL  |       |
|packing_quantity        |int(11)      | YES  |   | NULL  |       |
|ship_quantity           |int(11)      | YES  |   | NULL  |       |
|receive_quantity        |int(11)      | YES  |   | NULL  |       |
+------------------------+-------------+------+---+-------+-------+
15 rows in set (0.00 sec)
```

Finally, make sure that the **order_dim** table was removed by using this command.

```
mysql> show tables;
```

Here is the list of tables in the **dw** database.

```
+----------------------------+
| Tables_in_dw               |
+----------------------------+
| allocate_date_dim          |
| campaign_session_stg       |
| customer_dim               |
| customer_stg               |
| date_dim                   |
| month_dim                  |
| month_end_sales_order_fact |
| order_date_dim             |
```

```
| pa_customer_dim            |
| packing_date_dim           |
| product_dim                |
| product_stg                |
| promo_schedule_stg         |
| receive_date_dim           |
| request_delivery_date_dim  |
| sales_order_fact           |
| ship_date_dim              |
+----------------------------+
17 rows in set (0.00 sec)
```

Revising the Regular Population Script

Another thing you need to do after degenerating a dimension is revise the regular population script. The revised script needs to enter order numbers to the sales order fact and no longer needs to populate the order dimension.

Listing 17.2 shows the revised regular population script.

Listing 17.2: Revised daily DW regular population

```
/**********************************************************************/
/*                                                                    */
/* dw_regular_17.sql                                                  */
/*                                                                    */
/**********************************************************************/

USE dw;

/* CUSTOMER_DIM POPULATION                                            */

TRUNCATE customer_stg;

LOAD DATA INFILE 'customer.csv'
INTO TABLE customer_stg
FIELDS TERMINATED BY ','
OPTIONALLY ENCLOSED BY '"'
LINES TERMINATED BY '\r\n'
IGNORE 1 LINES
( customer_number
, customer_name
, customer_street_address
, customer_zip_code
```

```
, customer_city
, customer_state
, shipping_address
, shipping_zip_code
, shipping_city
, shipping_state )
;

/* SCD 2 ON ADDRESSES                                              */

UPDATE
  customer_dim a
, customer_stg b
SET
  a.expiry_date = SUBDATE(CURRENT_DATE, 1)
WHERE
  a.customer_number = b.customer_number
AND (   a.customer_street_address <> b.customer_street_address
     OR a.customer_city <> b.customer_city
     OR a.customer_zip_code <> b.customer_zip_code
     OR a.customer_state <> b.customer_state
     OR a.shipping_address <> b.shipping_address
     OR a.shipping_city <> b.shipping_city
     OR a.shipping_zip_code <> b.shipping_zip_code
     OR a.shipping_state <> b.shipping_state
     OR a.shipping_address IS NULL
     OR a.shipping_city IS NULL
     OR a.shipping_zip_code IS NULL
     OR a.shipping_state IS NULL)
AND expiry_date = '9999-12-31'
;

INSERT INTO customer_dim
SELECT
  NULL
, b.customer_number
, b.customer_name
, b.customer_street_address
, b.customer_zip_code
, b.customer_city
, b.customer_state
, b.shipping_address
, b.shipping_zip_code
, b.shipping_city
, b.shipping_state
```

```
, CURRENT_DATE
, '9999-12-31'
FROM
  customer_dim a
, customer_stg b
WHERE
    a.customer_number = b.customer_number
AND (   a.customer_street_address <> b.customer_street_address
     OR a.customer_city <> b.customer_city
     OR a.customer_zip_code <> b.customer_zip_code
     OR a.customer_state <> b.customer_state
     OR a.shipping_address <> b.shipping_address
     OR a.shipping_city <> b.shipping_city
     OR a.shipping_zip_code <> b.shipping_zip_code
     OR a.shipping_state <> b.shipping_state
     OR a.shipping_address IS NULL
     OR a.shipping_city IS NULL
     OR a.shipping_zip_code IS NULL
     OR a.shipping_state IS NULL)
AND EXISTS (
SELECT *
FROM customer_dim x
WHERE b.customer_number = x.customer_number
AND a.expiry_date = SUBDATE(CURRENT_DATE, 1))
AND NOT EXISTS (
SELECT *
FROM customer_dim y
WHERE     b.customer_number = y.customer_number
      AND y.expiry_date = '9999-12-31')
;

/* END OF SCD 2                                                       */

/* SCD 1 ON NAME                                                      */

UPDATE customer_dim a, customer_stg b
SET a.customer_name = b.customer_name
WHERE     a.customer_number = b.customer_number
      AND a.expiry_date = '9999-12-31'
      AND a.customer_name <> b.customer_name
;

/* ADD NEW CUSTOMER                                                   */

INSERT INTO customer_dim
SELECT
```

```
  NULL
, customer_number
, customer_name
, customer_street_address
, customer_zip_code
, customer_city
, customer_state
, shipping_address
, shipping_zip_code
, shipping_city
, shipping_state
, CURRENT_DATE
, '9999-12-31'
FROM customer_stg
WHERE customer_number NOT IN(
SELECT a.customer_number
FROM
  customer_dim a
, customer_stg b
WHERE b.customer_number = a.customer_number )
;

/* RE-BUILD PA CUSTOMER DIMENSION                                  */

TRUNCATE pa_customer_dim;

INSERT INTO pa_customer_dim
SELECT
  customer_sk
, customer_number
, customer_name
, customer_street_address
, customer_zip_code
, customer_city
, customer_state
, shipping_address
, shipping_zip_code
, shipping_city
, shipping_state
, effective_date
, expiry_date
FROM customer_dim
WHERE customer_state = 'PA'
;
```

```
/* END OF CUSTOMER_DIM POPULATION                                  */

/* PRODUCT_DIM POPULATION                                          */

TRUNCATE product_stg
;

LOAD DATA INFILE 'product.txt'
INTO TABLE product_stg
FIELDS TERMINATED BY ''
OPTIONALLY ENCLOSED BY ''
LINES TERMINATED BY '\r\n'
IGNORE 1 LINES
( product_code
, product_name
, product_category )
;

/* SCD2 ON PRODUCT NAME AND GROUP                                  */

UPDATE
  product_dim a
, product_stg b
SET
  expiry_date = SUBDATE(CURRENT_DATE, 1)
WHERE
    a.product_code = b.product_code
AND (   a.product_name <> b.product_name
     OR a.product_category <> b.product_category )
     AND expiry_date = '9999-12-31'
;

INSERT INTO product_dim
SELECT
  NULL
, b.product_code
, b.product_name
, b.product_category
, CURRENT_DATE
, '9999-12-31'
FROM
  product_dim a
, product_stg b
WHERE
    a.product_code = b.product_code
AND (   a.product_name <> b.product_name
```

```
     OR a.product_category <> b.product_category )
AND EXISTS (
SELECT *
FROM product_dim x
WHERE     b.product_code = x.product_code
      AND a.expiry_date = SUBDATE(CURRENT_DATE, 1))
AND NOT EXISTS (
SELECT *
FROM product_dim y
WHERE    b.product_code = y.product_code
     AND y.expiry_date = '9999-12-31')
;

/* END OF SCD 2                                                    */

/* ADD NEW PRODUCT                                                 */

INSERT INTO product_dim
SELECT
  NULL
, product_code
, product_name
, product_category
, CURRENT_DATE
, '9999-12-31'
FROM product_stg
WHERE product_code NOT IN(
SELECT y.product_code
FROM product_dim x, product_stg y
WHERE x.product_code = y.product_code )
;

/* END OF PRODUCT_DIM POPULATION                                   */

/* insert new orders                                               */

INSERT INTO sales_order_fact
SELECT
  customer_sk
, product_sk
, e.order_date_sk
, NULL
, NULL
, NULL
, NULL
```

```
, a.order_number
, f.request delivery_date_sk
, order_amount
, quantity
, NULL
, NULL
, NULL
, NULL
FROM
  source.sales_order a
, customer_dim c
, product_dim d
, order_date_dim e
, request_delivery_date_dim f
WHERE
    a.order_status = 'N'
AND a.customer_number = c.customer_number
AND a.status_date >= c.effective_date
AND a.status_date <= c.expiry_date
AND a.product_code = d.product_code
AND a.status_date >= d.effective_date
AND a.status_date <= d.expiry_date
AND a.status_date = e.order_date
AND a.request_delivery_date = f.request_delivery_date
AND a.entry_date = CURRENT_DATE
;

UPDATE
  sales_order_fact a
, source.sales_order b
, allocate_date_dim c
SET
  a.allocate_date_sk = c.allocate_date_sk
, a.allocate_quantity = b.quantity
WHERE
    order_status = 'A'
AND b.entry_date = CURRENT_DATE
AND b.order_number = a.order_number
AND c.allocate_date = b.status_date
;

UPDATE
  sales_order_fact a
, source.sales_order b
, packing_date_dim d
SET
```

```
  a.packing_date_sk = d.packing_date_sk
, a.packing_quantity = b.quantity
WHERE
    order_status = 'P'
AND b.entry_date = CURRENT_DATE
AND b.order_number = a.order_number
AND d.packing_date = b.status_date
;

UPDATE
  sales_order_fact a
, source.sales_order b
, ship_date_dim e
SET
  a.ship_date_sk = e.ship_date_sk
, a.ship_quantity = b.quantity
WHERE
    order_status = 'S'
AND b.entry_date = CURRENT_DATE
AND b.order_number = a.order_number
AND e.ship_date = b.status_date
;

UPDATE
  sales_order_fact a
, source.sales_order b
, receive_date_dim f
SET
  a.receive_date_sk = f.receive_date_sk
, a.receive_quantity = b.quantity
WHERE
    order_status = 'R'
AND b.entry_date = CURRENT_DATE
AND b.order_number = a.order_number
AND f.receive_date = b.status_date
;

/* end of script                                                    */
```

Testing the Revised Regular Population Script

In this section I explain how to test the revised regular population script shown in Listing 17.2. The test uses two new sales orders with delivery milestones Order, Allocate, Pack, Ship, and Receive. Therefore, you need to add five rows for each order. The script in Listing 17.3 adds ten new rows into the **sales_order** table in the **source** database.

Listing 17.3: Sales orders for testing degeneration

```
/**********************************************************************/
/*                                                                    */
/* sales_order_17.sql                                                 */
/*                                                                    */
/**********************************************************************/

USE source;

INSERT INTO sales_order VALUES
  (52, 1, 1, '2007-03-11', 'N', '2007-03-20', '2007-03-11', 7500,
       75)
, (53, 2, 2, '2007-03-11', 'N', '2007-03-20', '2007-03-11', 1000,
       10)
, (52, 1, 1, '2007-03-12', 'A', '2007-03-20', '2007-03-12', 7500,
       75)
, (53, 2, 2, '2007-03-12', 'A', '2007-03-20', '2007-03-12', 1000,
       10)
, (52, 1, 1, '2007-03-13', 'P', '2007-03-20', '2007-03-13', 7500,
       75)
, (53, 2, 2, '2007-03-13', 'P', '2007-03-20', '2007-03-13', 1000,
       10)
, (52, 1, 1, '2007-03-14', 'S', '2007-03-20', '2007-03-14', 7500,
       75)
, (53, 2, 2, '2007-03-14', 'S', '2007-03-20', '2007-03-14', 1000,
       10)
, (52, 1, 1, '2007-03-15', 'R', '2007-03-20', '2007-03-15', 7500,
       75)
, (53, 2, 2, '2007-03-15', 'R', '2007-03-20', '2007-03-15', 1000,
       10)
;

/* end of script                                                      */
```

Run the script in Listing 17.3 using this command.

```
mysql> \. c:\mysql\scripts\sales_order_17.sql
```

Here is the response on the console.

```
Database changed
Query OK, 10 rows affected (0.05 sec)
Records: 10  Duplicates: 0  Warnings: 0
```

Now set your MySQL date to March 11, 2007 and run the **dw_regular_17.sql** script again. Afterward, set your MySQL date to March 12 through March 15, 2005 and run the **dw_regular_17.sql** script for each date.

After running the script five times, query the two orders in the **sales_order_fact** table using this command.

```
mysql> select order_number od, order_date_sk od_sk, allocate_date_sk
       ad_sk,
    -> packing_date_sk pk_sk, ship_date_sk sd_sk, receive_date_sk
       rd_sk
    -> from sales_order_fact
    -> where order_number IN(52, 53);
```

You should get the following result.

```
+------+-------+-------+-------+-------+-------+
| od   | od_sk | ad_sk | pk_sk | sd_sk | rd_sk |
+------+-------+-------+-------+-------+-------+
|   52 |   741 |   742 |   743 |   744 |   745 |
|   53 |   741 |   742 |   743 |   744 |   745 |
+------+-------+-------+-------+-------+-------+
2 rows in set (0.00 sec)
```

Note

741 - 745 are March 11, 2007 - 15, 2007.

Summary

You learned the degenerate dimension technique in this chapter and applied the technique to degenerate the order dimension. In the next chapter you learn another technique for handling a special type of dimension called junk dimension.

Chapter 18
Junk Dimensions

A junk dimension is a dimension that contains data with a small number of possible values. The sales order, for example, might have more discrete data (yes-no type values), such as

- **verification_ind** (the value is yes if this order has been verified)
- **credit_check_flag** (indicating whether or not the customer credit status for this order has been checked)
- **new_customer_ind** (the value is yes if this is the first order of a new customer)
- **web_order_flag** (indicating whether or not this order was placed online)

This type of data may often be useful to enhance sales analysis and should be stored in a special type of dimension called junk dimension.

This chapter discusses junk dimensions.

Adding the Sales Order Attribute Junk Dimension

Let's add a sales order junk dimension to our data warehouse. First off, you need to add a dimension named **sales_order_attribute_dim**. Figure 18.1 shows our data warehouse schema after the addition. Note that only tables related to the **sales_order_attribute_dim** table are shown.

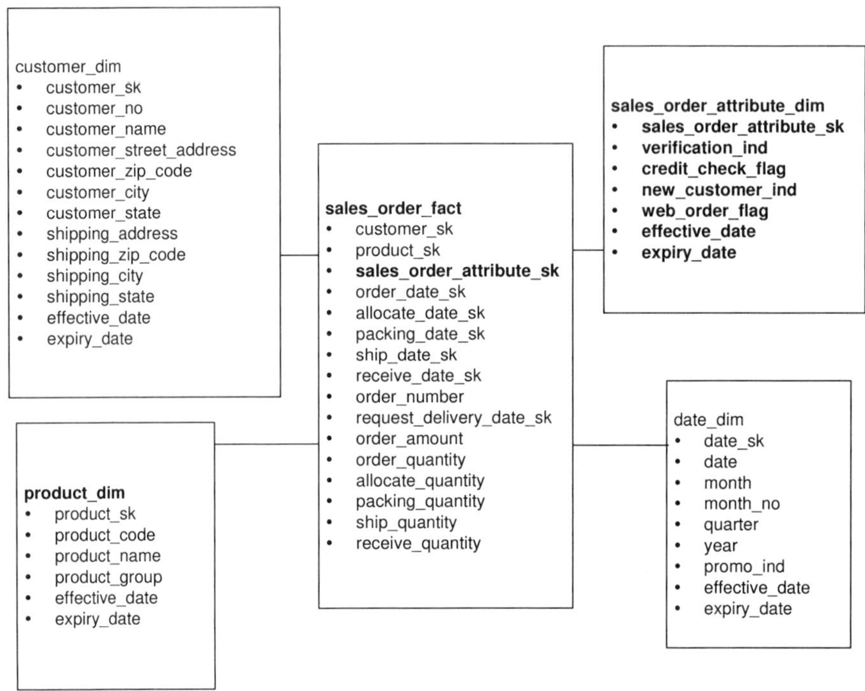

Figure 18.1: The schema with the sales_order_attribute_dim junk dimension

The new dimension contains four yes-no columns: **verification_ind**, **credit_check_flag**, **new_customer_ind**, and **web_order_flag**. Each of the four columns can have one of two possible values (Y or N), therefore the **sales_order_attribute_dim** can have a maximum of sixteen (2^4) rows. You can pre-populate the dimension and you need only do this once.

Note

If you know that a certain combination is not possible, you do not need to load that combination.

The script in Listing 18.1 creates the **sales_order_attribute_dim** table and pre-populate the table with its all sixteen possible combinations.

Listing 18.1: Pre-populating the sales_order_attribute_dim table

```
/*****************************************************************/
```

```
/*                                                                   */
/* junk_dim.sql                                                      */
/*                                                                   */
/*********************************************************************/

USE dw;

CREATE TABLE sales_order_attribute_dim
( sales_order_attribute_sk INT NOT NULL AUTO_INCREMENT PRIMARY KEY
, verification_ind CHAR(1)
, credit_check_flag CHAR(1)
, new_customer_ind CHAR(1)
, web_order_flag CHAR(1)
, effective_date DATE
, expiry_date DATE )
;

INSERT INTO sales_order_attribute_dim VALUES
  (NULL, 'Y', 'N', 'N', 'N', '0000-00-00', '9999-12-31')
, (NULL, 'Y', 'Y', 'N', 'N', '0000-00-00', '9999-12-31')
, (NULL, 'Y', 'Y', 'Y', 'N', '0000-00-00', '9999-12-31')
, (NULL, 'Y', 'Y', 'Y', 'Y', '0000-00-00', '9999-12-31')
, (NULL, 'Y', 'N', 'Y', 'N', '0000-00-00', '9999-12-31')
, (NULL, 'Y', 'N', 'Y', 'Y', '0000-00-00', '9999-12-31')
, (NULL, 'Y', 'N', 'N', 'Y', '0000-00-00', '9999-12-31')
, (NULL, 'Y', 'Y', 'N', 'Y', '0000-00-00', '9999-12-31')
, (NULL, 'N', 'N', 'N', 'N', '0000-00-00', '9999-12-31')
, (NULL, 'N', 'Y', 'N', 'N', '0000-00-00', '9999-12-31')
, (NULL, 'N', 'Y', 'Y', 'N', '0000-00-00', '9999-12-31')
, (NULL, 'N', 'Y', 'Y', 'Y', '0000-00-00', '9999-12-31')
, (NULL, 'N', 'N', 'Y', 'N', '0000-00-00', '9999-12-31')
, (NULL, 'N', 'N', 'Y', 'Y', '0000-00-00', '9999-12-31')
, (NULL, 'N', 'N', 'N', 'Y', '0000-00-00', '9999-12-31')
, (NULL, 'N', 'Y', 'N', 'Y', '0000-00-00', '9999-12-31')
;

/* end of script                                                     */
```

Run the script in Listing 18.1 using this command.

```
mysql> \. c:\mysql\scripts\junk_dim.sql
```

This is how the response on your console should look like.

```
Database changed
Query OK, 0 rows affected (0.14 sec)
```

```
Query OK, 16 rows affected (0.05 sec)
Records: 16  Duplicates: 0  Warnings: 0
```

Query the **sales_order_attribute_dim** table to confirm correct population.

```
mysql> select sales_order_attribute_sk soa_sk, verification_ind vi,
    -> credit_check_flag ccf, new_customer_ind nci, web_order_flag
       wof
    -> from sales_order_attribute_dim;
```

The query result is presented below.

```
+--------+------+------+------+------+
| soa_sk | vi   | ccf  | nci  | wof  |
+--------+------+------+------+------+
|      1 | Y    | N    | N    | N    |
|      2 | Y    | Y    | N    | N    |
|      3 | Y    | Y    | Y    | N    |
|      4 | Y    | Y    | Y    | Y    |
|      5 | Y    | N    | Y    | N    |
|      6 | Y    | N    | Y    | Y    |
|      7 | Y    | N    | N    | Y    |
|      8 | Y    | Y    | N    | Y    |
|      9 | N    | N    | N    | N    |
|     10 | N    | Y    | N    | N    |
|     11 | N    | Y    | Y    | N    |
|     12 | N    | Y    | Y    | Y    |
|     13 | N    | N    | Y    | N    |
|     14 | N    | N    | Y    | Y    |
|     15 | N    | N    | N    | Y    |
|     16 | N    | Y    | N    | Y    |
+--------+------+------+------+------+
16 rows in set (0.00 sec)
```

The next step is to add a sales order attribute surrogate key using the script in Listing 18.2.

Listing 18.2: Adding sales_order_attribute_sk

```
/**********************************************************************/
/*                                                                    */
/* sales_order_attribute_sk.sql                                       */
/*                                                                    */
/**********************************************************************/

USE dw;
```

```
ALTER TABLE sales_order_fact
ADD sales_order_attribute_sk INT AFTER product_sk
;

/* end of script                                                     */
```

Run the script in Listing 18.2 using this command.

```
mysql> \. c:\mysql\scripts\sales_order_attribute_sk.sql
```

You should see the following on your console.

```
Database changed
Query OK, 51 rows affected (0.36 sec)
Records: 51  Duplicates: 0  Warnings: 0
```

Confirm the **sales_order_attribute_sk** column was added to the **sales_order_fact** table by using this statement.

```
mysql> desc sales_order_fact;
```

Here is the description of the table.

```
+-------------------------+--------------+-----+----+--------+-----+
| Field                   | Type         | Null| Key| Default|Extra|
+-------------------------+--------------+-----+----+--------+-----+
| customer_sk             | int(11)      | YES |    | NULL   |     |
| product_sk              | int(11)      | YES |    | NULL   |     |
| sales_order_attribute_sk| int(11)      | YES |    | NULL   |     |
| order_date_sk           | int(11)      | YES |    | NULL   |     |
| allocate_date_sk        | int(11)      | YES |    | NULL   |     |
| packing_date_sk         | int(11)      | YES |    | NULL   |     |
| ship_date_sk            | int(11)      | YES |    | NULL   |     |
| receive_date_sk         | int(11)      | YES |    | NULL   |     |
| order_number            | int(11)      | YES |    | NULL   |     |
| request_delivery_date_sk| int(11)      | YES |    | NULL   |     |
| order_amount            | decimal(10,2)| YES |    | NULL   |     |
| order_quantity          | int(11)      | YES |    | NULL   |     |
| allocate_quantity       | int(11)      | YES |    | NULL   |     |
| packing_quantity        | int(11)      | YES |    | NULL   |     |
| ship_quantity           | int(11)      | YES |    | NULL   |     |
| receive_quantity        | int(11)      | YES |    | NULL   |     |
+-------------------------+--------------+-----+----+--------+-----+
16 rows in set (0.00 sec)
```

Revising the Regular Population Script

Since you now have a new dimension, you have to update the regular population script. Listing 18.3 shows the revised script.

Listing 18.3: Revised daily DW regular population

```
/**********************************************************************/
/*                                                                    */
/* dw_regular_18.sql                                                  */
/*                                                                    */
/**********************************************************************/

USE dw;

/* CUSTOMER_DIM POPULATION                                            */

TRUNCATE customer_stg;

LOAD DATA INFILE 'customer.csv'
INTO TABLE customer_stg
FIELDS TERMINATED BY ','
OPTIONALLY ENCLOSED BY '"'
LINES TERMINATED BY '\r\n'
IGNORE 1 LINES
( customer_number
, customer_name
, customer_street_address
, customer_zip_code
, customer_city
, customer_state
, shipping_address
, shipping_zip_code
, shipping_city
, shipping_state )
;

/* SCD 2 ON ADDRESSES                                                 */

UPDATE
  customer_dim a
, customer_stg b
SET
  a.expiry_date = SUBDATE(CURRENT_DATE, 1)
WHERE
```

```
  a.customer_number = b.customer_number
AND (   a.customer_street_address <> b.customer_street_address
     OR a.customer_city <> b.customer_city
     OR a.customer_zip_code <> b.customer_zip_code
     OR a.customer_state <> b.customer_state
     OR a.shipping_address <> b.shipping_address
     OR a.shipping_city <> b.shipping_city
     OR a.shipping_zip_code <> b.shipping_zip_code
     OR a.shipping_state <> b.shipping_state
     OR a.shipping_address IS NULL
     OR a.shipping_city IS NULL
     OR a.shipping_zip_code IS NULL
     OR a.shipping_state IS NULL)
AND expiry_date = '9999-12-31'
;

INSERT INTO customer_dim
SELECT
  NULL
, b.customer_number
, b.customer_name
, b.customer_street_address
, b.customer_zip_code
, b.customer_city
, b.customer_state
, b.shipping_address
, b.shipping_zip_code
, b.shipping_city
, b.shipping_state
, CURRENT_DATE
, '9999-12-31'
FROM
  customer_dim a
, customer_stg b
WHERE
    a.customer_number = b.customer_number
AND (   a.customer_street_address <> b.customer_street_address
     OR a.customer_city <> b.customer_city
     OR a.customer_zip_code <> b.customer_zip_code
     OR a.customer_state <> b.customer_state
     OR a.shipping_address <> b.shipping_address
     OR a.shipping_city <> b.shipping_city
     OR a.shipping_zip_code <> b.shipping_zip_code
     OR a.shipping_state <> b.shipping_state
     OR a.shipping_address IS NULL
```

```
     OR a.shipping_city IS NULL
     OR a.shipping_zip_code IS NULL
     OR a.shipping_state IS NULL)
AND EXISTS (
SELECT *
FROM customer_dim x
WHERE b.customer_number = x.customer_number
AND a.expiry_date = SUBDATE(CURRENT_DATE, 1))
AND NOT EXISTS (
SELECT *
FROM customer_dim y
WHERE     b.customer_number = y.customer_number
      AND y.expiry_date = '9999-12-31')
;

/* END OF SCD 2                                                    */

/* SCD 1 ON NAME                                                   */

UPDATE
  customer_dim a
, customer_stg b
SET a.customer_name = b.customer_name
WHERE     a.customer_number = b.customer_number
      AND a.expiry_date = '9999-12-31'
      AND a.customer_name <> b.customer_name
;

/* ADD NEW CUSTOMER                                                */

INSERT INTO customer_dim
SELECT
  NULL
, customer_number
, customer_name
, customer_street_address
, customer_zip_code
, customer_city
, customer_state
, shipping_address
, shipping_zip_code
, shipping_city
, shipping_state
, CURRENT_DATE
, '9999-12-31'
FROM customer_stg
```

```
WHERE customer_number NOT IN(
SELECT a.customer_number
FROM
  customer_dim a
, customer_stg b
WHERE b.customer_number = a.customer_number )
;

/* RE-BUILD PA CUSTOMER DIMENSION                                  */

TRUNCATE pa_customer_dim;

INSERT INTO pa_customer_dim
SELECT
  customer_sk
, customer_number
, customer_name
, customer_street_address
, customer_zip_code
, customer_city
, customer_state
, shipping_address
, shipping_zip_code
, shipping_city
, shipping_state
, effective_date
, expiry_date
FROM customer_dim
WHERE customer_state = 'PA'
;

/* END OF CUSTOMER_DIM POPULATION                                  */

/* PRODUCT_DIM POPULATION                                          */

TRUNCATE product_stg
;

LOAD DATA INFILE 'product.txt'
INTO TABLE product_stg
FIELDS TERMINATED BY ''
OPTIONALLY ENCLOSED BY ''
LINES TERMINATED BY '\r\n'
IGNORE 1 LINES
( product_code
```

```
, product_name
, product_category )
;

/* SCD2 ON PRODUCT NAME AND GROUP                                  */

UPDATE
  product_dim a
, product_stg b
SET
  expiry_date = SUBDATE(CURRENT_DATE, 1)
WHERE
    a.product_code = b.product_code
AND (   a.product_name <> b.product_name
     OR a.product_category <> b.product_category )
     AND expiry_date = '9999-12-31'
;

INSERT INTO product_dim
SELECT
  NULL
, b.product_code
, b.product_name
, b.product_category
, CURRENT_DATE
, '9999-12-31'
FROM
  product_dim a
, product_stg b
WHERE
    a.product_code = b.product_code
AND (   a.product_name <> b.product_name
     OR a.product_category <> b.product_category )
AND EXISTS (
SELECT *
FROM product_dim x
WHERE     b.product_code = x.product_code
      AND a.expiry_date = SUBDATE(CURRENT_DATE, 1))
AND NOT EXISTS (
SELECT *
FROM product_dim y
WHERE    b.product_code = y.product_code
     AND y.expiry_date = '9999-12-31')
;

/* END OF SCD 2                                                    */
```

```
/* ADD NEW PRODUCT                                                    */

INSERT INTO product_dim
SELECT
  NULL
, product_code
, product_name
, product_category
, CURRENT_DATE
, '9999-12-31'
FROM product_stg
WHERE product_code NOT IN(
SELECT y.product_code
FROM product_dim x, product_stg y
WHERE x.product_code = y.product_code )
;

/* END OF PRODUCT_DIM POPULATION                                      */

/* insert new orders                                                  */

INSERT INTO sales_order_fact
SELECT
  b.customer_sk
, c.product_sk
, f.sales_order_attribute_sk
, d.order_date_sk
, NULL
, NULL
, NULL
, NULL
, a.order_number
, e.request_delivery_date_sk
, order_amount
, quantity
, NULL
, NULL
, NULL
, NULL
FROM
  source.sales_order a
, customer_dim b
, product_dim c
, order_date_dim d
```

```
, request_delivery_date_dim e
, sales_order_attribute_dim f
WHERE
      order_status = 'N'
AND entry_date = CURRENT_DATE
AND a.customer_number = b.customer_number
AND a.status_date >= b.effective_date
AND a.status_date <= b.expiry_date
AND a.product_code = c.product_code
AND a.status_date >= c.effective_date
AND a.status_date <= c.expiry_date
AND a.status_date = d.order_date
AND a.request_delivery_date = e.request_delivery_date
AND a.verification_ind = f.verification_ind
AND a.credit_check_flag = f.credit_check_flag
AND a.new_customer_ind = f.new_customer_ind
AND a.web_order_flag = f.web_order_flag
AND a.status_date >= f.effective_date
AND a.status_date <= f.expiry_date
;

UPDATE
  sales_order_fact a
, source.sales_order b
, allocate_date_dim c
SET
  a.allocate_date_sk = c.allocate_date_sk
, a.allocate_quantity = b.quantity
WHERE
    order_status = 'A'
AND b.entry_date = CURRENT_DATE
AND b.order_number = a.order_number
AND c.allocate_date = b.status_date
;

UPDATE
  sales_order_fact a
, source.sales_order b
, packing_date_dim d
SET
  a.packing_date_sk = d.packing_date_sk
, a.packing_quantity = b.quantity
WHERE
    order_status = 'P'
AND b.entry_date = CURRENT_DATE
AND b.order_number = a.order_number
```

```
AND d.packing_date = b.status_date
;

UPDATE
  sales_order_fact a
, source.sales_order b
, ship_date_dim e
SET
  a.ship_date_sk = e.ship_date_sk
, a.ship_quantity = b.quantity
WHERE
    order_status = 'S'
AND b.entry_date = CURRENT_DATE
AND b.order_number = a.order_number
AND e.ship_date = b.status_date
;

UPDATE
  sales_order_fact a
, source.sales_order b
, receive_date_dim f
SET
  a.receive_date_sk = f.receive_date_sk
, a.receive_quantity = b.quantity
WHERE
    order_status = 'R'
AND b.entry_date = CURRENT_DATE
AND b.order_number = a.order_number
AND f.receive_date = b.status_date
;

/* end of script                                                  */
```

Before you can run the revised script, you need to change the **sales_order** source data by adding four attributes columns to it using the **sales_order_attributes.sql** script in Listing 18.4.

Listing 18.4: Adding Sales Order Attributes in the sales_order table

```
/******************************************************************/
/*                                                                */
/* sales_order_attributes.sql                                     */
/*                                                                */
/******************************************************************/
```

```
USE source;

ALTER TABLE sales_order
  ADD verification_ind CHAR(1) AFTER product_code
, ADD credit_check_flag CHAR(1) AFTER verification_ind
, ADD new_customer_ind CHAR(1) AFTER credit_check_flag
, ADD web_order_flag CHAR(1) AFTER new_customer_ind
;

/* end of script                                                    */
```

Run the script using this command.

```
mysql> \. c:\mysql\scripts\sales_order_attributes.sql
```

You can see the response on your console.

```
Database changed
Query OK, 67 rows affected (0.38 sec)
Records: 67  Duplicates: 0  Warnings: 0
```

Now, add more sales orders. You can use the script in Listing 18.5 to add eight orders.

Listing 18.5: Adding eight junk sales orders

```
/******************************************************************/
/*                                                                */
/* sales_order_18.sql                                             */
/*                                                                */
/******************************************************************/

USE source;

INSERT INTO sales_order VALUES
  (54, 1, 1, 'Y', 'Y', 'N', 'Y', '2007-03-16', 'N', '2007-03-20',
      '2007-03-16', 7500, 75)
, (55, 2, 2, 'N', 'N', 'N', 'N', '2007-03-16', 'N', '2007-03-20',
      '2007-03-16', 1000, 10)
, (56, 3, 3, 'Y', 'Y', 'N', 'N', '2007-03-16', 'N', '2007-03-20',
      '2007-03-16', 7500, 75)
, (57, 4, 4, 'Y', 'N', 'N', 'N', '2007-03-16', 'N', '2007-03-20',
      '2007-03-16', 1000, 10)
, (58, 11, 1, 'N', 'Y', 'Y', 'Y', '2007-03-16', 'N', '2007-03-20',
      '2007-03-16', 7500, 75)
, (59, 12, 2, 'N', 'Y', 'Y', 'N', '2007-03-16', 'N', '2007-03-20',
      '2007-03-16', 1000, 10)
```

```
, (60, 13, 3, 'Y', 'Y', 'Y', 'N', '2007-03-16', 'N', '2007-03-20',
      '2007-03-16', 7500, 75)
, (61, 14, 4, 'Y', 'N', 'Y', 'N', '2007-03-16', 'N', '2007-03-20',
      '2007-03-16', 1000, 10)
;

/* end of script                                                   */
```

Run the script using this command.

```
mysql> \. c:\mysql\scripts\sales_order_18.sql
```

The response should be as follows.

```
Database changed
Query OK, 8 rows affected (0.05 sec)
Records: 8  Duplicates: 0  Warnings: 0
```

To confirm that eight sales orders were loaded correctly, query the **sales_order** table in the **source** database.

```
mysql> select order_number, verification_ind vi, credit_check_flag
      ccf,
    -> new_customer_ind nci, web_order_flag wof
    -> from sales_order
    -> where order_number between 54 and 61;
```

Here is the content of the **sales_order** table.

```
+--------------+------+------+------+------+
| order_number | vi   | ccf  | nci  | wof  |
+--------------+------+------+------+------+
|           54 | Y    | Y    | N    | Y    |
|           55 | N    | N    | N    | N    |
|           56 | Y    | Y    | N    | N    |
|           57 | Y    | N    | N    | N    |
|           58 | N    | Y    | Y    | Y    |
|           59 | N    | Y    | Y    | N    |
|           60 | Y    | Y    | Y    | N    |
|           61 | Y    | N    | Y    | N    |
+--------------+------+------+------+------+
8 rows in set (0.43 sec)
```

Now, you're ready to run the revised regular loading script. Set your MySQL date to March 16, 2007 (the order date) and run the **dw_regular_18.sql** script.

```
mysql> \. c:\mysql\scripts\dw_regular_18.sql
```

You should see the following on your MySQL console.

```
Database changed
Query OK, 9 rows affected (0.06 sec)

Query OK, 9 rows affected (0.07 sec)
Records: 9  Deleted: 0  Skipped: 0  Warnings: 0

Query OK, 0 rows affected (0.00 sec)
Rows matched: 0  Changed: 0  Warnings: 0

Query OK, 0 rows affected (0.00 sec)
Records: 0  Duplicates: 0  Warnings: 0

Query OK, 0 rows affected (0.00 sec)
Rows matched: 0  Changed: 0  Warnings: 0

Query OK, 0 rows affected (0.00 sec)
Records: 0  Duplicates: 0  Warnings: 0

Query OK, 19 rows affected (0.07 sec)

Query OK, 19 rows affected (0.06 sec)
Records: 19  Duplicates: 0  Warnings: 0

Query OK, 4 rows affected (0.07 sec)

Query OK, 4 rows affected (0.06 sec)
Records: 4  Deleted: 0  Skipped: 0  Warnings: 0

Query OK, 0 rows affected (0.00 sec)
Rows matched: 0  Changed: 0  Warnings: 0

Query OK, 0 rows affected (0.00 sec)
Records: 0  Duplicates: 0  Warnings: 0

Query OK, 0 rows affected (0.00 sec)
Records: 0  Duplicates: 0  Warnings: 0

Query OK, 8 rows affected (0.15 sec)
Records: 8  Duplicates: 0  Warnings: 0

Query OK, 0 rows affected (0.01 sec)
Rows matched: 0  Changed: 0  Warnings: 0
```

```
Query OK, 0 rows affected (0.01 sec)
Rows matched: 0  Changed: 0  Warnings: 0

Query OK, 0 rows affected (0.01 sec)
Rows matched: 0  Changed: 0  Warnings: 0

Query OK, 0 rows affected (0.00 sec)
Rows matched: 0  Changed: 0  Warnings: 0
```

You can use the analytical query in Listing 18.6 to confirm correct loading. The query analyzes how many sales orders from new customers were checked for credit statuses.

Listing 18.6: An example attributes analysis

```
/**********************************************************************/
/*                                                                    */
/* new_customer_credit_check.sql                                      */
/*                                                                    */
/**********************************************************************/

USE dw;

SELECT CONCAT( ROUND( checked / ( checked + not_checked )*100 ), '
      %' )
FROM
( SELECT COUNT(*) checked FROM sales_order_fact a,
      sales_order_attribute_dim b
  WHERE new_customer_ind = 'Y' and credit_check_flag = 'Y'
  AND a.sales_order_attribute_sk = b.sales_order_attribute_sk)  x
,
(SELECT COUNT(*) not_checked
FROM sales_order_fact a, sales_order_attribute_dim b
WHERE new_customer_ind = 'Y' and credit_check_flag = 'N'
AND a.sales_order_attribute_sk = b.sales_order_attribute_sk)  y;

/* end of script                                                      */
```

Run the query using this command.

```
mysql> \. c:\mysql\scripts\new_customer_credit_check.sql
```

You should get the following output.

```
Database changed
```

```
+---------------------------------------------------------------------+
| CONCAT( ROUND( checked / ( checked + not_checked )*100 ), ' %' ) |
+---------------------------------------------------------------------+
| 75 %                                                                |
+---------------------------------------------------------------------+
1 row in set (0.01 sec)
```

Summary

In this chapter you learned a technique called junk dimension and used it on the sales attributes junk dimension. In the next chapter you will learn to extend your data warehouse by adding another star to the existing schema.

Chapter 19
Multi-Star Schemas

Starting from Chapter 10, "Adding Columns" you have been growing your data warehouse by adding columns and tables, and in Chapter 14, "Snapshots" you added a second fact table, the **month_end_sales_order_fact** table. After the addition, your schema has had two fact tables (the first is the **sales_order_fact** table you created at the start of the data warehouse). With two fact tables, the data warehouse is officially a two-star schema.

In this chapter you will add a new star to the existing stars of the dimensional data warehouse. Unlike the existing stars that are related to sales, the new star addresses the needs of the production business area. The new star, which has one fact table and one dimension table, stores the production data in the data warehouse.

The New Star Schema

Figure 19.1 is the extended schema of our data warehouse. The schema has three stars. The **sales_order_fact** table is the first star's fact table. In the same schema are the **customer_dim**, **product_dim**, and **date_dim** tables.

The **month_end_sales_order_fact** table is the second star's fact table. The **product_dim** and **month_dim** tables are its corresponding dimension tables. The first and the second stars share the **product_dim** table. You might recall that data in the second star's fact and month dimension are derived from the first star's fact and **date_dim**, respectively. They don't get their data from the data source.

The third star's fact table is a new **production_fact** table. Its dimensions are stored in the existing **date_dim** and the **product_dim** tables as well as in a new **factory_dim** table. The third star's data comes from the data source.

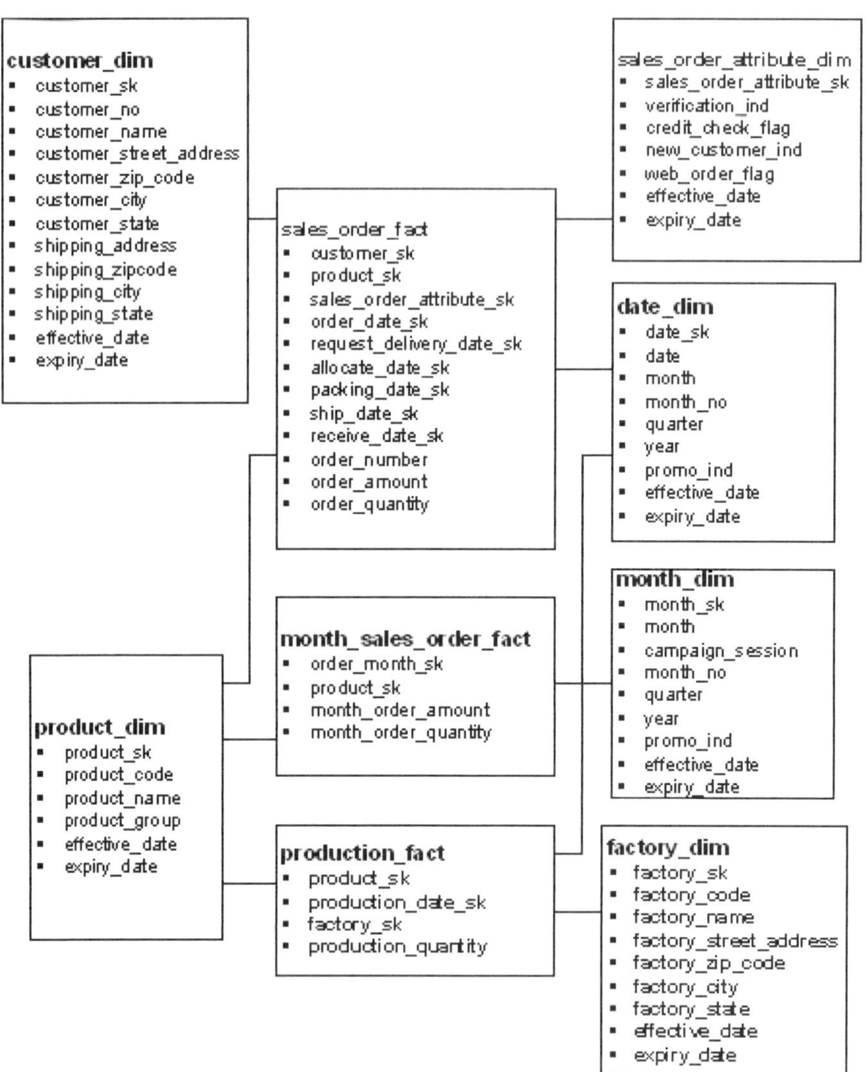

Figure 19.1: A three-star dimensional data warehouse schema

You create the third star's new tables using the script in Listing 19.1.

Listing 19.1: Creating the third star's tables

```
/******************************************************************/
/*                                                                */
/* third_star_tables.sql                                          */
```

```
/*                                                                */
/******************************************************************/

/* default to dw                                                  */

USE dw;

CREATE TABLE factory_dim (
  factory_sk INT NOT NULL AUTO_INCREMENT PRIMARY KEY
, factory_code INT
, factory_name CHAR(30)
, factory_street_address CHAR(50)
, factory_zip_code INT(5)
, factory_city CHAR(30)
, factory_state CHAR(2)
, effective_date DATE
, expiry_date DATE
)
;

CREATE TABLE production_fact (
  product_sk INT
, production_date_sk INT
, factory_sk INT
, production_quantity INT
)
;

/* end of script                                                  */
```

Now run the script in Listing 19.1.

```
mysql> \. c:\mysql\scripts\third_star_tables.sql
```

Populating the New Star's Tables

In this section, I show you how to populate the tables of the third star.

Let's assume that the **factory_dim** table stores information about factories and gets its data from a MySQL table called **factory_master**. You can create the **factory_master** table in the **source** database using the script in Listing 19.2 and populate it using the script in Listing 19.3.

Listing 19.2: Creating the factory_master table

```
/**********************************************************************/
/*                                                                    */
/* factory_master.sql                                                 */
/*                                                                    */
/**********************************************************************/

USE source;

CREATE TABLE factory_master
( factory_code INT
, factory_name CHAR(30)
, factory_street_address CHAR(50)
, factory_zip_code INT(5)
, factory_city CHAR(30)
, factory_state CHAR(2) )
;

/* end of script                                                      */
```

Listing 19.3: Factory_dim initial population

```
/**********************************************************************/
/*                                                                    */
/* factory_ini.sql                                                    */
/*                                                                    */
/**********************************************************************/

USE dw;

INSERT INTO factory_dim
SELECT
  NULL
, factory_code
, factory_name
, factory_street_address
, factory_zip_code
, factory_city
, factory_state
, CURRENT_DATE
, '9999-12-31'
FROM source.factory_master
;

/* end of script                                                      */
```

Run the **factory_master.sql** script in Listing 19.2 using this command.

```
mysql> \. c:\mysql\scripts\factory_master.sql
```

Run the **factory_ini.sql** script in Listing 19.3 using this command.

```
mysql> \. c:\mysql\scripts\factory_ini.sql
```

Note
You do not need to change anything on the existing first and second stars.

Changes to factories are rare, so you can expect the users to provide any new information regarding the factories in a CSV file. Here are some sample factories in a **factory.csv** file.

```
FACTORY_CODE,NAME,STREET_ADDRESS,ZIP_CODE,CITY,STATE
2,Second Factory,24242 Bunty La.,17055,Pittsburgh,PA
3,Third Factory,37373 Burbank Dr.,17050,Mechanicsburg,PA
```

Like other CSV source files, you need a staging table to load the **factory.csv** file. Use the script in Listing 19.4 to create the staging table.

Listing 19.4: Creating the factory staging table

```
/******************************************************************/
/*                                                                */
/* factory_stg.sql                                                */
/*                                                                */
/******************************************************************/

USE dw;

CREATE TABLE factory_stg
( factory_code INT
, factory_name CHAR(30)
, factory_street_address CHAR(50)
, factory_zip_code INT(5)
, factory_city CHAR(30)
, factory_state CHAR(2) )
;

/* end of script                                                  */
```

Run the **factory_stg.sql** script by using this command.

```
mysql> \. c:\mysql\scripts\factory_stg.sql
```

The first dimension table in the third star, the **product_dim** table, gets its data from a **daily_production** table in the source database. The script in Listing 19.5 creates this table.

Listing 19.5: Creating the daily production table

```
/**************************************************************/
/*                                                            */
/* daily_production.sql                                       */
/*                                                            */
/**************************************************************/

USE source;

CREATE TABLE daily_production
( product_code INT
, production_date DATE
, factory_code INT
, production_quantity INT )
;

/* end of script                                              */
```

Run the script in Listing 19.5 using this command.

```
mysql> \. c:\mysql\scripts\daily_production.sql
```

Assuming the users agree that the fact table will start its population on the date you implement it, you can use the script in Listing 19.6 to regularly populate the factory dimension and fact tables.

> **Note**
> You apply SCD1 to all columns in the **factory_dim** table. You run this script daily to load today's production data.

Listing 19.6: Production regular population

```
/**************************************************************/
/*                                                            */
/* production_regular.sql                                     */
/*                                                            */
/**************************************************************/
USE dw;

TRUNCATE factory_stg;
```

```
LOAD DATA INFILE 'factory.csv'
INTO TABLE factory_stg
FIELDS TERMINATED BY ','
OPTIONALLY ENCLOSED BY '"'
LINES TERMINATED BY '\r\n'
IGNORE 1 LINES
( factory_code
, factory_name
, factory_street_address
, factory_zip_code
, factory_city
, factory_state )
;

/* SCD1                                                                   */

UPDATE
  factory_dim a
, factory_stg b
SET
  a.factory_name = b.factory_name
, a.factory_street_address = b.factory_street_address
, a.factory_zip_code = b.factory_zip_code
, a.factory_city = b.factory_city
, a.factory_state = b.factory_state
WHERE a.factory_code = b.factory_code
;

/* add new factory                                                        */

INSERT INTO factory_dim
SELECT
  NULL
, factory_code
, factory_name
, factory_street_address
, factory_zip_code
, factory_city
, factory_state
, CURRENT_DATE
, '9999-12-31'
FROM factory_stg
WHERE factory_code NOT IN (
SELECT y.factory_code
```

```
FROM factory_dim x, factory_stg y
WHERE x.factory_code = y.factory_code )
;

INSERT INTO production_fact
SELECT
  b.product_sk
, c.date_sk
, d.factory_sk
, production_quantity
FROM
  source.daily_production a
, product_dim b
, date_dim c
, factory_dim d
WHERE
    production_date = CURRENT_DATE
AND a.product_code = b.product_code
AND a.production_date >= b.effective_date
AND a.production_date <= b.expiry_date
AND a.production_date = c.date
AND a.factory_code = d.factory_code
;

/* end of script                                                    */
```

Testing

Now that we've discussed all the tables in the third star, we're ready to do some testing.

First of all, you need some factories. The script in Listing 19.7 loads four factories into the **factory_master** table in the **source** database.

Listing 19.7: Factories in the factory_master source table

```
/**********************************************************************/
/*                                                                    */
/* factory_master_source.sql                                          */
/*                                                                    */
/**********************************************************************/

USE source;
```

```
INSERT INTO factory_master VALUES
  ( 1, 'First Factory', '11111 Lichtman St.', 17050,
       'Mechanicsburg', 'PA' )
, ( 2, 'Second Factory', '22222 Stobosky Ave.', 17055, 'Pittsburgh',
       'PA' )
, ( 3, 'Third Factory', '33333 Fritze Rd.', 17050, 'Mechanicsburg',
       'PA' )
, ( 4, 'Fourth Factory', '44444 Jenzen Blvd.', 17055, 'Pittsburgh',
       'PA' )
;

/* end of script                                                  */
```

Run the script in Listing 19.7 using this command.

```
mysql> \. c:\mysql\scripts\factory_master_source.sql
```

You'll see the following on your console.

```
Database changed
Query OK, 4 rows affected (0.06 sec)
Records: 4  Duplicates: 0  Warnings: 0
```

After you run the script in Listing 19.7, you need to set your MySQL date to any date later than the date you set in Chapter 18, "Junk Dimensions." (In Chapter 18 you set your MySQL date to March 16, 2007) To follow the exercise in this chapter, however, you must set your MySQL date to March 18, 2007. After that, run the **factory_ini.sql** script in Listing 19.3 to load the four factories in the **factory_master** table to the **factory_dim** table. You can invoke the **factory_ini.sql** script using this command.

```
mysql> \. c:\mysql\scripts\factory_ini.sql
```

MySQL will indicate that 4 records are affected by the query.

```
Database changed
Query OK, 4 rows affected (0.04 sec)
Records: 4  Duplicates: 0  Warnings: 0
```

Now query the **factory_dim** table to confirm correct population using this statement.

```
mysql> select * from factory_dim \G
```

Here is the query result.

```
*************************** 1. row ***************************
             factory_sk: 1
           factory_code: 1
           factory_name: First Factory
factory_street_address: 11111 Lichtman St.
       factory_zip_code: 17050
           factory_city: Mechanicsburg
          factory_state: PA
         effective_date: 2007-03-18
            expiry_date: 9999-12-31
*************************** 2. row ***************************
             factory_sk: 2
           factory_code: 2
           factory_name: Second Factory
factory_street_address: 22222 Stobosky Ave.
       factory_zip_code: 17055
           factory_city: Pittsburgh
          factory_state: PA
         effective_date: 2007-03-18
            expiry_date: 9999-12-31
*************************** 3. row ***************************
             factory_sk: 3
           factory_code: 3
           factory_name: Third Factory
factory_street_address: 33333 Fritze Rd.
       factory_zip_code: 17050
           factory_city: Mechanicsburg
          factory_state: PA
         effective_date: 2007-03-18
            expiry_date: 9999-12-31
*************************** 4. row ***************************
             factory_sk: 4
           factory_code: 4
           factory_name: Fourth Factory
factory_street_address: 44444 Jenzen Blvd.
       factory_zip_code: 17055
           factory_city: Pittsburgh
          factory_state: PA
         effective_date: 2007-03-18
            expiry_date: 9999-12-31
4 rows in set (0.00 sec)
```

Next, prepare the **factory.csv** file below.

```
FACTORY_CODE,NAME,STREET_ADDRESS,ZIP_CODE,CITY,STATE
2,Second Factory,24242 Bunty La.,17055,Pittsburgh,PA
```

```
3,Third Factory,37373 Burbank Dr.,17050,Mechanicsburg,PA
```

Note

This CSV file contains the changes to factory codes 2 and 3 to test the SCD1 on the factory dimension.

You can use the script in Listing 19.8 to load data to the **daily_production** table in the source database.

Listing 19.8: Daily production data

```
/**********************************************************************/
/*                                                                    */
/* daily_production_data.sql                                          */
/*                                                                    */
/**********************************************************************/

USE source;

INSERT INTO daily_production VALUES
  ( 1, CURRENT_DATE, 4, 100 )
, ( 2, CURRENT_DATE, 3, 200 )
, ( 3, CURRENT_DATE, 2, 300 )
, ( 4, CURRENT_DATE, 1, 400 )
, ( 1, CURRENT_DATE, 1, 400 )
, ( 2, CURRENT_DATE, 2, 300 )
, ( 3, CURRENT_DATE, 3, 200 )
, ( 4, CURRENT_DATE, 4, 100 )
;

/* end of script                                                      */
```

Run the script in Listing 19.8 by using this command.

```
mysql> \. c:\mysql\scripts\daily_production_data.sql
```

Here is what should be printed on your console.

```
Database changed
Query OK, 8 rows affected (0.05 sec)
Records: 8  Duplicates: 0  Warnings: 0
```

Now you're ready to test the production regular loading. Your MySQL date must have been set to March 18, 2005 before you run the **production_regular.sql** script. To run the script, use the following command.

```
mysql> \. c:\mysql\scripts\production_regular.sql
```

Here is the response from MySQL.

```
Database changed
Query OK, 1 rows affected (0.07 sec)

Query OK, 2 rows affected (0.03 sec)
Records: 2  Deleted: 0  Skipped: 0  Warnings: 0

Query OK, 2 rows affected (0.00 sec)
Rows matched: 2  Changed: 0  Warnings: 0

Query OK, 0 rows affected (0.00 sec)
Records: 0  Duplicates: 0  Warnings: 0

Query OK, 8 rows affected (0.07 sec)
Records: 8  Duplicates: 0  Warnings: 0
```

Using the following SQL statement, query the **production_fact** table to confirm a successful regular load of the daily production data.

```
mysql> select * from production_fact;
```

Here is the query result.

```
+-----------+------------------+-----------+---------------------+
| product_sk| production_date_sk| factory_sk | production_quantity |
+-----------+------------------+-----------+---------------------+
|         1 |              748 |          4 |                 100 |
|         2 |              748 |          3 |                 200 |
|         4 |              748 |          2 |                 300 |
|         5 |              748 |          1 |                 400 |
|         1 |              748 |          1 |                 400 |
|         2 |              748 |          2 |                 300 |
|         4 |              748 |          3 |                 200 |
|         5 |              748 |          4 |                 100 |
+-----------+------------------+-----------+---------------------+
8 rows in set (0.00 sec)
```

To confirm that SCD1 has been applied successfully on the factory dimension, query the **factory_dim** table using this statement.

```
mysql> select * from factory_dim \G
```

You will see the following records as the result.

```
*************************** 1. row ***************************
            factory_sk: 1
          factory_code: 1
          factory_name: First Factory
factory_street_address: 11111 Lichtman St.
      factory_zip_code: 17050
          factory_city: Mechanicsburg
         factory_state: PA
        effective_date: 2007-03-18
           expiry_date: 9999-12-31
*************************** 2. row ***************************
            factory_sk: 2
          factory_code: 2
          factory_name: Second Factory
factory_street_address: 24242 Bunty La.
      factory_zip_code: 17055
          factory_city: Pittsburgh
         factory_state: PA
        effective_date: 2007-03-18
           expiry_date: 9999-12-31
*************************** 3. row ***************************
            factory_sk: 3
          factory_code: 3
          factory_name: Third Factory
factory_street_address: 37373 Burbank Dr.
      factory_zip_code: 17050
          factory_city: Mechanicsburg
         factory_state: PA
        effective_date: 2007-03-18
           expiry_date: 9999-12-31
*************************** 4. row ***************************
            factory_sk: 4
          factory_code: 4
          factory_name: Fourth Factory
factory_street_address: 44444 Jenzen Blvd.
      factory_zip_code: 17055
          factory_city: Pittsburgh
         factory_state: PA
        effective_date: 2007-03-18
           expiry_date: 9999-12-31
4 rows in set (0.00 sec)
```

Note
The Second and Third factories have their addresses changed correctly.

Summary

In this final chapter of Part III, you learned to extend the data warehouse by adding a new star. The techniques to extend the initial data warehouse you learned in Part III are those to solve the most commonly encountered growth cases.

In Part IV you will learn additional techniques to deal with advanced growth cases.

Part IV
Advanced Techniques

Part IV, the final part of the book, explores six advanced techniques in dimensional data warehousing that you may need to use to meet user requirements. The six techniques are

- Non-straight sources
- Fact-less facts
- Late arrival facts
- Dimension consolidation
- Accumulated measures
- Band dimensions

Chapter 20
Non-straight Sources

In this chapter you learn how to handle non-straight data sources, which are data sources that you cannot load directly to the data warehouse because they have different granularities than the dimension tables. This chapter starts by presenting examples of non-straight sources. It then lets you try to handle non-straight sources in the data warehouse you've been building since Chapter 1, "Basic Components."

Overview

Let me explain how you can handle non-straight sources by revisiting the campaign source data in Chapter 16, "Muti-Path and Ragged Hierarchies" here.

```
CAMPAIGN SESSION,MONTH,YEAR
2006 First Campaign,1,2006
2006 First Campaign,2,2006
2006 First Campaign,3,2006
2006 First Campaign,4,2006
2006 Second Campaign,5,2006
2006 Second Campaign,6,2006
2006 Second Campaign,7,2006
2006 Third Campaign,8,2006
2006 Last Campaign,9,2006
2006 Last Campaign,10,2006
2006 Last Campaign,11,2006
2006 Last Campaign,12,2006
```

The granularity of the campaign data source is month because every row has a month element. Also a campaign may last more than a month, as shown by the 2006 First Campaign that ran for four months. This means, the source data repeats this campaign four times. That is four rows.

Let's say your user wants to simplify the campaign source data preparation and prepare a maximum of one row for a campaign, regardless how long it runs. The new data format will have to be changed to the following.

```
CAMPAIGN_SESSION,START_MONTH,START_YEAR,END_MONTH,END_YEAR
2006 First Campaign,1,2006,4,2006
2006 Second Campaign,5,2006,7,2006
2006 Third Campaign,8,2006,8,2006
2006 Last Campaign,9,2006,12,2006
```

The data source is now much simpler than before it was reformatted. Each campaign is only represented by one row.

This is how you handle non-straight sources, by changing their formats so that they can be loaded to their dimension tables.

Revising the Campaign Population Script

In the overview I explained how you could simplify the campaign data in Chapter 16. In this section I explain how you can update the campaign population script for the non-straight data source.

First of all, you need a different campaign staging table. Use the script in Listing 20.1 to create one.

Listing 20.1: Creating a new staging table for the non-straight campaign population

```
/**********************************************************************/
/*                                                                    */
/* campaign_stg_20.sql                                                */
/*                                                                    */
/**********************************************************************/

USE dw;

CREATE TABLE non_straight_campaign_stg
 ( campaign_session CHAR(30)
, start_month CHAR(9)
, start_year INT(4)
, end_month CHAR(9)
, end_year INT(4)
)
```

```
;

/* end of script                                                    */
```

Run the script in Listing 20.1 using this command.

```
mysql> \. c:\mysql\scripts\campaign_stg_20.sql
```

You'll see the following message on your console.

```
Database changed
Query OK, 0 rows affected (0.12 sec)
```

Note that the new staging table has both the start month/year and end month/year columns.

The revised campaign population script is given in Listing 20.2. It updates the month dimension twice. The first update is for the start and the end month of every campaign. The second update is for the months between the start and end months of each campaign.

Listing 20.2: Revised campaign population script

```
/******************************************************************/
/*                                                                */
/* campaign_session_20.sql                                        */
/*                                                                */
/******************************************************************/

TRUNCATE non_straight_campaign_stg;

LOAD DATA INFILE 'non_straight_campaign.csv'
INTO TABLE non_straight_campaign_stg
FIELDS TERMINATED BY ','
OPTIONALLY ENCLOSED BY '"'
LINES TERMINATED BY '\r\n'
IGNORE 1 LINES
(
  campaign_session
, start_month
, start_year
, end_month
, end_year
)
;
```

```
/* for the start and end months                                    */

UPDATE month_dim p,
(
SELECT
  a.month
, a.year
, b.campaign_session
FROM
month_dim a LEFT OUTER JOIN
( SELECT
    campaign_session
  , month
  , year
  FROM
  (SELECT
     campaign_session
   , start_month month
   , start_year year
   FROM non_straight_campaign_stg

   UNION ALL

  SELECT
    campaign_session
  , end_month month
  , end_year year
  FROM non_straight_campaign_stg) x

  ORDER BY year, month) b

ON     a.year = b.year
   AND a.month = b.month ) q

SET p.campaign_session = q.campaign_session
WHERE
    q.campaign_session IS NOT NULL
AND p.month = q.month
AND p.year = q.year
;

/* end of the start and end months                                 */

/* for the in-between months                                       */

UPDATE
```

```
  month_dim p
, month_dim q,

(SELECT
  MIN(a.month) minmo
, MIN(a.year) minyear
, a.campaign_session campaign_session
, MAX(b.month) maxmo
, MAX(b.year) maxyear
FROM
  month_dim a
, month_dim b
WHERE a.campaign_session IS NOT NULL
AND b.campaign_session IS NOT NULL
AND a.month = b.month
AND a.year = b.year
GROUP BY
  a.campaign_session
, b.campaign_session
) r

SET p.campaign_session = r.campaign_session

WHERE
  p.month > r.minmo
AND p.year = r.minyear
AND q.month < r.maxmo
AND q.year = r.maxyear
AND p.month = q.month
AND p.year = q.year
;

/* end of the in-between months                                    */

/* end of script                                                   */
```

Now let's test the new script. The campaign data can be found in the **non_straight_campaign.csv** file (printed below).

```
CAMPAIGN_SESSION,START_MONTH,START_YEAR,END_MONTH,END_YEAR
2006 First Campaign,1,2006,4,2006
2006 Second Campaign,5,2006,7,2006
2006 Third Campaign,8,2006,8,2006
2006 Last Campaign,9,2006,12,2006
```

Before you run the revised campaign population script, however, you need to remove the campaign sessions you loaded in Chapter 16 using the script in Listing 20.3.

Listing 20.3: Removing campaign

```
/**********************************************************************/
/*                                                                    */
/* remove_campaign.sql                                                */
/*                                                                    */
/**********************************************************************/

USE dw;

UPDATE month_dim
SET campaign_session = NULL
;

/* end of script                                                      */
```

Run the script in Listing 20.3 by using this command.

```
mysql> \. c:\mysql\scripts\remove_campaign.sql
```

You'll be notified that there are 12 rows affected.

```
Database changed
Query OK, 12 rows affected (0.06 sec)
Rows matched: 96  Changed: 12  Warnings: 0
```

Now run the **campaign_session_20.sql** script in Listing 20.2.

```
mysql> \. c:\mysql\scripts\campaign_session_20.sql
```

You'll see these messages on the console.

```
Query OK, 1 row affected (0.10 sec)

Query OK, 4 rows affected (0.05 sec)
Records: 4  Deleted: 0  Skipped: 0  Warnings: 0

Query OK, 7 rows affected (0.06 sec)
Rows matched: 7  Changed: 7  Warnings: 0

Query OK, 5 rows affected (0.05 sec)
Rows matched: 5  Changed: 5  Warnings: 0
```

Now query the **month_dim** table to confirm it was correctly populated.

```
mysql> select month_sk m_sk, month_name, month m, campaign_session,
    -> quarter q, year
    -> from month_dim where year = 2006;
```

The result is given below.

```
+------+------------+------+----------------------+------+------+
| m_sk | month_name | m    | campaign_session     | q    | year |
+------+------------+------+----------------------+------+------+
|   11 | January    |    1 | 2006 First Campaign  |    1 | 2006 |
|   12 | February   |    2 | 2006 First Campaign  |    1 | 2006 |
|   13 | March      |    3 | 2006 First Campaign  |    1 | 2006 |
|   14 | April      |    4 | 2006 First Campaign  |    2 | 2006 |
|   15 | May        |    5 | 2006 Second Campaign |    2 | 2006 |
|   16 | June       |    6 | 2006 Second Campaign |    2 | 2006 |
|   17 | July       |    7 | 2006 Second Campaign |    3 | 2006 |
|   18 | August     |    8 | 2006 Third Campaign  |    3 | 2006 |
|   19 | September  |    9 | 2006 Last Campaign   |    3 | 2006 |
|   20 | October    |   10 | 2006 Last Campaign   |    4 | 2006 |
|   21 | November   |   11 | 2006 Last Campaign   |    4 | 2006 |
|   22 | December   |   12 | 2006 Last Campaign   |    4 | 2006 |
+------+------------+------+----------------------+------+------+
12 rows in set (0.00 sec)
```

The two hierarchical queries from Chapter 16, **quarter_path.sql** and **campaign_session_path.sql**, do not need to change. If you run them again you'll get the same results as before.

Summary

In this chapter, you learned how to handle non-straight data sources and adjust your regular population script to adapt to the source change. In the next chapter we'll discuss another advanced technique, whereby a fact does not have any measure from its source data.

Chapter 21
Factless Facts

This chapter teaches you how to deal with a requirement for a measure that is not available in the source data. For example, the product source data (the **product.txt** file you used in Chapter 2, "Dimension History" and Chapter 8, "Regular Population") do not contain product count information. If you need to know the number of products in your system, clearly you cannot simply pull this out of your data warehouse.

The factless fact technique can help. By using this technique, you can count the number of products by keeping track of product launches. You can create a factless fact table that has only surrogate keys from the product (what you count) and the date (when the count occurs) dimensions. We call the table a factless table because the table itself does not have a measure.

This chapter shows you how to apply the factless fact technique in your data warehouse.

Product Launch Factless Facts

In this section, I explain how to implement a product launch factless fact, including adding and initially populating the factless **product_count_fact** table.

The data warehouse schema to track the number of product launches is shown in Figure 21.1. Only the tables related to the **product_count_fact** table are shown.

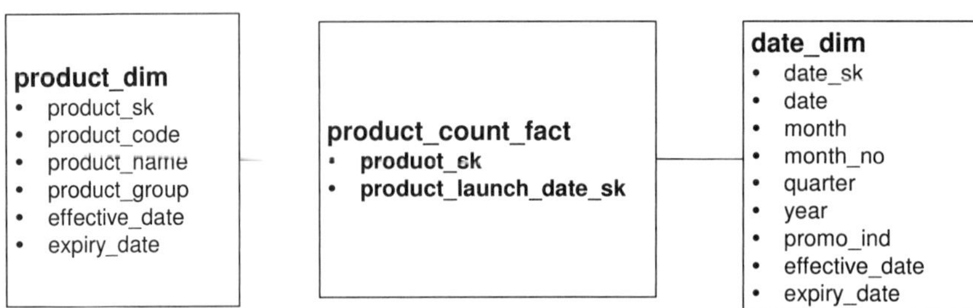

Figure 21.1: Fact-less fact table

Use the script in Listing 21.1 to create the factless fact table.

Listing 21.1: Creating the product_count_fact table

```
/**********************************************************************/
/*                                                                    */
/* product_count.sql                                                  */
/*                                                                    */
/**********************************************************************/

USE dw;

CREATE TABLE product_count_fact
( product_sk INT
, product_launch_date_sk INT )
;

/* end of script                                                      */
```

Run the script by using the following command.

```
mysql> \. c:\mysql\scripts\product_count.sql
```

Now you need to create a product launch date view on the date dimension. You do that by applying role-playing on the date dimension. (Dimension role-playing was discussed in Chapter 13, "Dimension Role Playing.") The view only gets product effective dates, not all dates in the date dimension. The **product_launch_date_dim** dimension is a subset dimension. The script in Listing 21.2 creates the required **product_launch_date** view.

Listing 21.2: Creating the product_launch_date view

```
/**********************************************************************/
/*                                                                    */
/* product_launch_date_dim.sql                                        */
```

```
/*                                                                  */
/********************************************************************/

USE dw;

CREATE VIEW product_launch_date_dim (
  product_launch_date_sk
, product_launch_date
, month_name
, month
, quarter
, year
, promo_ind
, effective_date
, expiry_date
)
AS SELECT
DISTINCT
  date_sk
, date
, month_name
, month
, quarter
, year
, promo_ind
, b.effective_date
, b.expiry_date
FROM
  product_dim a
, date_dim b
WHERE
    a.effective_date = b.date
;

/* end of script                                                    */
```

Run the script to create the **product_launch_date_dim** view using this command.

```
mysql> \. c:\mysql\scripts\product_launch_date_dim.sql
```

You can verify that the views were created successfully by issuing the show full tables command, like this.

```
mysql> show full tables like 'product_%date_dim';
```

The query result is as follows.

```
+-------------------------------+------------+
| Tables_in_dw (product_%date_dim) | Table_type |
+----------------------------------+------------+
| product_launch_date_dim          | VIEW       |
+----------------------------------+------------+
1 row in set (0.00 sec)
```

Next, confirm that you have the product launch dates in the view.

```
mysql> select * from product_launch_date_dim \G
```

The result of the query is as follows.

```
*************************** 1. row ***************************
product_launch_date_sk: 1
   product_launch_date: 2005-03-01
            month_name: March
                 month: 3
               quarter: 1
                  year: 2005
             promo_ind: NULL
        effective_date: 0000-00-00
           expiry_date: 9999-12-31
*************************** 2. row ***************************
product_launch_date_sk: 731
   product_launch_date: 2007-03-01
            month_name: March
                 month: 3
               quarter: 1
                  year: 2007
             promo_ind: NULL
        effective_date: 0000-00-00
           expiry_date: 9999-12-31
2 rows in set (0.01 sec)
```

Note

The query output has two product launch dates (March 1, 2005 and March 1, 2007), which is correct since the product's effective date in the **product_dim** table is either one of these two dates.

You now need to initially populate the **product_count_fact** table. The script in Listing 21.4 loads the existing product launches to the **product_count_fact** table from the **product_dim** table. The script has two Insert statements. The first Insert adds the products that have not been updated. No SCD2 is applied.

The second Insert handles products that have been through SCD2. Note that the Select statement returns the earliest inserted rows when you do a GROUP BY, so it correctly picks up the effective date of a product when it is launched, not the product's effective date of an SCD2 row.

Listing 21.4: The script for initially populating the product count

```
/**********************************************************************/
/*                                                                    */
/* product_count_ini.sql                                              */
/*                                                                    */
/**********************************************************************/

USE dw;

/* for new products                                                  */

INSERT INTO product_count_fact
(product_sk, product_launch_date_sk)
SELECT
  a.product_sk
, b.date_sk
FROM
  product_dim a
, date_dim b
WHERE
a.effective_date = b.date
GROUP BY product_code
HAVING COUNT(product_code) = 1
;

/* for products that have been updated by SCD2                        */

INSERT INTO product_count_fact (product_sk, product_launch_date_sk)
SELECT
  a.product_sk
, b.date_sk
FROM
  product_dim a
, date_dim b
WHERE
a.effective_date = b.date
GROUP BY product_code
HAVING COUNT(product_code) > 1
;
```

```
/* end of script                                                      */
```

Run the script in Listing 21.4 using this command.

```
mysql> \. c:\mysql\scripts\product_count_ini.sql
```

You will see this message on the console.

```
Database changed
Query OK, 3 rows affected (0.12 sec)
Records: 3  Duplicates: 0  Warnings: 0

Query OK, 1 row affected (0.07 sec)
Records: 1  Duplicates: 0  Warnings: 0
```

Then, confirm that the initial population was successful by querying the **product_count_fact** table using this statement.

```
mysql> select * from product_count_fact;
```

Here is the query result.

```
+------------+------------------------+
| product_sk | product_launch_date_sk |
+------------+------------------------+
|          2 |                      1 |
|          5 |                    731 |
|          1 |                      1 |
|          3 |                      1 |
+------------+------------------------+
4 rows in set (0.06 sec)
```

Revising the DW Regular Population Script

Since the schema has changed, you need to revise the regular population script as well. You need the script to also populate the **product_count_fact** table right after the **product_dim** table gets populated. Listing 23.5 shows the revised regular population script.

Listing 21.5: The revised daily DW regular population script

```
/**********************************************************************/
/*                                                                    */
/* dw_regular_21.sql                                                  */
```

```
/*                                                                  */
/********************************************************************/

USE dw;

/* CUSTOMER_DIM POPULATION                                          */

TRUNCATE customer_stg;

LOAD DATA INFILE 'customer.csv'
INTO TABLE customer_stg
FIELDS TERMINATED BY ','
OPTIONALLY ENCLOSED BY '"'
LINES TERMINATED BY '\r\n'
IGNORE 1 LINES
( customer_number
, customer_name
, customer_street_address
, customer_zip_code
, customer_city
, customer_state
, shipping_address
, shipping_zip_code
, shipping_city
, shipping_state )
;

/* SCD 2 ON ADDRESSES                                               */

UPDATE
  customer_dim a
, customer_stg b
SET
  a.expiry_date = SUBDATE(CURRENT_DATE, 1)
WHERE
  a.customer_number = b.customer_number
AND (   a.customer_street_address <> b.customer_street_address
     OR a.customer_city <> b.customer_city
     OR a.customer_zip_code <> b.customer_zip_code
     OR a.customer_state <> b.customer_state
     OR a.shipping_address <> b.shipping_address
     OR a.shipping_city <> b.shipping_city
     OR a.shipping_zip_code <> b.shipping_zip_code
     OR a.shipping_state <> b.shipping_state
     OR a.shipping_address IS NULL
```

```
     OR a.shipping_city IS NULL
     OR a.shipping_zip_code IS NULL
     OR a.shipping_state IS NULL)
AND expiry_date = '9999-12-31'
;

INSERT INTO customer_dim
SELECT
  NULL
, b.customer_number
, b.customer_name
, b.customer_street_address
, b.customer_zip_code
, b.customer_city
, b.customer_state
, b.shipping_address
, b.shipping_zip_code
, b.shipping_city
, b.shipping_state
, CURRENT_DATE
, '9999-12-31'
FROM
  customer_dim a
, customer_stg b
WHERE
    a.customer_number = b.customer_number
AND (   a.customer_street_address <> b.customer_street_address
     OR a.customer_city <> b.customer_city
     OR a.customer_zip_code <> b.customer_zip_code
     OR a.customer_state <> b.customer_state
     OR a.shipping_address <> b.shipping_address
     OR a.shipping_city <> b.shipping_city
     OR a.shipping_zip_code <> b.shipping_zip_code
     OR a.shipping_state <> b.shipping_state
     OR a.shipping_address IS NULL
     OR a.shipping_city IS NULL
     OR a.shipping_zip_code IS NULL
     OR a.shipping_state IS NULL)
AND EXISTS (
SELECT *
FROM customer_dim x
WHERE b.customer_number = x.customer_number
AND a.expiry_date = SUBDATE(CURRENT_DATE, 1))
AND NOT EXISTS (
SELECT *
FROM customer_dim y
```

```
WHERE     b.customer_number = y.customer_number
      AND y.expiry_date = '9999-12-31')
;

/* END OF SCD 2                                                    */

/* SCD 1 ON NAME                                                   */

UPDATE customer_dim a, customer_stg b
SET a.customer_name = b.customer_name
WHERE     a.customer_number = b.customer_number
      AND a.expiry_date = '9999-12-31'
      AND a.customer_name <> b.customer_name
;

/* ADD NEW CUSTOMER                                                */

INSERT INTO customer_dim
SELECT
  NULL
, customer_number
, customer_name
, customer_street_address
, customer_zip_code
, customer_city
, customer_state
, shipping_address
, shipping_zip_code
, shipping_city
, shipping_state
, CURRENT_DATE
, '9999-12-31'
FROM customer_stg
WHERE customer_number NOT IN(
SELECT a.customer_number
FROM
  customer_dim a
, customer_stg b
WHERE b.customer_number = a.customer_number )
;

/* RE-BUILD PA CUSTOMER DIMENSION                                  */

TRUNCATE pa_customer_dim;
```

```
INSERT INTO pa_customer_dim
SELECT
  customer_sk
, customer_number
, customer_name
, customer_street_address
, customer_zip_code
, customer_city
, customer_state
, shipping_address
, shipping_zip_code
, shipping_city
, shipping_state
, effective_date
, expiry_date
FROM customer_dim
WHERE customer_state = 'PA'
;

/* END OF CUSTOMER_DIM POPULATION                                 */

/* PRODUCT_DIM POPULATION                                         */

TRUNCATE product_stg
;

LOAD DATA INFILE 'product.txt'
INTO TABLE product_stg
FIELDS TERMINATED BY ''
OPTIONALLY ENCLOSED BY ''
LINES TERMINATED BY '\r\n'
IGNORE 1 LINES
( product_code
, product_name
, product_category )
;

/* SCD2 ON PRODUCT NAME AND GROUP                                 */

UPDATE
  product_dim a
, product_stg b
SET
  expiry_date = SUBDATE(CURRENT_DATE, 1)
WHERE
    a.product_code = b.product_code
```

```
AND (   a.product_name <> b.product_name
     OR a.product_category <> b.product_category )
     AND expiry_date = '9999-12-31'
;

INSERT INTO product_dim
SELECT
  NULL
, b.product_code
, b.product_name
, b.product_category
, CURRENT_DATE
, '9999-12-31'
FROM
  product_dim a
, product_stg b
WHERE
    a.product_code = b.product_code
AND (   a.product_name <> b.product_name
     OR a.product_category <> b.product_category )
AND EXISTS (
SELECT *
FROM product_dim x
WHERE     b.product_code = x.product_code
            AND a.expiry_date = SUBDATE(CURRENT_DATE, 1))
AND NOT EXISTS (
SELECT *
FROM product_dim y
WHERE    b.product_code = y.product_code
     AND y.expiry_date = '9999-12-31')
;

/* END OF SCD 2                                                     */

/* ADD NEW PRODUCT                                                  */

INSERT INTO product_dim
SELECT
  NULL
, product_code
, product_name
, product_category
, CURRENT_DATE
, '9999-12-31'
FROM product_stg
```

```
WHERE product_code NOT IN(
SELECT y.product_code
FROM product_dim x, product_stg y
WHERE x.product_code = y.product_code )
;

/* END OF PRODUCT_DIM POPULATION                                    */

/* PRODUCT_COUNT_FACT POPULATION                                    */

TRUNCATE product_count_fact
;

INSERT INTO product_count_fact
(product_sk, product_launch_date_sk)
SELECT
  a.product_sk
, b.date_sk
FROM
  product_dim a
, date_dim b
WHERE
a.effective_date = b.date
GROUP BY product_code
HAVING COUNT(product_code) = 1
;

/* for products that have been updated by SCD2                      */

INSERT INTO product_count_fact
(product_sk, product_launch_date_sk)
SELECT
  a.product_sk
, b.date_sk
FROM
  product_dim a
, date_dim b
WHERE
a.effective_date = b.date
GROUP BY product_code
HAVING COUNT(product_code) > 1
;

/* END OF PRODUCT_COUNT_FACT POPULATION                             */

/* insert new orders                                                */
```

```
INSERT INTO sales_order_fact
SELECT
  b.customer_sk
, c.product_sk
, f.sales_order_attribute_sk
, d.order_date_sk
, NULL
, NULL
, NULL
, NULL
, a.order_number
, e.request_delivery_date_sk
, order_amount
, quantity
, NULL
, NULL
, NULL
, NULL
FROM
  source.sales_order a
, customer_dim b
, product_dim c
, order_date_dim d
, request_delivery_date_dim e
, sales_order_attribute_dim f
WHERE
      order_status = 'N'
AND entry_date = CURRENT_DATE
AND a.customer_number = b.customer_number
AND a.status_date >= b.effective_date
AND a.status_date <= b.expiry_date
AND a.product_code = c.product_code
AND a.status_date >= c.effective_date
AND a.status_date <= c.expiry_date
AND a.status_date = d.order_date
AND a.request_delivery_date = e.request_delivery_date
AND a.verification_ind = f.verification_ind
AND a.credit_check_flag = f.credit_check_flag
AND a.new_customer_ind = f.new_customer_ind
AND a.web_order_flag = f.web_order_flag
AND a.status_date >= f.effective_date
AND a.status_date <= f.expiry_date
;
```

```
UPDATE sales_order_fact a, source.sales_order b, allocate_date_dim c
SET
  a.allocate_date_sk = c.allocate_date_sk
, a.allocate quantity = b.quantity
WHERE
    order_status = 'A'
AND b.entry_date = CURRENT_DATE
AND b.order_number = a.order_number
AND c.allocate_date = b.status_date
;

UPDATE sales_order_fact a, source.sales_order b, packing_date_dim d
SET
  a.packing_date_sk = d.packing_date_sk
, a.packing_quantity = b.quantity
WHERE
    order_status = 'P'
AND b.entry_date = CURRENT_DATE
AND b.order_number = a.order_number
AND d.packing_date = b.status_date
;

UPDATE sales_order_fact a, source.sales_order b, ship_date_dim e
SET
  a.ship_date_sk = e.ship_date_sk
, a.ship_quantity = b.quantity
WHERE
    order_status = 'S'
AND b.entry_date = CURRENT_DATE
AND b.order_number = a.order_number
AND e.ship_date = b.status_date
;

UPDATE sales_order_fact a, source.sales_order b, receive_date_dim f
SET
  a.receive_date_sk = f.receive_date_sk
, a.receive_quantity = b.quantity
WHERE
    order_status = 'R'
AND b.entry_date = CURRENT_DATE
AND b.order_number = a.order_number
AND f.receive_date = b.status_date
;

/* end of script                                                  */
```

Before you can test the revised regular population script, you need to do two things. First, you need to prepare a product text file. Use the previous product text file, but change the name of Product code 1 to 'Regular Hard Disk Drive' and add a new product 'High End Hard Disk Drive' (product code 5), as shown here:

```
PRODUCT CODE,PRODUCT NAME,PRODUCT GROUP
1          Regular Hard Disk Drive      Storage
2          Floppy Drive                 Storage
3          Flat Panel                   Monitor
4          Keyboard                     Peripheral
5          High End Hard Disk Drive     Storage
```

Second, you need to set your MySQL date to March 20, 2007 (a date later than March 16, 2007, which is the last date you ran the regular population script in Chapter 18). Now run the dw_regular_21.sql script:

```
mysql> \. c:\mysql\scripts\dw_regular_21.sql
```

You'll see the following message on your console.

```
Database changed
Query OK, 9 rows affected (0.10 sec)

Query OK, 9 rows affected (0.14 sec)
Records: 9  Deleted: 0  Skipped: 0  Warnings: 0

Query OK, 0 rows affected (0.00 sec)
Rows matched: 0  Changed: 0  Warnings: 0

Query OK, 0 rows affected (0.00 sec)
Records: 0  Duplicates: 0  Warnings: 0

Query OK, 0 rows affected (0.01 sec)
Rows matched: 0  Changed: 0  Warnings: 0

Query OK, 0 rows affected (0.00 sec)
Records: 0  Duplicates: 0  Warnings: 0

Query OK, 19 rows affected (0.04 sec)

Query OK, 19 rows affected (0.11 sec)
Records: 19  Duplicates: 0  Warnings: 0

Query OK, 4 rows affected (0.09 sec)
```

```
Query OK, 5 rows affected (0.06 sec)
Records: 5  Deleted: 0  Skipped: 0  Warnings: 0

Query OK, 1 row affected (0.04 sec)
Rows matched: 1  Changed: 1  Warnings: 0

Query OK, 1 row affected (0.06 sec)
Records: 1  Duplicates: 0  Warnings: 0

Query OK, 1 row affected (0.05 sec)
Records: 1  Duplicates: 0  Warnings: 0

Query OK, 2 rows affected (0.10 sec)
Records: 2  Duplicates: 0  Warnings: 0

Query OK, 1 row affected (0.08 sec)
Rows matched: 1  Changed: 1  Warnings: 0

Query OK, 0 rows affected (0.00 sec)
Records: 0  Duplicates: 0  Warnings: 0

Query OK, 0 rows affected (0.01 sec)
Rows matched: 0  Changed: 0  Warnings: 0

Query OK, 0 rows affected (0.00 sec)
Rows matched: 0  Changed: 0  Warnings: 0

Query OK, 0 rows affected (0.01 sec)
Rows matched: 0  Changed: 0  Warnings: 0

Query OK, 0 rows affected (0.01 sec)
Rows matched: 0  Changed: 0  Warnings: 0
```

You can confirm that the regular population is correct by querying the **product_count_fact** table:

```
mysql> SELECT c.product_sk psk, c.product_code pc,
       b.product_launch_date_sk plsk,
    -> b.product_launch_date pld
    -> FROM product_count_fact a, product_launch_date_dim b,
    -> product_dim c
    -> WHERE a.product_launch_date_sk = b.product_launch_date_sk
    -> AND a.product_sk = c.product_sk
    -> ORDER BY product_code, product_launch_date;
```

Here is the correct result.

```
+-----+------+------+------------+
| psk | pc   | plsk | pld        |
+-----+------+------+------------+
|   1 |    1 |    1 | 2005-03-01 |
|   2 |    2 |    1 | 2005-03-01 |
|   3 |    3 |    1 | 2005-03-01 |
|   5 |    4 |  731 | 2007-03-01 |
|   7 |    5 |  750 | 2007-03-20 |
+-----+------+------+------------+
5 rows in set (0.01 sec)
```

Note

The launch date of the new product code (March 20, 200) was added. The change on the name of Product code 1 did not impact the launch date.

Summary

In this chapter you learned the factless fact technique and applied it to product counting in the sales data warehouse. In the next chapter you will learn another advanced technique called the late-arrival fact.

Chapter 22
Late Arrival Facts

A fact is late if it is loaded at a later date than its effective date. Take as an example a sales order that is entered into the source data later than its order date. When the sales order is then loaded into its fact table, the loading date takes place after its order date and the sales order is therefore a late arrival fact.

Late arrival facts affect the population of periodic snapshot fact tables, such as the **month_end_sales_order_fact** table discussed in Chapter 14, "Snapshots." For instance, if the month end snapshot sales order amount of March 2007 has been calculated and stored in the **month_end_sales_order_fact** table, and a late sales order with a March 10 order date is loaded, the March 2007 snapshot amount must be re-calculated to account for the late fact.

This chapter teaches you how to handle late arrival fact.

Handling Late Arrival Facts

In this section I explain how to handle late arrival sales orders when populating the **month_end_sales_order_fact** table.

First of all, in order for you to know if a sales order is late, you need to load the entry date from the sales order source to the **sales_order_fact** table. Since you don't have a column for the entry date, you need to add a new one to the fact table. Similar to adding the request delivery date in Chapter 13, "Dimension Role Playing," you apply the dimension role playing technique to add the entry date. Therefore, add a date surrogate key column in the sales order fact table named **entry_date_sk** and create a database view from the date dimension table called **entry_date_dim**. The script in Listing 22.1 creates the **entry_date_dim** view and add the **entry_date_sk** surrogate key column in the **sales_order_fact** table.

Note

You might want to review the dimension role-playing technique in Chapter 13 to understand why you need to add the surrogate key column and create a database view.

Listing 22.1: Adding the entry_date column

```
/******************************************************************/
/*                                                                */
/* entry_date.sql                                                 */
/*                                                                */
/******************************************************************/

USE dw;

CREATE VIEW entry_date_dim (
  entry_date_sk
, entry_date
, month_name
, month
, quarter
, year
, promo_ind
, effective_date
, expiry_date
)
AS SELECT
  date_sk
, date
, month_name
, month
, quarter
, year
, promo_ind
, effective_date
, expiry_date
FROM date_dim
;

ALTER TABLE sales_order_fact
ADD entry_date_sk INT AFTER receive_date_sk
;

/* end of script                                                  */
```

To run the script in Listing 22.1, type in the following command into the MySQL console.

```
mysql> \. c:\mysql\scripts\entry_date.sql
```

You will see the following as the response.

```
Database changed
Query OK, 0 rows affected (0.02 sec)

Query OK, 59 rows affected (0.49 sec)
Records: 59  Duplicates: 0  Warnings: 0
```

After creating the **entry_date_dim** view and adding the **entry_date_sk** column to the **sales_order_fact** table, you now need to revise the data warehouse regular population script to include the entry date. Listing 22.2 shows the revised regular population script. Note that the **sales_order** source already contains entry dates, but we did not previously load it into the data warehouse.

Listing 22.2: The revised daily DW regular population

```
/******************************************************************/
/*                                                                */
/* dw_regular_22.sql                                              */
/*                                                                */
/******************************************************************/

USE dw;

/* CUSTOMER_DIM POPULATION                                        */

TRUNCATE customer_stg;

LOAD DATA INFILE 'customer.csv'
INTO TABLE customer_stg
FIELDS TERMINATED BY ','
OPTIONALLY ENCLOSED BY '"'
LINES TERMINATED BY '\r\n'
IGNORE 1 LINES
( customer_number
, customer_name
, customer_street_address
, customer_zip_code
, customer_city
```

```
, customer_state
, shipping_address
, shipping_zip_code
, shipping_city
, shipping_state )
;

/* SCD 2 ON ADDRESSES                                              */

UPDATE
  customer_dim a
, customer_stg b
SET
  a.expiry_date = SUBDATE(CURRENT_DATE, 1)
WHERE
  a.customer_number = b.customer_number
AND (   a.customer_street_address <> b.customer_street_address
     OR a.customer_city <> b.customer_city
     OR a.customer_zip_code <> b.customer_zip_code
     OR a.customer_state <> b.customer_state
     OR a.shipping_address <> b.shipping_address
     OR a.shipping_city <> b.shipping_city
     OR a.shipping_zip_code <> b.shipping_zip_code
     OR a.shipping_state <> b.shipping_state
     OR a.shipping_address IS NULL
     OR a.shipping_city IS NULL
     OR a.shipping_zip_code IS NULL
     OR a.shipping_state IS NULL)
AND expiry_date = '9999-12-31'
;

INSERT INTO customer_dim
SELECT
  NULL
, b.customer_number
, b.customer_name
, b.customer_street_address
, b.customer_zip_code
, b.customer_city
, b.customer_state
, b.shipping_address
, b.shipping_zip_code
, b.shipping_city
, b.shipping_state
, CURRENT_DATE
, '9999-12-31'
```

```
FROM
  customer_dim a
, customer_stg b
WHERE
    a.customer_number = b.customer_number
AND (   a.customer_street_address <> b.customer_street_address
     OR a.customer_city <> b.customer_city
     OR a.customer_zip_code <> b.customer_zip_code
     OR a.customer_state <> b.customer_state
     OR a.shipping_address <> b.shipping_address
     OR a.shipping_city <> b.shipping_city
     OR a.shipping_zip_code <> b.shipping_zip_code
     OR a.shipping_state <> b.shipping_state
     OR a.shipping_address IS NULL
     OR a.shipping_city IS NULL
     OR a.shipping_zip_code IS NULL
     OR a.shipping_state IS NULL)
AND EXISTS (
SELECT *
FROM customer_dim x
WHERE b.customer_number = x.customer_number
AND a.expiry_date = SUBDATE(CURRENT_DATE, 1))
AND NOT EXISTS (
SELECT *
FROM customer_dim y
WHERE     b.customer_number = y.customer_number
      AND y.expiry_date = '9999-12-31')
;

/* END OF SCD 2                                                        */

/* SCD 1 ON NAME                                                       */

UPDATE customer_dim a, customer_stg b
SET a.customer_name = b.customer_name
WHERE     a.customer_number = b.customer_number
      AND a.expiry_date = '9999-12-31'
      AND a.customer_name <> b.customer_name
;

/* ADD NEW CUSTOMER                                                    */

INSERT INTO customer_dim
SELECT
  NULL
```

```
, customer_number
, customer_name
, customer_street_address
, customer_zip_code
, customer_city
, customer_state
, shipping_address
, shipping_zip_code
, shipping_city
, shipping_state
, CURRENT_DATE
, '9999-12-31'
FROM customer_stg
WHERE customer_number NOT IN(
SELECT a.customer_number
FROM
  customer_dim a
, customer_stg b
WHERE b.customer_number = a.customer_number )
;

/* RE-BUILD PA CUSTOMER DIMENSION                                   */

TRUNCATE pa_customer_dim;

INSERT INTO pa_customer_dim
SELECT
  customer_sk
, customer_number
, customer_name
, customer_street_address
, customer_zip_code
, customer_city
, customer_state
, shipping_address
, shipping_zip_code
, shipping_city
, shipping_state
, effective_date
, expiry_date
FROM customer_dim
WHERE customer_state = 'PA'
;

/* END OF CUSTOMER_DIM POPULATION                                   */
```

```
/* PRODUCT_DIM POPULATION                                         */

TRUNCATE product_stg
;

LOAD DATA INFILE 'product.txt'
INTO TABLE product_stg
FIELDS TERMINATED BY ''
OPTIONALLY ENCLOSED BY ''
LINES TERMINATED BY '\r\n'
IGNORE 1 LINES
( product_code
, product_name
, product_category )
;

/* SCD2 ON PRODUCT NAME AND GROUP                                 */

UPDATE
  product_dim a
, product_stg b
SET
  expiry_date = SUBDATE(CURRENT_DATE, 1)
WHERE
    a.product_code = b.product_code
AND (   a.product_name <> b.product_name
     OR a.product_category <> b.product_category )
     AND expiry_date = '9999-12-31'
;

INSERT INTO product_dim
SELECT
  NULL
, b.product_code
, b.product_name
, b.product_category
, CURRENT_DATE
, '9999-12-31'
FROM
  product_dim a
, product_stg b
WHERE
    a.product_code = b.product_code
AND (   a.product_name <> b.product_name
     OR a.product_category <> b.product_category )
```

```
AND EXISTS (
SELECT *
FROM product_dim x
WHERE     b.product_code = x.product_code
      AND a.expiry_date = SUBDATE(CURRENT_DATE, 1))
AND NOT EXISTS (
SELECT *
FROM product_dim y
WHERE    b.product_code = y.product_code
     AND y.expiry_date = '9999-12-31')
;

/* END OF SCD 2                                                   */

/* ADD NEW PRODUCT                                                */

INSERT INTO product_dim
SELECT
  NULL
, product_code
, product_name
, product_category
, CURRENT_DATE
, '9999-12-31'
FROM product_stg
WHERE product_code NOT IN(
SELECT y.product_code
FROM product_dim x, product_stg y
WHERE x.product_code = y.product_code )
;

/* END OF PRODUCT_DIM POPULATION                                  */

/* PRODUCT_COUNT_FACT POPULATION                                  */

TRUNCATE product_count_fact
;

INSERT INTO product_count_fact
(product_sk, product_launch_date_sk)
SELECT
  a.product_sk
, b.date_sk

FROM
  product_dim a
```

```
, date_dim b

WHERE
a.effective_date = b.date
GROUP BY product_code
HAVING COUNT(product_code) = 1
;

/* for products that have been updated by SCD2                        */

INSERT INTO product_count_fact (product_sk, product_launch_date_sk)
SELECT
  a.product_sk
, b.date_sk

FROM
  product_dim a
, date_dim b

WHERE
a.effective_date = b.date
GROUP BY product_code
HAVING COUNT(product_code) > 1
;

/* END OF PRODUCT_COUNT_FACT POPULATION                               */

/* INSERT NEW ORDERS                                                  */

INSERT INTO sales_order_fact
SELECT
  b.customer_sk
, c.product_sk
, f.sales_order_attribute_sk
, d.order_date_sk
, NULL
, NULL
, NULL
, NULL
, g.entry_date_sk
, a.order_number
, e.request_delivery_date_sk
, order_amount
, quantity
, NULL
```

```
, NULL
, NULL
, NULL
FROM
  source.sales_order a
, customer_dim b
, product_dim c
, order_date_dim d
, request_delivery_date_dim e
, sales_order_attribute_dim f
, entry_date_dim g
WHERE
      order_status = 'N'
AND a.entry_date = CURRENT_DATE
AND a.customer_number = b.customer_number
AND a.status_date >= b.effective_date
AND a.status_date <= b.expiry_date
AND a.product_code = c.product_code
AND a.status_date >= c.effective_date
AND a.status_date <= c.expiry_date
AND a.status_date = d.order_date
AND a.entry_date = g.entry_date
AND a.request_delivery_date = e.request_delivery_date
AND a.verification_ind = f.verification_ind
AND a.credit_check_flag = f.credit_check_flag
AND a.new_customer_ind = f.new_customer_ind
AND a.web_order_flag = f.web_order_flag
AND a.status_date >= f.effective_date
AND a.status_date <= f.expiry_date
;

UPDATE
  sales_order_fact a
, source.sales_order b
, allocate_date_dim c
SET
  a.allocate_date_sk = c.allocate_date_sk
, a.allocate_quantity = b.quantity
WHERE
    order_status = 'A'
AND b.entry_date = CURRENT_DATE
AND b.order_number = a.order_number
AND c.allocate_date = b.status_date
;

UPDATE
```

```
  sales_order_fact a
, source.sales_order b
, packing_date_dim d
SET
  a.packing_date_sk = d.packing_date_sk
, a.packing_quantity = b.quantity
WHERE
    order_status = 'P'
AND b.entry_date = CURRENT_DATE
AND b.order_number = a.order_number
AND d.packing_date = b.status_date
;

UPDATE
  sales_order_fact a
, source.sales_order b
, ship_date_dim e
SET
  a.ship_date_sk = e.ship_date_sk
, a.ship_quantity = b.quantity
WHERE
    order_status = 'S'
AND b.entry_date = CURRENT_DATE
AND b.order_number = a.order_number
AND e.ship_date = b.status_date
;

UPDATE
  sales_order_fact a
, source.sales_order b
, receive_date_dim f
SET
  a.receive_date_sk = f.receive_date_sk
, a.receive_quantity = b.quantity
WHERE
    order_status = 'R'
AND b.entry_date = CURRENT_DATE
AND b.order_number = a.order_number
AND f.receive_date = b.status_date
;

/* end of script                                                      */
```

You must also revise the month end population script. The revised script, presented in listing 22.3, has three parts. The first part handles sales orders that are not late. The second part adds incoming sales amounts to the existing rows that have the same product and month as the incoming sales orders. The third part adds new rows for the incoming sales orders.

Listing 22.3: Revised Month End Sales Order population

```
/******************************************************************/
/*                                                                */
/* month_end_sales_order_22.sql                                   */
/*                                                                */
/******************************************************************/

USE dw;

/* normal (order_date = entry_date)                               */

INSERT INTO month_end_sales_order_fact
SELECT
  d.month_sk
, a.product_sk
, SUM(order_amount)
, SUM(order_quantity)
FROM
  sales_order_fact a
, order_date_dim b
, entry_date_dim c
, month_dim d
WHERE
    a.order_date_sk = b.order_date_sk
AND a.entry_date_sk = c.entry_date_sk
AND b.order_date = c.entry_date
AND c.month = MONTH(CURRENT_DATE)
AND c.year = YEAR(CURRENT_DATE)
AND b.month = d.month
AND b.year = d.year
GROUP BY d.month, d.year, product_sk
;

/* late arrival, amount & quantity already exist for the past months
*/

UPDATE
   month_end_sales_order_fact a

, (SELECT
  y.month
```

```
, y.year
, w.product_sk
, SUM(order_amount) order_amount
, SUM(order_quantity) order_quantity
FROM
  sales_order_fact x
, order_date_dim y
, entry_date_dim z
, product_dim w
WHERE
    x.order_date_sk = y.order_date_sk
AND x.entry_date_sk = z.entry_date_sk
AND order_date <> entry_date
AND MONTH(entry_date) = MONTH(CURRENT_DATE)
AND YEAR(entry_date) = YEAR(CURRENT_DATE)
AND x.product_sk = w.product_sk
GROUP BY y.month, y.year, product_sk) b

, month_dim c

SET month_order_amount = month_order_amount + b.order_amount
, month_order_quantity = month_order_quantity + b.order_quantity
WHERE
    a.month_order_sk = c.month_sk
AND b.month = c.month
AND b.year = c.year
AND a.product_sk = b.product_sk
;

/* late arrival but amount & quantity not exist for the past months
*/

INSERT INTO month_end_sales_order_fact
SELECT
  d.month_sk
, a.product_sk
, SUM(order_amount)
, SUM(order_quantity)
FROM
  sales_order_fact a
, order_date_dim b
, entry_date_dim c
, month_dim d
WHERE
    a.order_date_sk = b.order_date_sk
```

```
AND a.entry_date_sk = c.entry_date_sk
AND b.order_date <> c.entry_date
AND c.month = MONTH(CURRENT_DATE)
AND c.year = YEAR(CURRENT_DATE)
AND b.month = d.month
AND b.year = d.year
AND NOT EXISTS
(SELECT * FROM
  month_end_sales_order_fact p
, sales_order_fact q
, month_dim s
WHERE
    p.month_order_sk = s.month_sk
AND s.month = d.month
AND s.year = d.year
AND p.product_sk = a.product_sk )
GROUP BY
  d.month
, d.year
, a.product_sk
;

/* end of script                                                    */
```

Testing

This section explains the steps you need to do before running the revised scripts in Listings 22.2 and 22.3.

The first step is to load the entry dates for March sales orders by executing the following SQL statement. This SQL statement updates the sales orders' **entry_date_sk** that have the same values as their **order_date_sk**. These March entry dates are later required to test the population of March month-end snapshot.

```
UPDATE sales_order_fact
SET entry_date_sk = order_date_sk
WHERE order_date_sk BETWEEN 731 AND 754
;
```

You can then query the **month_end_sales_order_fact** table before running the regular population script. Later, you use this 'before' data to compare with the 'after' date to confirm correct regular population.

Here is the statement you can use to query the **month_end_sales_order_fact** table.

```
mysql> select year, month, product_name, month_order_amount amt,
    -> month_order_quantity qty
    -> from month_end_sales_order_fact a, month_dim b,
    -> product_dim c
    -> where a.month_order_sk = b.month_sk
    -> and a.product_sk = c.product_sk
    -> order by year, month, product_name;
```

The query result is given below.

```
+------+-------+-----------------+---------+------+
| year | month | product_name    | amt     | qty  |
+------+-------+-----------------+---------+------+
| 2006 |     1 | LCD Panel       | 1000.00 | NULL |
| 2006 |     2 | Hard Disk Drive | 1000.00 | NULL |
| 2006 |     3 | Floppy Drive    | 2000.00 | NULL |
| 2006 |     4 | LCD Panel       | 2500.00 | NULL |
| 2006 |     5 | Hard Disk Drive | 3000.00 | NULL |
| 2006 |     6 | Floppy Drive    | 3500.00 | NULL |
| 2006 |     7 | LCD Panel       | 4000.00 | NULL |
| 2006 |     8 | Hard Disk Drive | 4500.00 | NULL |
| 2006 |     9 | Floppy Drive    | 1000.00 | NULL |
| 2006 |    10 | LCD Panel       | 1000.00 | NULL |
| 2007 |     2 | Floppy Drive    | 4000.00 | NULL |
| 2007 |     2 | LCD Panel       | 4000.00 | NULL |
+------+-------+-----------------+---------+------+
12 rows in set (0.00 sec)
```

To compare the 'before' and 'after' dates, query the sales_order_fact table using this statement.

```
mysql> SELECT product_name, SUM(order_amount)
    -> FROM sales_order_fact a, product_dim b
    -> WHERE order_date_sk > 730
    -> AND a.product_sk = b.product_sk
    -> GROUP BY a.product_sk
    -> ORDER BY product_name;
```

The result should be similar to the following.

```
+-----------------+-------------------+
| product_name    | SUM(order_amount) |
+-----------------+-------------------+
```

```
| Flat Panel      |          47000.00 |
| Floppy Drive    |          25000.00 |
| Hard Disk Drive |          46500.00 |
| Keyboard        |          27000.00 |
+-----------------+-------------------+
4 rows in set (0.00 sec)
```

The next step is to prepare sales orders test data by running the script in Listing 22.4. The scripts loads two sales orders into the sales order source data, one that is late and one that is not late.

Listing 22.4: Adding two sales orders

```
/******************************************************************/
/*                                                                */
/* sales_order_22.sql                                             */
/*                                                                */
/******************************************************************/

USE source;

INSERT INTO sales_order VALUES

/* late arrival                                                   */

  (62, 6, 2, 'Y', 'Y', 'Y', 'N', '2007-02-25', 'N', '2007-03-30',
      '2007-03-26', 1000, 10)

/* normal                                                         */

, (63, 12, 5, 'Y', 'N', 'Y', 'N', '2007-03-26', 'N', '2007-03-30',
      '2007-03-26', 2000, 20)
;

/* end of script                                                  */
```

Run the above script by using this command.

```
mysql> \. c:\mysql\scripts\sales_order_22.sql
```

You will see the following response on your MySQL console.

```
Database changed
Query OK, 2 rows affected (0.07 sec)
Records: 2  Duplicates: 0  Warnings: 0
```

Before you run the new month end sales order population script, you must first load the two new sales orders into the **sales_order_fact** table. Set your MySQL date to March 26, 2005, which is the entry date the two sales orders in your test data, then run the dw_regular_22.sql script using this command.

```
mysql> \. c:\mysql\scripts\dw_regular_22.sql
```

You should see this on your console.

```
Database changed
Query OK, 9 rows affected (0.08 sec)

Query OK, 9 rows affected (0.07 sec)
Records: 9  Deleted: 0  Skipped: 0  Warnings: 0

Query OK, 0 rows affected (0.00 sec)
Rows matched: 0  Changed: 0  Warnings: 0

Query OK, 0 rows affected (0.00 sec)
Records: 0  Duplicates: 0  Warnings: 0

Query OK, 0 rows affected (0.00 sec)
Rows matched: 0  Changed: 0  Warnings: 0

Query OK, 0 rows affected (0.00 sec)
Records: 0  Duplicates: 0  Warnings: 0

Query OK, 19 rows affected (0.09 sec)

Query OK, 19 rows affected (0.06 sec)
Records: 19  Duplicates: 0  Warnings: 0

Query OK, 5 rows affected (0.06 sec)

Query OK, 5 rows affected (0.05 sec)
Records: 5  Deleted: 0  Skipped: 0  Warnings: 0

Query OK, 0 rows affected (0.00 sec)
Rows matched: 0  Changed: 0  Warnings: 0

Query OK, 0 rows affected (0.00 sec)
Records: 0  Duplicates: 0  Warnings: 0

Query OK, 0 rows affected (0.00 sec)
Records: 0  Duplicates: 0  Warnings: 0
```

```
Query OK, 3 rows affected (0.02 sec)
Records: 3  Duplicates: 0  Warnings: 0

Query OK, 2 rows affected (0.01 sec)
Records: 2  Duplicates: 0  Warnings: 0

Query OK, 2 rows affected (0.09 sec)
Records: 2  Duplicates: 0  Warnings: 0

Query OK, 0 rows affected (0.01 sec)
Rows matched: 0  Changed: 0  Warnings: 0

Query OK, 0 rows affected (0.01 sec)
Rows matched: 0  Changed: 0  Warnings: 0

Query OK, 0 rows affected (0.01 sec)
Rows matched: 0  Changed: 0  Warnings: 0

Query OK, 0 rows affected (0.00 sec)
Rows matched: 0  Changed: 0  Warnings: 0
```

You're now ready to run the revised month end snapshot population. Set your MySQL date to March 31, 2007 (end of the March month) and run the **month_end_sales_order_22.sql** script to populate the March 2007 snapshot:

```
mysql> \. c:\mysql\scripts\month_end_sales_order_22.sql
```

Here is what you should see on your console.

```
Database changed
Query OK, 1 row affected (0.09 sec)
Records: 1  Duplicates: 0  Warnings: 0

Query OK, 1 row affected (0.07 sec)
Rows matched: 1  Changed: 1  Warnings: 0

Query OK, 0 rows affected (3.48 sec)
Records: 0  Duplicates: 0  Warnings: 0
```

Finally, run the same query to get the 'after' data of the month end sales orders.

```
mysql> select year, month, product_name, month_order_amount amt,
    -> month_order_quantity qty
    -> from month_end_sales_order_fact a, month_dim b,
```

```
    -> product_dim c
    -> where a.month_order_sk = b.month_sk
    -> and a.product_sk = c.product_sk
    -> order by year, month, product_name;
```

Here is the query result.

```
+------+-------+--------------------------+----------+------+
| year | month | product_name             | amt      | qty  |
+------+-------+--------------------------+----------+------+
| 2006 |     1 | LCD Panel                |  1000.00 | NULL |
| 2006 |     2 | Hard Disk Drive          |  1000.00 | NULL |
| 2006 |     3 | Floppy Drive             |  2000.00 | NULL |
| 2006 |     4 | LCD Panel                |  2500.00 | NULL |
| 2006 |     5 | Hard Disk Drive          |  3000.00 | NULL |
| 2006 |     6 | Floppy Drive             |  3500.00 | NULL |
| 2006 |     7 | LCD Panel                |  4000.00 | NULL |
| 2006 |     8 | Hard Disk Drive          |  4500.00 | NULL |
| 2006 |     9 | Floppy Drive             |  1000.00 | NULL |
| 2006 |    10 | LCD Panel                |  1000.00 | NULL |
| 2007 |     2 | Floppy Drive             |  5000.00 | NULL |
| 2007 |     2 | LCD Panel                |  4000.00 | NULL |
| 2007 |     3 | Flat Panel               | 47000.00 |  275 |
| 2007 |     3 | Floppy Drive             | 25000.00 |  120 |
| 2007 |     3 | Hard Disk Drive          | 46500.00 |  420 |
| 2007 |     3 | High End Hard Disk Drive |  4000.00 |   40 |
| 2007 |     3 | Keyboard                 | 27000.00 |   90 |
+------+-------+--------------------------+----------+------+
17 rows in set (0.00 sec)
```

If you compare the results of the 'before' and 'after' queries, you can see that

- The Floppy Drive's sales amount in February 2007 has been correctly increased from 4,000 to 5,000, thanks to the addition of the late arrival product sales order with the amount of 1,000 amount.
- All March sales orders are summarized. These include the High End Hard Disk Drive sales orders that you just added when you ran the **sales_order_22.sql** script earlier in this chapter.

Summary

In this chapter you learned how to handle late arrival facts. You revised and tested the month end sales order population to specifically handle late arrival sales orders.

In the next chapter you will learn how to consolidate common data among existing dimensions.

Chapter 23
Dimension Consolidation

When the number of dimensions in your data warehouse increases, you might find some common data in more than one dimension. For example, the zip code, city, and state are in the customer and shipping addresses of the customer dimension as well as in the factory dimensions. This chapter explains how you can consolidate the zip code from the three dimensions into a new zip code dimension.

Revising the Data Warehouse Schema

To consolidate dimensions, you need to change the data warehouse schema. The revised schema is shown in Figure 23.1. A new **zip_code_dim** table has been added, and the structures of the **sales_order_fact** and **production_fact** tables have been changed. Note that only the tables related to the zip code are shown.

The **zip_code_dim** table is related to the two fact tables. The relationships replace those from the customer and factory dimensions. You need two relationships to the **sales_order_fact** table, one for the customer address and one for the shipping address. There is only one relationship to the **production_fact** table, therefore only the factory zip code surrogate key was added in this fact table.

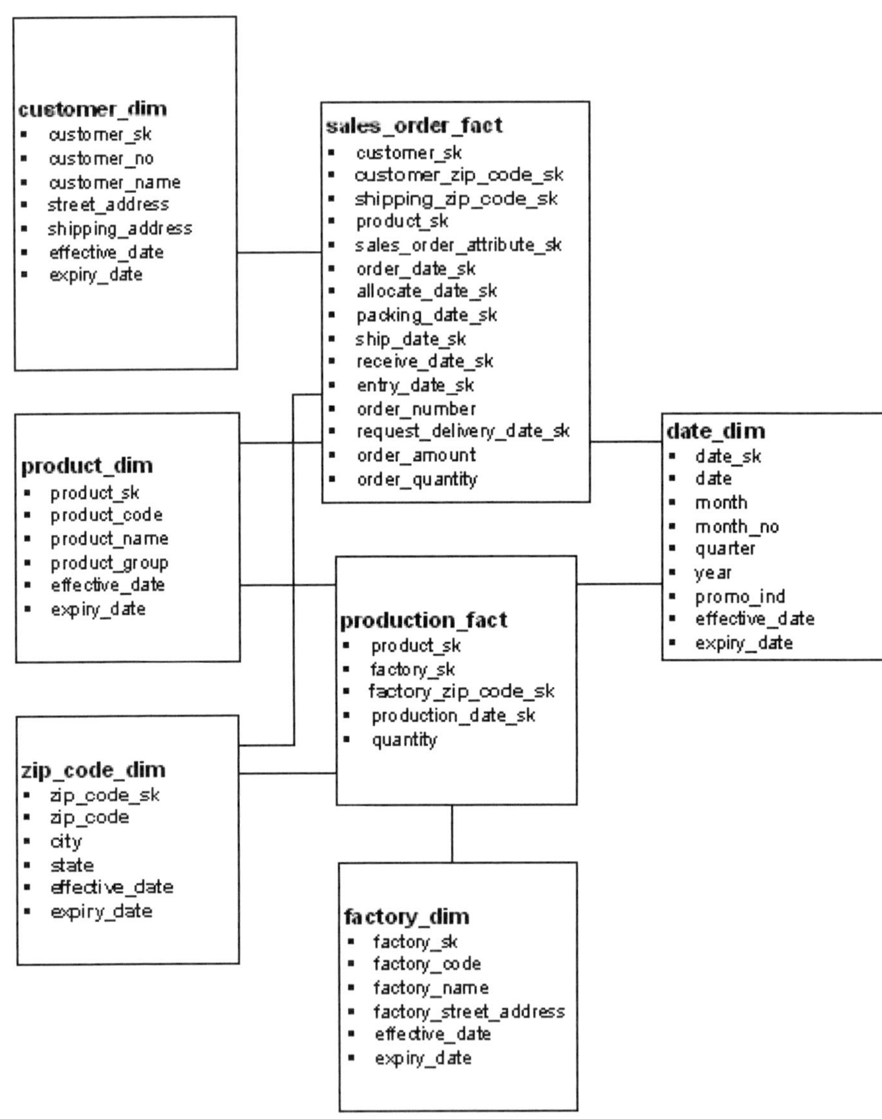

Figure 23.1: The schema after zip_code_dim is added

The script in Listing 23.1 can be used to create the **zip_code_dim** table.

Listing 23.1: Creating the zip_code_dim table

```
/******************************************************************/
/*                                                                */
```

```
/* zip_code_dim.sql                                                  */
/*                                                                   */
/*********************************************************************/

/* default to dw                                                     */

USE dw;

CREATE TABLE zip_code_dim (
  zip_code_sk INT NOT NULL AUTO_INCREMENT PRIMARY KEY
, zip_code INT(5)
, city CHAR(30)
, state CHAR(2)
, effective_date DATE
, expiry_date DATE
)
;

/* end of script                                                     */
```

Run the script in Listing 23.1 to create the **zip_code_dim** table:

```
mysql> \. c:\mysql\scripts\zip_code_dim.sql
```

Then, you need to populate the **zip_code_dim** table. I have provided the necessary zip code information in the **zip_code.csv** file below.

```
ZIP CODE,CITY,STATE
17050,PITTSBURGH,PA
17051,MC VEYTOWN,PA
17052,MAPLETON DEPOT,PA
17053,MARYSVILLE,PA
17054,MATTAWANA,PA
17055,MECHANICSBURG,PA
44102,CLEVELAND,OH
```

As usual, you load data from a CSV file to a staging table. The script in Listing 23.2 can be used to create a staging table called **zip_code_stg**.

Listing 23.2: Creating the zip_code_stg table

```
/*********************************************************************/
/*                                                                   */
/* zip_code_stg.sql                                                  */
/*                                                                   */
/*********************************************************************/
```

```
/* default to dw                                                        */

USE dw;

CREATE TABLE zip_code_stg (
  zip_code INT(5)
, city CHAR(30)
, state CHAR(2)
)
;

/* end of script                                                        */
```

Run the script in Listing 23.2 to create the staging table.

```
mysql> \. c:\mysql\scripts\zip_code_stg.sql
```

Assuming the **zip_code.csv** file contains the complete postal codes and these codes never change, you need to load the zip code file to the data warehouse once only. This is a type of pre-population called one-time population.

The script in Listing 23.3 contains the script for loading the zip code data into the **zip_code_stg** staging table.

Listing 23.3: Zip_code_dim population

```
/**********************************************************************/
/*                                                                    */
/* zip_code_population.sql                                            */
/*                                                                    */
/**********************************************************************/

/* default to dw                                                      */

USE dw;

TRUNCATE zip_code_stg;

LOAD DATA INFILE 'zip_code.csv'
INTO TABLE zip_code_stg
FIELDS TERMINATED BY ','
OPTIONALLY ENCLOSED BY ''
LINES TERMINATED BY '\r\n'
IGNORE 1 LINES
( zip_code
, city
```

```
, state      )
;

INSERT INTO zip_code_dim
SELECT
  NULL
, zip_code
, city
, state
, '0000-00-00'
, '9999-12-31'
FROM zip_code_stg
;

/* end of script                                                    */
```

Run the script in Listing 23.3 to populate the **zip_code_dim** table.

```
mysql> \. c:\mysql\scripts\zip_code_population.sql
```

Here is the message that you will see as the response to the query.

```
Database changed
Query OK, 1 row affected (0.09 sec)

Query OK, 7 rows affected (0.08 sec)
Records: 7  Deleted: 0  Skipped: 0  Warnings: 0

Query OK, 7 rows affected (0.07 sec)
Records: 7  Duplicates: 0  Warnings: 0
```

You can query the **zip_code_dim** table to confirm correct population using this statement.

```
mysql> select zip_code_sk sk, zip_code zip, city, state from
       zip_code_dim;
```

The query result is as follows.

```
+----+-------+----------------+-------+
| sk | zip   | city           | state |
+----+-------+----------------+-------+
|  1 | 17050 | PITTSBURGH     | PA    |
|  2 | 17051 | MC VEYTOWN     | PA    |
|  3 | 17052 | MAPLETON DEPOT | PA    |
|  4 | 17053 | MARYSVILLE     | PA    |
```

```
|  5 | 17054 | MATTAWANA      | PA     |
|  6 | 17055 | MECHANICSBURG  | PA     |
|  7 | 44102 | CLEVELAND      | OH     |
+----+-------+----------------+-------+
7 rows in set (0.41 sec)
```

Now you need to revise the **sales_order_fact** table and the other tables. Here are the five steps you need to do to update the database structure.

1. Create a **customer_zip_code_dim** view and a **shipping_zip_code_dim** based on the **zip_code_dim** table.
2. Add the **customer_zip_code_sk** and **shipping_zip_code_sk** columns to the **sales_order_fact** table.
3. Initially load the two zip code surrogate key columns based on the existing customer and shipping zip codes.
4. Remove the customer and shipping codes as well as their cities and states from the **customer_dim** table
5. Remove the customer city, state, and zip code from the **pa_customer_dim** table

The script in Listing 23.4 implements the above five revisions.

Listing 23.4: The revised sales_order_fact script

```
/******************************************************************/
/*                                                                */
/* sales_order_fact_23.sql                                        */
/*                                                                */
/******************************************************************/

USE dw;

CREATE VIEW customer_zip_code_dim
( customer_zip_code_sk
, customer_zip_code
, customer_city
, customer_state
, effective_date
, expiry_date )
AS SELECT
  zip_code_sk
, zip_code
, city
, state
, effective_date
```

```
, expiry_date
FROM zip_code_dim
;

CREATE VIEW shipping_zip_code_dim
( shipping_zip_code_sk
, shipping_zip_code
, shipping_city
, shipping_state
, effective_date
, expiry_date )
AS SELECT
  zip_code_sk
, zip_code
, city
, state
, effective_date
, expiry_date
FROM zip_code_dim
;

ALTER TABLE sales_order_fact
  ADD customer_zip_code_sk INT AFTER customer_sk
, ADD shipping_zip_code_sk INT AFTER customer_zip_code_sk
;

UPDATE sales_order_fact a, customer_dim b, customer_zip_code_dim c
SET
  a.customer_zip_code_sk = c.customer_zip_code_sk
WHERE
    a.customer_sk = b.customer_sk
AND b.customer_zip_code = c.customer_zip_code
;

UPDATE
  sales_order_fact a
, customer_dim b
, shipping_zip_code_dim c
SET
  a.shipping_zip_code_sk = c.shipping_zip_code_sk
WHERE
    a.customer_sk = b.customer_sk
AND b.shipping_zip_code = c.shipping_zip_code
;
```

```
ALTER TABLE customer_dim
  DROP customer_zip_code
, DROP customer_city
, DROP customer_state
, DROP shipping_zip_code
, DROP shipping_city
, DROP shipping_state
;

ALTER TABLE pa_customer_dim
  DROP customer_zip_code
, DROP customer_city
, DROP customer_state
, DROP shipping_zip_code
, DROP shipping_city
, DROP shipping_state
;

/* end of script                                                 */
```

Testing the Zip Code Dimension Implementation

Before you run the sales_order_fact_23.sql script in Listing 23.4 to modify the data warehouse structure, I'd like you to query the **customer_dim** table using this statement.

```
mysql> select customer_sk sk, customer_zip_code czip,
       shipping_zip_code szip from customer_dim;
```

The query result is presented here.

```
+----+-------+-------+
| sk | czip  | szip  |
+----+-------+-------+
|  1 | 17050 |  NULL |
|  2 | 17055 |  NULL |
|  3 | 17055 |  NULL |
|  4 | 17050 |  NULL |
|  5 | 17050 |  NULL |
|  6 | 17055 |  NULL |
|  7 | 17050 |  NULL |
|  8 | 17055 |  NULL |
|  9 | 17055 |  NULL |
| 10 | 17050 | 17050 |
```

```
| 11 | 17055 | 17055 |
| 12 | 17055 | 17055 |
| 13 | 17050 | 17050 |
| 14 | 17050 | 17050 |
| 15 | 17055 | 17055 |
| 16 | 17050 | 17050 |
| 17 | 17055 | 17055 |
| 18 | 17055 | 17055 |
| 19 | 44102 | 44102 |
| 20 | 44102 | 44102 |
| 21 | 44102 | 44102 |
| 22 | 17050 | 17050 |
| 23 | 44102 | 44102 |
+----+-------+-------+
23 rows in set (0.00 sec)
```

Now run the **sales_order_fact_23.sql** script in Listing 23.4.

```
mysql> \. c:\mysql\scripts\sales_order_fact_23.sql
```

You'll see this response on your console.

```
Database changed
Query OK, 0 rows affected (0.04 sec)

Query OK, 0 rows affected (0.00 sec)

Query OK, 62 rows affected (0.40 sec)
Records: 62  Duplicates: 0  Warnings: 0

Query OK, 62 rows affected (0.09 sec)
Rows matched: 62  Changed: 62  Warnings: 0

Query OK, 26 rows affected (0.05 sec)
Rows matched: 26  Changed: 26  Warnings: 0

Query OK, 23 rows affected (0.33 sec)
Records: 23  Duplicates: 0  Warnings: 0

Query OK, 19 rows affected (0.42 sec)
Records: 19  Duplicates: 0  Warnings: 0
```

You can confirm that the splitting of the zip code has been successful by querying the **customer_zip_code_dim**, **shipping_code_dim**, and **sales_order_fact** tables:

```
mysql> select customer_zip_code_sk sk, customer_zip_code zip,
       customer_city city, customer_state state
    -> from customer_zip_code_dim;
```

The query result is as follows.

```
+----+-------+----------------+-------+
| sk | zip   | city           | state |
+----+-------+----------------+-------+
|  1 | 17050 | PITTSBURGH     | PA    |
|  2 | 17051 | MC VEYTOWN     | PA    |
|  3 | 17052 | MAPLETON DEPOT | PA    |
|  4 | 17053 | MARYSVILLE     | PA    |
|  5 | 17054 | MATTAWANA      | PA    |
|  6 | 17055 | MECHANICSBURG  | PA    |
|  7 | 44102 | CLEVELAND      | OH    |
+----+-------+----------------+-------+
7 rows in set (0.00 sec)
```

The shipping zip codes should be the same as the customer zip codes. Prove it using this query.

```
mysql> select shipping_zip_code_sk sk, shipping_zip_code zip,
       shipping_city city, shipping_state sta
    -> from shipping_zip_code_dim;
```

The query result is should be the same as the following.

```
+----+-------+----------------+-------+
| sk | zip   | city           | state |
+----+-------+----------------+-------+
|  1 | 17050 | PITTSBURGH     | PA    |
|  2 | 17051 | MC VEYTOWN     | PA    |
|  3 | 17052 | MAPLETON DEPOT | PA    |
|  4 | 17053 | MARYSVILLE     | PA    |
|  5 | 17054 | MATTAWANA      | PA    |
|  6 | 17055 | MECHANICSBURG  | PA    |
|  7 | 44102 | CLEVELAND      | OH    |
+----+-------+----------------+-------+
7 rows in set (0.00 sec)
```

Now, query the sales orders:

```
mysql> select order_date_sk odsk, customer_sk csk,
    -> customer_zip_code_sk czsk, shipping_zip_code_sk szsk
    -> from sales_order_fact order by order_date_sk;
```

You should get the following result.

```
+------+------+------+------+
| odsk | csk  | czsk | szsk |
+------+------+------+------+
|    1 |    3 |    6 | NULL |
|   46 |    4 |    1 | NULL |
|   81 |    5 |    1 | NULL |
|  152 |    6 |    6 | NULL |
|  185 |    7 |    1 | NULL |
|  255 |    1 |    1 | NULL |
|  311 |    2 |    6 | NULL |
|  347 |    3 |    6 | NULL |
|  380 |    4 |    1 | NULL |
|  416 |    5 |    1 | NULL |
|  456 |    6 |    6 | NULL |
|  458 |    7 |    1 | NULL |
|  502 |    1 |    1 | NULL |
|  548 |    2 |    6 | NULL |
|  554 |    3 |    6 | NULL |
|  584 |    4 |    1 | NULL |
|  681 |    5 |    1 | NULL |
|  722 |    6 |    6 | NULL |
|  727 |    6 |    6 | NULL |
|  730 |    7 |    1 | NULL |
|  731 |    3 |    6 | NULL |
|  731 |    4 |    1 | NULL |
|  731 |    5 |    1 | NULL |
|  731 |    8 |    6 | NULL |
|  731 |    7 |    1 | NULL |
|  731 |    9 |    6 | NULL |
|  731 |    2 |    6 | NULL |
|  731 |    1 |    1 | NULL |
|  731 |    9 |    6 | NULL |
|  731 |    1 |    1 | NULL |
|  731 |    2 |    6 | NULL |
|  731 |    3 |    6 | NULL |
|  731 |    4 |    1 | NULL |
|  731 |    5 |    1 | NULL |
|  731 |    8 |    6 | NULL |
|  731 |    7 |    1 | NULL |
|  732 |   18 |    6 |    6 |
|  732 |   17 |    6 |    6 |
|  732 |   16 |    1 |    1 |
|  732 |   15 |    6 |    6 |
```

```
| 732 | 14 | 1 | 1 |
| 732 | 13 | 1 | 1 |
| 732 | 12 | 6 | 6 |
| 732 | 11 | 6 | 6 |
| 732 | 10 | 1 | 1 |
| 734 | 12 | 6 | 6 |
| 734 | 11 | 6 | 6 |
| 734 | 10 | 1 | 1 |
| 735 | 10 | 1 | 1 |
| 735 | 11 | 6 | 6 |
| 741 | 10 | 1 | 1 |
| 741 | 11 | 6 | 6 |
| 746 | 23 | 7 | 7 |
| 746 | 22 | 1 | 1 |
| 746 | 21 | 7 | 7 |
| 746 | 20 | 7 | 7 |
| 746 | 13 | 1 | 1 |
| 746 | 12 | 6 | 6 |
| 746 | 11 | 6 | 6 |
| 746 | 10 | 1 | 1 |
| 756 | 21 | 7 | 7 |
| 756 | 21 | 7 | 7 |
+------+------+------+------+
62 rows in set (0.00 sec)
```

Note
The early sales orders do not have shipping zip codes (NULL) because the customers didn't have shipping zip codes at the time they placed the sales orders. You added the shipping zip codes in Chapter 10, "Adding Columns."

Revising the production_fact Table

Similar to what you have done to the customer and shipping zip codes, you need to do the following five steps for the factory zip code:

1. Create a **factory_zip_code_dim** view based on the **zip_code_dim** table.
2. Add the **factory_zip_code_sk** column to the **production_fact** table
3. Load the **factory_zip_code_sk** values from the existing factory zip codes.

4. Define **factory_code** as the primary key of the **factory_stg** table and populate the **factory_stg** with the factories from the **factory_dim** table. You need the complete data (including the zip code, city, and state) of all factories in the staging for the production regular population. The primary key is required to maintain the factory data in the factory_stg table.
5. Remove the factory zip code, and their cities and states from the **factory_dim** table

The script in Listing 23.5 implements the above five steps.

Listing 23.5: production_fact with zip_code_dim intial loading

```
/******************************************************************/
/*                                                                */
/* production_fact_23.sql                                         */
/*                                                                */
/******************************************************************/

USE dw;

CREATE VIEW factory_zip_code_dim
( factory_zip_code_sk
, factory_zip_code
, factory_city
, factory_state
, effective_date
, expiry_date )
AS SELECT
  zip_code_sk
, zip_code
, city
, state
, effective_date
, expiry_date
FROM zip_code_dim
;

ALTER TABLE production_fact
  ADD factory_zip_code_sk INT AFTER factory_sk
;

UPDATE
  production_fact a
```

```
, factory_dim b
, factory_zip_code_dim c
SET
  a.factory_zip_code_sk = c.factory_zip_code_sk
WHERE
    a.factory_sk = b.factory_sk
AND b.factory_zip_code = c.factory_zip_code
;

TRUNCATE factory_stg;

ALTER TABLE factory_stg
ADD PRIMARY KEY (factory_code)
;

INSERT INTO factory_stg
SELECT
  factory_code
, factory_name
, factory_street_address
, factory_zip_code
, factory_city
, factory_state
FROM factory_dim
;

ALTER TABLE factory_dim
  DROP factory_zip_code
, DROP factory_city
, DROP factory_state
;

/* end of script                                              */
```

Testing the Factory Zip Codes

Before you run the product_fact_23.sql script in Listing 23.5 to modify the data warehouse structure, I'd like you to query the **factory_dim** table using this statement.

```
mysql> select factory_sk, factory_zip_code from factory_dim;
```

Here is the query result.

```
+------------+---------------------+
| factory_sk | customer_zip_code_sk |
+------------+---------------------+
|          1 |               17050 |
|          2 |               17055 |
|          3 |               17050 |
|          4 |               17055 |
+------------+---------------------+
```

Now run the **production_fact_23.sql** script in Listing 23.5.

```
mysql> \. c:\mysql\scripts\production_fact_23.sql
```

You will see something similar to this on your console.

```
Database changed
Query OK, 0 rows affected (0.00 sec)

Query OK, 8 rows affected (0.46 sec)
Records: 8  Duplicates: 0  Warnings: 0

Query OK, 8 rows affected (0.09 sec)
Rows matched: 8  Changed: 8  Warnings: 0

Query OK, 2 rows affected (0.13 sec)

Query OK, 0 rows affected (0.32 sec)
Records: 0  Duplicates: 0  Warnings: 0

Query OK, 4 rows affected (0.06 sec)
Records: 4  Duplicates: 0  Warnings: 0

Query OK, 4 rows affected (0.35 sec)
Records: 4  Duplicates: 0  Warnings: 0
```

If you query the **factory_zip_code_dim** table, it will return the seven zip codes in the **factory_zip_code_dim** table.

```
mysql> select factory_zip_code_sk sk, factory_zip_code zip,
       factory_city city, factory_state state
    -> from factory_zip_code_dim;
+----+-------+----------------+-------+
| sk | zip   | city           | state |
+----+-------+----------------+-------+
|  1 | 17050 | PITTSBURGH     | PA    |
|  2 | 17051 | MC VEYTOWN     | PA    |
```

```
|  3 | 17052 | MAPLETON DEPOT | PA    |
|  4 | 17053 | MARYSVILLE     | PA    |
|  5 | 17054 | MATTAWANA      | PA    |
|  6 | 17055 | MECHANICSBURG  | PA    |
|  7 | 44102 | CLEVELAND      | OH    |
+----+-------+----------------+-------+
7 rows in set (0.00 sec)
```

To confirm that the **factory_zip_code_sk** column in the **prodction_fact** table has been populated correctly, send this statement to MySQL.

```
mysql> select product_sk psk, production_date_sk pdsk, factory_sk
       fsk,
    -> factory_zip_code_sk fzsk, production_quantity qty
    -> from production_fact;
```

You should see the following result on the console.

```
+------+------+------+------+------+
| psk  | pdsk | fsk  | fzsk | qty  |
+------+------+------+------+------+
|    1 |  711 |    4 |    6 |  100 |
|    2 |  711 |    3 |    1 |  200 |
|    4 |  711 |    2 |    6 |  300 |
|    5 |  711 |    1 |    1 |  400 |
|    1 |  711 |    1 |    1 |  400 |
|    2 |  711 |    2 |    6 |  300 |
|    4 |  711 |    3 |    1 |  200 |
|    5 |  711 |    4 |    6 |  100 |
+------+------+------+------+------+
8 rows in set (0.00 sec)
```

Revising the Regular Population Script

Since you've modified the database structure, you will also need to revise the regular population script. There are changes in three areas:

- You need to remove all zip code related columns in the customer dimension population, as the customer addresses and shipping zip codes are no longer in the customer dimension
- You need to use the surrogate keys from the customer zip code and shipping zip code dimension views. (Shown in bold in the script in Listing 23.6)

- You need to move the **pa_customer_dim** population after the **sales_order_fact** population because to get the customer zip code you need to go to the **customer_zip_code_sk** in sales order fact table.

The regular population script in Listing 23.6 implements these three changes.

Listing 23.6: Revised daily population

```
/*****************************************************************/
/*                                                               */
/* dw_regular_23.sql                                             */
/*                                                               */
/*****************************************************************/

USE dw;

/* CUSTOMER_DIM POPULATION                                       */

TRUNCATE customer_stg;

LOAD DATA INFILE 'customer.csv'
INTO TABLE customer_stg
FIELDS TERMINATED BY ','
OPTIONALLY ENCLOSED BY '"'
LINES TERMINATED BY '\r\n'
IGNORE 1 LINES
( customer_number
, customer_name
, customer_street_address
, customer_zip_code
, customer_city
, customer_state
, shipping_address
, shipping_zip_code
, shipping_city
, shipping_state )
;

/* SCD 2 ON ADDRESSES                                            */

UPDATE
  customer_dim a
, customer_stg b
SET
  a.expiry_date = SUBDATE(CURRENT_DATE, 1)
```

```
WHERE
  a.customer_number = b.customer_number
AND (   a.customer_street_address <> b.customer_street_address
     OR a.shipping_address <> b.shipping_address
     OR a.shipping_address IS NULL )
AND expiry_date = '9999-12-31'
;

INSERT INTO customer_dim
SELECT
  NULL
, b.customer_number
, b.customer_name
, b.customer_street_address
, b.shipping_address
, CURRENT_DATE
, '9999-12-31'
FROM
  customer_dim a
, customer_stg b
WHERE
    a.customer_number = b.customer_number
AND (   a.customer_street_address <> b.customer_street_address
     OR a.shipping_address <> b.shipping_address
     OR a.shipping_address IS NULL )
AND EXISTS (
SELECT *
FROM customer_dim x
WHERE b.customer_number = x.customer_number
AND a.expiry_date = SUBDATE(CURRENT_DATE, 1))
AND NOT EXISTS (
SELECT *
FROM customer_dim y
WHERE     b.customer_number = y.customer_number
      AND y.expiry_date = '9999-12-31')
;

/* END OF SCD 2                                                   */

/* SCD 1 ON NAME                                                  */

UPDATE customer_dim a, customer_stg b
SET a.customer_name = b.customer_name
WHERE     a.customer_number = b.customer_number
      AND a.expiry_date = '9999-12-31'
      AND a.customer_name <> b.customer_name
```

```
;

/* ADD NEW CUSTOMER                                                    */

INSERT INTO customer_dim
SELECT
  NULL
, customer_number
, customer_name
, customer_street_address
, shipping_address
, CURRENT_DATE
, '9999-12-31'
FROM customer_stg
WHERE customer_number NOT IN(
SELECT a.customer_number
FROM
  customer_dim a
, customer_stg b
WHERE b.customer_number = a.customer_number )
;

/* END OF CUSTOMER_DIM POPULATION                                      */

/* PRODUCT_DIM POPULATION                                              */

TRUNCATE product_stg
;

LOAD DATA INFILE 'product.txt'
INTO TABLE product_stg
FIELDS TERMINATED BY ''
OPTIONALLY ENCLOSED BY ''
LINES TERMINATED BY '\r\n'
IGNORE 1 LINES
( product_code
, product_name
, product_category )
;

/* SCD2 ON PRODUCT NAME AND GROUP                                      */

UPDATE
  product_dim a
, product_stg b
```

```
SET
  expiry_date = SUBDATE(CURRENT_DATE, 1)
WHERE
    a.product_code = b.product_code
AND (   a.product_name <> b.product_name
     OR a.product_category <> b.product_category )
     AND expiry_date = '9999-12-31'
;

INSERT INTO product_dim
SELECT
  NULL
, b.product_code
, b.product_name
, b.product_category
, CURRENT_DATE
, '9999-12-31'
FROM
  product_dim a
, product_stg b
WHERE
    a.product_code = b.product_code
AND (   a.product_name <> b.product_name
     OR a.product_category <> b.product_category )
AND EXISTS (
SELECT *
FROM product_dim x
WHERE     b.product_code = x.product_code
      AND a.expiry_date = SUBDATE(CURRENT_DATE, 1))
AND NOT EXISTS (
SELECT *
FROM product_dim y
WHERE    b.product_code = y.product_code
     AND y.expiry_date = '9999-12-31')
;

/* END OF SCD 2                                                  */

/* ADD NEW PRODUCT                                               */

INSERT INTO product_dim
SELECT
  NULL
, product_code
, product_name
, product_category
```

```
, CURRENT_DATE
, '9999-12-31'
FROM product_stg
WHERE product_code NOT IN(
SELECT y.product_code
FROM product_dim x, product_stg y
WHERE x.product_code = y.product_code )
;

/* END OF PRODUCT_DIM POPULATION                                    */

/* PRODUCT_COUNT_FACT POPULATION                                    */

TRUNCATE product_count_fact
;

INSERT INTO product_count_fact
(product_sk, product_launch_date_sk)
SELECT
  a.product_sk
, b.date_sk
FROM
  product_dim a
, date_dim b
WHERE
a.effective_date = b.date
GROUP BY product_code
HAVING COUNT(product_code) = 1
;

/* for products that have been updated by SCD2                      */

INSERT INTO product_count_fact (product_sk, product_launch_date_sk)
SELECT
  a.product_sk
, b.date_sk

FROM
  product_dim a
, date_dim b

WHERE
a.effective_date = b.date
GROUP BY product_code
HAVING COUNT(product_code) > 1
```

```
;

/* END OF PRODUCT_COUNT_FACT POPULATION                              */

/* INSERT NEW ORDERS                                                  */

INSERT INTO sales_order_fact
SELECT
  b.customer_sk
, h.customer_zip_code_sk
, i.shipping_zip_code_sk
, c.product_sk
, f.sales_order_attribute_sk
, d.order_date_sk
, NULL
, NULL
, NULL
, NULL
, g.entry_date_sk
, a.order_number
, e.request_delivery_date_sk
, order_amount
, quantity
, NULL
, NULL
, NULL
, NULL
FROM
  source.sales_order a
, customer_dim b
, product_dim c
, order_date_dim d
, request_delivery_date_dim e
, sales_order_attribute_dim f
, entry_date_dim g
, customer_zip_code_dim h
, shipping_zip_code_dim i
, customer_stg j
WHERE
      order_status = 'N'
AND a.entry_date = CURRENT_DATE
AND a.customer_number = b.customer_number
AND a.status_date >= b.effective_date
AND a.status_date <= b.expiry_date
AND a.customer_number = j.customer_number
AND j.customer_zip_code = h.customer_zip_code
```

```
AND a.status_date >= h.effective_date
AND a.status_date <= h.expiry_date
AND j.shipping_zip_code = i.shipping_zip_code
AND a.status_date >= i.effective_date
AND a.status_date <= i.expiry_date
AND a.product_code = c.product_code
AND a.status_date >= c.effective_date
AND a.status_date <= c.expiry_date
AND a.status_date = d.order_date
AND a.entry_date = g.entry_date
AND a.request_delivery_date = e.request_delivery_date
AND a.verification_ind = f.verification_ind
AND a.credit_check_flag = f.credit_check_flag
AND a.new_customer_ind = f.new_customer_ind
AND a.web_order_flag = f.web_order_flag
AND a.status_date >= f.effective_date
AND a.status_date <= f.expiry_date
;

/* RE-BUILD PA CUSTOMER DIMENSION                                  */

TRUNCATE pa_customer_dim;

INSERT INTO pa_customer_dim
SELECT DISTINCT a.*
FROM
  customer_dim a
, sales_order_fact b
, customer_zip_code_dim c
WHERE
    c.customer_state = 'PA'
AND b.customer_zip_code_sk = c.customer_zip_code_sk
AND a.customer_sk = b.customer_sk
;

UPDATE
  sales_order_fact a
, source.sales_order b
, allocate_date_dim c
SET
  a.allocate_date_sk = c.allocate_date_sk
, a.allocate_quantity = b.quantity
WHERE
    order_status = 'A'
AND b.entry_date = CURRENT_DATE
```

```
AND b.order_number = a.order_number
AND c.allocate_date = b.status_date
;

UPDATE
  sales_order_fact a
, source.sales_order b
, packing_date_dim d
SET
  a.packing_date_sk = d.packing_date_sk
, a.packing_quantity = b.quantity
WHERE
    order_status = 'P'
AND b.entry_date = CURRENT_DATE
AND b.order_number = a.order_number
AND d.packing_date = b.status_date
;

UPDATE sales_order_fact a, source.sales_order b, ship_date_dim e
SET
  a.ship_date_sk = e.ship_date_sk
, a.ship_quantity = b.quantity
WHERE
    order_status = 'S'
AND b.entry_date = CURRENT_DATE
AND b.order_number = a.order_number
AND e.ship_date = b.status_date
;

UPDATE
  sales_order_fact a
, source.sales_order b
, receive_date_dim f
SET
  a.receive_date_sk = f.receive_date_sk
, a.receive_quantity = b.quantity
WHERE
    order_status = 'R'
AND b.entry_date = CURRENT_DATE
AND b.order_number = a.order_number
AND f.receive_date = b.status_date
;

/* end of script                                                   */
```

Testing the Revised Regular Population Script

Before you can run the revised regular population script, there are a few things you need to prepare. First, you need to prepare the following **customer.csv** file, which contains two changes from the **customer.csv** in Chapter 10:

- The street and shipping addresses of customer number 4 changes from zip code 17050 to 17055
- A new customer number 15 is added.

Here is the content of the revised **customer.csv** file.

```
CUSTOMER NO,CUSTOMER NAME,STREET ADDRESS,ZIP
      CODE,CITY,STATE,SHIPPING ADDRESS,ZIP CODE,CITY,STATE
1,Really Large Customers,7500 Louise Dr.,17050,Mechanicsburg,PA,7500
      Louise Dr.,17050,Mechanicsburg,PA
2,Small Stores,2500 Woodland St.,17055,Pittsburgh,PA,2500 Woodland
      St.,17055,Pittsburgh,PA
3,Medium Retailers,1111 Ritter Rd.,17055,Pittsburgh,PA,1111 Ritter
      Rd.,17055,Pittsburgh,PA
4,Good Companies,9999 Louise Dr.,17055,Pittsburgh,PA,9999 Louise
      Dr.,17055,Pittsburgh,PA
5,Wonderful Shops,3333 Rossmoyne Rd.,17050,Mechanicsburg,PA,3333
      Rossmoyne Rd.,17050,Mechanicsburg,PA
6,Extremely Loyal Clients,7777 Ritter Rd.,17055,Pittsburgh,PA,7777
      Ritter Rd.,17055,Pittsburgh,PA
7,Distinguished Agencies,9999 Scott St.,17050,Mechanicsburg,PA,9999
      Scott St.,17050,Mechanicsburg,PA
8,Subsidiaries,10000 Wetline Blvd.,17055,Pittsburgh,PA,10000 Wetline
      Blvd.,17055,Pittsburgh,PA
9,E-Distributors,2323 Louise Dr.,17055,Pittsburgh,PA,2323 Louise
      Dr.,17055,Pittsburgh,PA
10,Bigger Customers,7777 Ridge Rd.,44102,Cleveland,OH,7777 Ridge
      Rd.,44102,Cleveland,OH
11,Smaller Stores,8888 Jennings Fwy.,44102,Cleveland,OH,8888
      Jennings Fwy.,44102,Cleveland,OH
12,Small-Medium Retailers,9999 Memphis Ave.,44102,Cleveland,OH,9999
      Memphis Ave.,44102,Cleveland,OH
13,PA Customer,1111 Louise Dr.,17050,Mechanicsburg,PA,1111 Louise
      Dr.,17050,Mechanicsburg,PA
14,OH Customer,6666 Ridge Rd.,44102,Cleveland,OH,6666 Ridge
      Rd.,44102,Cleveland,OH
```

```
15,Super Stores,1000 Woodland St.,17055,Pittsburgh,PA,1000 Woodland
      St.,17055,Pittsburgh,PA
```

Now query the latest customer and shipping zip codes before you load the new customer data. Later you can compare this query output with the one after the changes.

```
mysql> SELECT order_date_sk odsk, customer_number cn,
    -> customer_zip_code czc, shipping_zip_code szc
    -> FROM customer_zip_code_dim a, shipping_zip_code_dim b,
    -> sales_order_fact c, customer_dim d
    -> WHERE a.customer_zip_code_sk = c.customer_zip_code_sk
    -> AND b.shipping_zip_code_sk = c.shipping_zip_code_sk
    -> AND d.customer_sk = c.customer_sk
    -> GROUP BY customer_number
    -> HAVING MAX(order_date_sk);
```

```
+------+------+-------+-------+
| odsk | cn   | czc   | szc   |
+------+------+-------+-------+
|  732 |    1 | 17050 | 17050 |
|  732 |    2 | 17055 | 17055 |
|  732 |    3 | 17055 | 17055 |
|  732 |    4 | 17050 | 17050 |
|  732 |    5 | 17050 | 17050 |
|  732 |    6 | 17055 | 17055 |
|  732 |    7 | 17050 | 17050 |
|  732 |    8 | 17055 | 17055 |
|  732 |    9 | 17055 | 17055 |
|  746 |   11 | 44102 | 44102 |
|  746 |   12 | 44102 | 44102 |
|  746 |   13 | 17050 | 17050 |
|  746 |   14 | 44102 | 44102 |
+------+------+-------+-------+
13 rows in set (0.42 sec)
```

Next, use the script in Listing 23.7 to add two sales orders.

- customer number 4 whose address has recently changed
- new customer number 15

Listing 23.7: Adding two sales orders

```
/**********************************************************************/
/*                                                                    */
/* sales_order_23.sql                                                 */
/*                                                                    */
```

```
/******************************************************************/

USE source;

INSERT INTO sales_order VALUES

  (64, 4, 3, 'Y', 'Y', 'Y', 'N', '2007-03-27', 'N', '2007-03-31',
      '2007-03-27', 10000, 100)
, (65, 15, 4, 'Y', 'N', 'Y', 'N', '2007-03-27', 'N', '2007-03-31',
      '2007-03-27', 20000, 200)
;

/* end of script                                                  */
```

Run the script in Listing 23.7 using this command.

```
mysql> \. c:\mysql\scripts\sales_order_23.sql
```

You will see the following response on the console.

```
Database changed
Query OK, 2 rows affected (0.06 sec)
Records: 2  Duplicates: 0  Warnings: 0
```

You're now ready to test the revised regular population. You must set your MySQL date to March 27, 2007 (the entry date of the two sales orders above) and run the dw_regular_23 script:

```
mysql> \. c:\mysql\scripts\dw_regular_23.sql
```

You should see something similar to the following on your console.

```
Database changed
Query OK, 9 rows affected (0.10 sec)

Query OK, 15 rows affected (0.05 sec)
Records: 15  Deleted: 0  Skipped: 0  Warnings: 0

Query OK, 1 row affected (0.06 sec)
Rows matched: 1  Changed: 1  Warnings: 0

Query OK, 1 row affected (0.06 sec)
Records: 1  Duplicates: 0  Warnings: 0

Query OK, 1 row affected (0.05 sec)
Rows matched: 1  Changed: 1  Warnings: 0
```

```
Query OK, 1 row affected (0.06 sec)
Records: 1  Duplicates: 0  Warnings: 0

Query OK, 5 rows affected (0.07 sec)

Query OK, 5 rows affected (0.06 sec)
Records: 5  Deleted: 0  Skipped: 0  Warnings: 0

Query OK, 0 rows affected (0.00 sec)
Rows matched: 0  Changed: 0  Warnings: 0

Query OK, 0 rows affected (0.00 sec)
Records: 0  Duplicates: 0  Warnings: 0

Query OK, 0 rows affected (0.00 sec)
Records: 0  Duplicates: 0  Warnings: 0

Query OK, 0 rows affected (0.00 sec)

Query OK, 3 rows affected (0.02 sec)
Records: 3  Duplicates: 0  Warnings: 0

Query OK, 2 rows affected (0.01 sec)
Records: 2  Duplicates: 0  Warnings: 0

Query OK, 2 rows affected (0.16 sec)
Records: 2  Duplicates: 0  Warnings: 0

Query OK, 19 rows affected (0.05 sec)

Query OK, 21 rows affected (0.08 sec)
Records: 21  Duplicates: 0  Warnings: 0

Query OK, 0 rows affected (0.00 sec)
Rows matched: 0  Changed: 0  Warnings: 0

Query OK, 0 rows affected (0.00 sec)
Rows matched: 0  Changed: 0  Warnings: 0

Query OK, 0 rows affected (0.01 sec)
Rows matched: 0  Changed: 0  Warnings: 0

Query OK, 0 rows affected (0.01 sec)
Rows matched: 0  Changed: 0  Warnings: 0
```

Confirm that the two customer changes, customer number 4 and 15, have been loaded correctly by querying the **customer_dim** table.

```
mysql> select * from customer_dim where customer_number in(4,15) \G
```

Here is the query result.

```
************************** 1. row **************************
            customer_sk: 4
        customer_number: 4
          customer_name: Good Companies
customer_street_address: 9500 Scott St.
       shipping_address: NULL
         effective_date: 2005-03-01
            expiry_date: 2007-03-01
************************** 2. row **************************
            customer_sk: 13
        customer_number: 4
          customer_name: Good Companies
customer_street_address: 9500 Scott St.
       shipping_address: 9500 Scott St.
         effective_date: 2007-03-02
            expiry_date: 2007-03-26
************************** 3. row **************************
            customer_sk: 24
        customer_number: 4
          customer_name: Good Companies
customer_street_address: 9999 Louise Dr.
       shipping_address: 9999 Louise Dr.
         effective_date: 2007-03-27
            expiry_date: 9999-12-31
************************** 4. row **************************
            customer_sk: 25
        customer_number: 15
          customer_name: Super Stores
customer_street_address: 1000 Woodland St.
       shipping_address: 1000 Woodland St.
         effective_date: 2007-03-27
            expiry_date: 9999-12-31
4 rows in set (0.00 sec)
```

To confirm the zip codes have been correctly loaded, query the **sales_order_fact** table on the two new sales orders using this SQL statement.

```
mysql> select * from sales_order_fact where order_number IN(64,65)
       \G
```

You should get the following result.

```
*************************** 1. row ***************************
            customer_sk: 24
    customer_zip_code_sk: 6
    shipping_zip_code_sk: 6
             product_sk: 4
sales_order_attribute_sk: 3
          order_date_sk: 757
       allocate_date_sk: NULL
        packing_date_sk: NULL
           ship_date_sk: NULL
        receive_date_sk: NULL
          entry_date_sk: 757
           order_number: 64
request_delivery_date_sk: 761
           order_amount: 10000.00
         order_quantity: 100
      allocate_quantity: NULL
       packing_quantity: NULL
          ship_quantity: NULL
       receive_quantity: NULL
*************************** 2. row ***************************
            customer_sk: 25
    customer_zip_code_sk: 6
    shipping_zip_code_sk: 6
             product_sk: 5
sales_order_attribute_sk: 5
          order_date_sk: 757
       allocate_date_sk: NULL
        packing_date_sk: NULL
           ship_date_sk: NULL
        receive_date_sk: NULL
          entry_date_sk: 757
           order_number: 65
request_delivery_date_sk: 761
           order_amount: 20000.00
         order_quantity: 200
      allocate_quantity: NULL
       packing_quantity: NULL
          ship_quantity: NULL
       receive_quantity: NULL
2 rows in set (0.00 sec)
```

Note

The output confirms correct population of the **sales_order_fact** table. The **zip_code_sk** 6 is Mechanicsburg, which is the correct zip code of the customer and shipping addresses.

Revising the Production Regular Population Script

Similar to what you've done to the regular data warehouse population script, you need to remove all zip code related columns from the factory dimension population and apply the factory zip code surrogate key in the production fact population.

Note that you are not going to truncate the **factory_stg** table as you only get incremental factory sources in the **factory.csv** file. You must maintain the complete existing factory data (including the zip code, city, state) in the staging. Therefore, use the REPLACE option in the LOAD DATA INFILE command (shown in bold in the script in Listing 23.9)

Listing 23.9: The revised production regular population script

```
/******************************************************************/
/*                                                                */
/* production_regular_23.sql                                      */
/*                                                                */
/******************************************************************/
USE dw;

LOAD DATA INFILE 'factory.csv'
REPLACE
INTO TABLE factory_stg
FIELDS TERMINATED BY ','
OPTIONALLY ENCLOSED BY '"'
LINES TERMINATED BY '\r\n'
IGNORE 1 LINES
( factory_code
, factory_name
, factory_street_address
, factory_zip_code
, factory_city
, factory_state )
```

```
;

/* SCD1                                                        */

UPDATE factory_dim a, factory_stg b
SET
  a.factory_name = b.factory_name
, a.factory_street_address = b.factory_street_address
WHERE a.factory_code = b.factory_code
;

/* add new factory                                             */

INSERT INTO factory_dim
SELECT
  NULL
, factory_code
, factory_name
, factory_street_address
, CURRENT_DATE
, '9999-12-31'
FROM factory_stg
WHERE factory_code NOT IN (
SELECT y.factory_code
FROM factory_dim x, factory_stg y
WHERE x.factory_code = y.factory_code )
;

INSERT INTO production_fact
SELECT
  b.product_sk
, c.date_sk
, d.factory_sk
, e.factory_zip_code_sk
, production_quantity
FROM
  source.daily_production a
, product_dim b
, date_dim c
, factory_dim d
, factory_zip_code_dim e
, factory_stg f
WHERE
    production_date = CURRENT_DATE
AND a.product_code = b.product_code
AND a.production_date >= b.effective_date
```

```
AND a.production_date <= b.expiry_date
AND a.factory_code = f.factory_code
AND f.factory_zip_code = e.factory_zip_code
AND a.production_date >= e.effective_date
AND a.production_date <= e.expiry_date
AND a.production_date = c.date
AND a.factory_code = d.factory_code
;

/* end of script                                                  */
```

Testing the Revised Production Regular Population Script

Before you can run the script in Listing 23.9, you need to prepare the factory source and the daily production data source. The following **factory.csv** file contains the new factory that needs to be added to the factory dimension when you run the **production_regular_23.sql** script.

```
FACTORY_CODE,NAME,STREET_ADDRESS,ZIP_CODE,CITY,STATE
5,Fifth Factory,90909 McNicholds Blvd.,17055,Pittsburgh,PA
```

Then, add three daily production records into the **daily_production** table using the script in Listing 23.10.

Listing 23.10: Adding three daily production records

```
/******************************************************************/
/*                                                                */
/* daily_production_23.sql                                        */
/*                                                                */
/******************************************************************/

USE source;

INSERT INTO daily_production VALUES
  ( 1, CURRENT_DATE, 3, 400 )
, ( 3, CURRENT_DATE, 4, 200 )
, ( 5, CURRENT_DATE, 5, 100 )
;

/* end of script                                                  */
```

Make sure that your MySQL date is March 27, 2007 and run the script in Listing 23.10.

```
mysql> \. c:\mysql\scripts\daily_production_23.sql
```

Next, run the production fact regular population script in Listing 23.9:

```
mysql> \. c:\mysql\scripts\production_regular_23.sql
```

You will see the following response on the console.

```
Database changed
Query OK, 1 row affected (0.06 sec)
Records: 1  Deleted: 0  Skipped: 0  Warnings: 0

Query OK, 0 rows affected (0.00 sec)
Rows matched: 4  Changed: 0  Warnings: 0

Query OK, 1 row affected (0.07 sec)
Records: 1  Duplicates: 0  Warnings: 0

Query OK, 3 rows affected (0.08 sec)
Records: 3  Duplicates: 0  Warnings: 0
```

To confirm correct population, query the **factory_dim** and the **sales_order_fact** tables.

```
mysql> select * from factory_dim \G
```

Here is the result.

```
*************************** 1. row ***************************
             factory_sk: 1
           factory_code: 1
           factory_name: First Factory
factory_street_address: 11111 Lichtman St.
         effective_date: 2007-03-18
            expiry_date: 9999-12-31
*************************** 2. row ***************************
             factory_sk: 2
           factory_code: 2
           factory_name: Second Factory
factory_street_address: 24242 Bunty La.
         effective_date: 2007-03-18
            expiry_date: 9999-12-31
*************************** 3. row ***************************
             factory_sk: 3
```

```
          factory_code: 3
          factory_name: Third Factory
factory_street_address: 37373 Burbank Dr.
        effective_date: 2007-03-18
           expiry_date: 9999-12-31
*************************** 4. row ***************************
            factory_sk: 4
          factory_code: 4
          factory_name: Fourth Factory
factory_street_address: 44444 Jenzen Blvd.
        effective_date: 2007-03-18
           expiry_date: 9999-12-31
*************************** 5. row ***************************
            factory_sk: 5
          factory_code: 5
          factory_name: Fifth Factory
factory_street_address: 90909 McNicholds Blvd.
        effective_date: 2007-03-27
           expiry_date: 9999-12-31
5 rows in set (0.00 sec)
```

Note

The fifth factory was correctly added.

Query the **production_fact** table to confirm that the three new daily productions are correctly loaded:

```
mysql> select product_sk psk, production_date_sk pdsk,
    -> factory_sk fsk, factory_zip_code_sk fzsk, production_quantity
       qty
    -> from production_fact;
```

You should see the following result on your console.

```
+------+------+------+------+------+
| psk  | pdsk | fsk  | fzsk | qty  |
+------+------+------+------+------+
|    1 |  748 |    4 |    6 |  100 |
|    2 |  748 |    3 |    1 |  200 |
|    4 |  748 |    2 |    6 |  300 |
|    5 |  748 |    1 |    1 |  400 |
|    1 |  748 |    1 |    1 |  400 |
|    2 |  748 |    2 |    6 |  300 |
|    4 |  748 |    3 |    1 |  200 |
|    5 |  748 |    4 |    6 |  100 |
```

```
|    6 |  757 |    3 |    1 |  400 |
|    4 |  757 |    4 |    6 |  200 |
|    7 |  757 |    5 |    6 |  100 |
+------+------+------+------+------+
11 rows in set (0.00 sec)
```

Summary

In this chapter you learned how to consolidate common data in existing dimensions. In particular, you consolidated zip codes from the customer and factory dimensions into a new zip code dimension. In the next chapter you will learn how to accumulate measures.

Chapter 24
Accumulated Measures

This chapter teaches you how to accumulate measures in a fact table, something you have to do if, say, your data warehouse users want to track month after month measures. In this chapter you also learn that accumulated measures are semi-additive and that its initial population is much more complex than any of those you've done in the previous chapters.

Note
The opposite of semi-additive measures are fully-additive measures, which were covered in Chapter 3, "Measure Additivity."

In this chapter I show you how to implement an accumulated month-end balance and how to change our data warehouse schema and initial and regular population scripts.

The Revised Schema

The first you need to do is set up a new fact table that stores the accumulated month-end balance of sales order amounts. Call this table **month_end_balance_fact**. Figure 24.1 shows a sample of an accumulated balance. The sample starts the accumulation in January 2006. The January order for Floppy Drive is 1000, so its accumulated month-end balance is 1000. There is sales order for Floppy Drive in February 2006, so its February accumulated month-end balance does not change. Its March order is 500, so its accumulated balance is 1500, and so on. The balances are reset at the beginning of each year.

The **month_end_balance_fact** table creates an additional star in your schema. The new star consists of this new fact table and two existing dimension tables from another star, **product_dim** and **month_dim**. Figure 24.1 shows the new schema. Note that only related tables are shown.

Month	Product Name	Order in the Month	Month-End Balance (Accumulated Sales Order Amount)
January 2006	Floppy Drive	1000	1000
January 2006	Hard Drive	9000	9000
February 2006	Floppy Drive	0	1000
February 2006	Hard Drive	12000	21000
March 2006	Floppy Drive	500	1500
March 2006	Hard Drive	15000	36000
…	…	…	…
December 2006	…	…	…
January 2007	Hard Drive	9000	9000
January 2007	Floppy Drive	0	0
February 2007	Hard Drive	15000	24000
February 2007	Floppy Drive	0	0
March 2007	…	…	…
…	…	…	…
December 2007	…	…	…

Table 24.1: Month end balance prepared data

The script in Listing 24.1 can be used to create the **month_end_balance_fact** table.

Figure 24.1: The month_end_balance_fact, product_dim, and month_dim tables create a new star

Listing 24.1: Creating the month_end_balance_fact table

```
/**************************************************************/
/*                                                            */
/* month_end_balance_fact.sql                                 */
/*                                                            */
/**************************************************************/

USE dw;

CREATE TABLE month_end_balance_fact
(month_sk INT
, product_sk INT
, month_end_amount_balance DEC(10,2)
```

```
, month_end_quantity_balance INT )
;

/* end of script                                                        */
```

Run the script in Listing 24.1 to create the new fact table.

```
mysql> \. c:\mysql\scripts\month_end_balance_fact.sql
```

Initial Population

You populate the **month_end_balance_fact** table with data in the **month_end_sales_order_fact** table. Listing 24.2 is the script to initially populate the **month_end_balance_fact** table.

The script loads the month end sales orders month by month. As you must reset the balance at the beginning of each year, for January the script needs only one Insert that adds the January balance to the **month_end_balance_fact** table. Starting from February it needs three Insert statements. The first adds the month sales amount of a product to its previous month's if there is a sales order for that product in the previous month. The second Insert statement handles the case when there is no sales record for the product in the previous month. The third Insert statement inserts a copy of the previous month product sales if there's no sales record for the product in the current month.

The last month of the month end sales data you have in the **month_end_sales_order_fact** table is March 2007.

Listing 24.2: Month end balance initial population

```
/**********************************************************************/
/*                                                                    */
/* month_end_balance_initial.sql                                      */
/*                                                                    */
/**********************************************************************/

USE dw;

/* January                                                            */

INSERT INTO month_end_balance_fact
SELECT m.*
```

```
FROM
   month_end_sales_order_fact m
, month_dim n
WHERE
    month = 1
AND m.month_order_sk = n.month_sk
;


/* February                                                    */

INSERT INTO month_end_balance_fact
SELECT n.month_order_sk, n.product_sk, (n.month_order_amount +
       m.month_end_amount_balance), (n.month_order_quantity +
       m.month_end_quantity_balance)
FROM
  month_end_balance_fact m
,  month_end_sales_order_fact n
, month_dim o
, month_dim p
WHERE
    o.month = 1
AND p.month = 2
AND m.month_sk = o.month_sk AND n.month_order_sk = p.month_sk
AND o.year = p.year
AND m.product_sk = n.product_sk
;

INSERT INTO month_end_balance_fact
SELECT m.*
FROM
   month_end_sales_order_fact m
, month_dim n
WHERE
    n.month = 2
AND m.month_order_sk = n.month_sk
AND m.product_sk NOT IN (
 SELECT x.product_sk
 FROM month_end_balance_fact x, month_dim y
 WHERE x.month_sk = y.month_sk AND y.month = 1
 AND y.year = n.year )
;

INSERT INTO month_end_balance_fact
```

```
SELECT o.month_sk, m.product_sk, m.month_end_amount_balance,
       m.month_end_quantity_balance
FROM
  month_end_balance_fact m
, month_dim n
, month_dim o
WHERE
    n.month = 1
AND m.month_sk = n.month_sk
AND o.month = 2
AND n.year = o.year
AND m.product_sk NOT IN (
SELECT x.product_sk
FROM  month_end_sales_order_fact x, month_dim y
WHERE x.month_order_sk = y.month_sk AND y.month = 2
AND y.year = n.year)
;

/* March                                                              */

INSERT INTO month_end_balance_fact
SELECT n.month_order_sk, n.product_sk, (n.month_order_amount +
       m.month_end_amount_balance), (n.month_order_quantity +
       m.month_end_quantity_balance)
FROM
  month_end_balance_fact m
,  month_end_sales_order_fact n
, month_dim o
, month_dim p
WHERE
    o.month = 2
AND p.month = 3
AND m.month_sk = o.month_sk AND n.month_order_sk = p.month_sk
AND o.year = p.year
AND m.product_sk = n.product_sk
AND (p.year <= 2007)
;

INSERT INTO month_end_balance_fact
SELECT m.*
FROM
   month_end_sales_order_fact m
, month_dim n
WHERE
    n.month = 3
AND m.month_order_sk = n.month_sk
```

```
AND m.product_sk NOT IN (
 SELECT x.product_sk
 FROM month_end_balance_fact x, month_dim y
 WHERE x.month_sk = y.month_sk AND y.month = 2
 AND y.year = n.year )
AND (n.year <= 2007)
;

INSERT INTO month_end_balance_fact
SELECT o.month_sk, m.product_sk, m.month_end_amount_balance,
       m.month_end_quantity_balance
FROM
  month_end_balance_fact m
, month_dim n
, month_dim o
WHERE
    n.month = 2
AND m.month_sk = n.month_sk
AND o.month = 3
AND n.year = o.year
AND m.product_sk NOT IN (
SELECT x.product_sk
FROM  month_end_sales_order_fact x, month_dim y
WHERE x.month_order_sk = y.month_sk AND y.month = 3
AND y.year = n.year)
AND (o.year <= 2007)
;

/* April                                                      */

INSERT INTO month_end_balance_fact
SELECT n.month_order_sk, n.product_sk, (n.month_order_amount +
       m.month_end_amount_balance), (n.month_order_quantity +
       m.month_end_quantity_balance)
FROM
  month_end_balance_fact m
,  month_end_sales_order_fact n
, month_dim o
, month_dim p
WHERE
    o.month = 3
AND p.month = 4
AND m.month_sk = o.month_sk AND n.month_order_sk = p.month_sk
AND o.year = p.year
AND m.product_sk = n.product_sk
```

```
AND (p.year <= 2007)
;

INSERT INTO month_end_balance_fact
SELECT m.*
FROM
   month_end_sales_order_fact m
, month_dim n
WHERE
    n.month = 4
AND m.month_order_sk = n.month_sk
AND m.product_sk NOT IN (
 SELECT x.product_sk
 FROM month_end_balance_fact x, month_dim y
 WHERE x.month_sk = y.month_sk AND y.month = 3
 AND y.year = n.year )
AND (n.year <= 2007)
;

INSERT INTO month_end_balance_fact
SELECT o.month_sk, m.product_sk, m.month_end_amount_balance,
       m.month_end_quantity_balance
FROM
  month_end_balance_fact m
, month_dim n
, month_dim o
WHERE
    n.month = 3
AND m.month_sk = n.month_sk
AND o.month = 4
AND n.year = o.year
AND m.product_sk NOT IN (
SELECT x.product_sk
FROM  month_end_sales_order_fact x, month_dim y
WHERE x.month_order_sk = y.month_sk AND y.month = 4
AND y.year = n.year)
AND (o.year <= 2007)
;

/* May                                                              */

INSERT INTO month_end_balance_fact
SELECT n.month_order_sk, n.product_sk, (n.month_order_amount +
       m.month_end_amount_balance), (n.month_order_quantity +
       m.month_end_quantity_balance)
FROM
```

```
  month_end_balance_fact m
,  month_end_sales_order_fact n
, month_dim o
, month_dim p
WHERE
    o.month = 4
AND p.month = 5
AND m.month_sk = o.month_sk AND n.month_order_sk = p.month_sk
AND o.year = p.year
AND m.product_sk = n.product_sk
AND (p.year < 2007)
;

INSERT INTO month_end_balance_fact
SELECT m.*
FROM
   month_end_sales_order_fact m
, month_dim n
WHERE
    n.month = 5
AND m.month_order_sk = n.month_sk
AND m.product_sk NOT IN (
 SELECT x.product_sk
 FROM month_end_balance_fact x, month_dim y
 WHERE x.month_sk = y.month_sk AND y.month = 4
 AND y.year = n.year )
AND (n.year < 2007)
;

INSERT INTO month_end_balance_fact
SELECT o.month_sk, m.product_sk, m.month_end_amount_balance,
       m.month_end_quantity_balance
FROM
  month_end_balance_fact m
, month_dim n
, month_dim o
WHERE
    n.month = 4
AND m.month_sk = n.month_sk
AND o.month = 5
AND n.year = o.year
AND m.product_sk NOT IN (
SELECT x.product_sk
FROM  month_end_sales_order_fact x, month_dim y
WHERE x.month_order_sk = y.month_sk AND y.month = 5
```

```
AND y.year = n.year)
AND (o.year < 2007)
;

/* June                                                                  */

INSERT INTO month_end_balance_fact
SELECT n.month_order_sk, n.product_sk, (n.month_order_amount +
      m.month_end_amount_balance), (n.month_order_quantity +
      m.month_end_quantity_balance)
FROM
  month_end_balance_fact m
,  month_end_sales_order_fact n
, month_dim o
, month_dim p
WHERE
    o.month = 5
AND p.month = 6
AND m.month_sk = o.month_sk AND n.month_order_sk = p.month_sk
AND o.year = p.year
AND m.product_sk = n.product_sk
AND (p.year < 2007)
;

INSERT INTO month_end_balance_fact
SELECT m.*
FROM
   month_end_sales_order_fact m
, month_dim n
WHERE
    n.month = 6
AND m.month_order_sk = n.month_sk
AND m.product_sk NOT IN (
 SELECT x.product_sk
 FROM month_end_balance_fact x, month_dim y
 WHERE x.month_sk = y.month_sk AND y.month = 5
 AND y.year = n.year )
AND (n.year < 2007)
;

INSERT INTO month_end_balance_fact
SELECT o.month_sk, m.product_sk, m.month_end_amount_balance,
      m.month_end_quantity_balance
FROM
  month_end_balance_fact m
, month_dim n
```

```
, month_dim o
WHERE
    n.month = 5
AND m.month_sk = n.month_sk
AND o.month = 6
AND n.year = o.year
AND m.product_sk NOT IN (
SELECT x.product_sk
FROM  month_end_sales_order_fact x, month_dim y
WHERE x.month_order_sk = y.month_sk AND y.month = 6
AND y.year = n.year)
AND (o.year < 2007)
;

/* July                                                              */

INSERT INTO month_end_balance_fact
SELECT n.month_order_sk, n.product_sk, (n.month_order_amount +
      m.month_end_amount_balance), (n.month_order_quantity +
      m.month_end_quantity_balance)
FROM
  month_end_balance_fact m
,  month_end_sales_order_fact n
, month_dim o
, month_dim p
WHERE
    o.month = 6
AND p.month = 7
AND m.month_sk = o.month_sk AND n.month_order_sk = p.month_sk
AND o.year = p.year
AND m.product_sk = n.product_sk
AND (p.year < 2007)
;

INSERT INTO month_end_balance_fact
SELECT m.*
FROM
   month_end_sales_order_fact m
, month_dim n
WHERE
    n.month = 7
AND m.month_order_sk = n.month_sk
AND m.product_sk NOT IN (
 SELECT x.product_sk
 FROM month_end_balance_fact x, month_dim y
```

```
 WHERE x.month_sk = y.month_sk AND y.month = 6
 AND y.year = n.year )
AND (n.year < 2007)
;

INSERT INTO month_end_balance_fact
SELECT o.month_sk, m.product_sk, m.month_end_amount_balance,
       m.month_end_quantity_balance
FROM
  month_end_balance_fact m
, month_dim n
, month_dim o
WHERE
    n.month = 6
AND m.month_sk = n.month_sk
AND o.month = 7
AND n.year = o.year
AND m.product_sk NOT IN (
SELECT x.product_sk
FROM  month_end_sales_order_fact x, month_dim y
WHERE x.month_order_sk = y.month_sk AND y.month = 7
AND y.year = n.year)
AND (o.year < 2007)
;

/* August                                                        */

INSERT INTO month_end_balance_fact
SELECT n.month_order_sk, n.product_sk, (n.month_order_amount +
       m.month_end_amount_balance), (n.month_order_quantity +
       m.month_end_quantity_balance)
FROM
  month_end_balance_fact m
,  month_end_sales_order_fact n
, month_dim o
, month_dim p
WHERE
    o.month = 7
AND p.month = 8
AND m.month_sk = o.month_sk AND n.month_order_sk = p.month_sk
AND o.year = p.year
AND m.product_sk = n.product_sk
AND (p.year < 2007)
;

INSERT INTO month_end_balance_fact
```

```
SELECT m.*
FROM
   month_end_sales_order_fact m
, month_dim n
WHERE
    n.month = 8
AND m.month_order_sk = n.month_sk
AND m.product_sk NOT IN (
 SELECT x.product_sk
 FROM month_end_balance_fact x, month_dim y
 WHERE x.month_sk = y.month_sk AND y.month = 7
 AND y.year = n.year )
AND (n.year < 2007)
;

INSERT INTO month_end_balance_fact
SELECT o.month_sk, m.product_sk, m.month_end_amount_balance,
       m.month_end_quantity_balance
FROM
  month_end_balance_fact m
, month_dim n
, month_dim o
WHERE
    n.month = 7
AND m.month_sk = n.month_sk
AND o.month = 8
AND n.year = o.year
AND m.product_sk NOT IN (
SELECT x.product_sk
FROM  month_end_sales_order_fact x, month_dim y
WHERE x.month_order_sk = y.month_sk AND y.month = 8
AND y.year = n.year)
AND (o.year < 2007)
;

/* September                                                   */

INSERT INTO month_end_balance_fact
SELECT n.month_order_sk, n.product_sk, (n.month_order_amount +
       m.month_end_amount_balance), (n.month_order_quantity +
       m.month_end_quantity_balance)
FROM
  month_end_balance_fact m
,  month_end_sales_order_fact n
, month_dim o
```

```
, month_dim p
WHERE
    o.month = 8
AND p.month = 9
AND m.month_sk = o.month_sk AND n.month_order_sk = p.month_sk
AND o.year = p.year
AND m.product_sk = n.product_sk
AND (p.year < 2007)
;

INSERT INTO month_end_balance_fact
SELECT m.*
FROM
   month_end_sales_order_fact m
, month_dim n
WHERE
    n.month = 9
AND m.month_order_sk = n.month_sk
AND m.product_sk NOT IN (
 SELECT x.product_sk
 FROM month_end_balance_fact x, month_dim y
 WHERE x.month_sk = y.month_sk AND y.month = 8
 AND y.year = n.year )
AND (n.year < 2007)
;

INSERT INTO month_end_balance_fact
SELECT o.month_sk, m.product_sk, m.month_end_amount_balance,
       m.month_end_quantity_balance
FROM
  month_end_balance_fact m
, month_dim n
, month_dim o
WHERE
    n.month = 8
AND m.month_sk = n.month_sk
AND o.month = 9
AND n.year = o.year
AND m.product_sk NOT IN (
SELECT x.product_sk
FROM  month_end_sales_order_fact x, month_dim y
WHERE x.month_order_sk = y.month_sk AND y.month = 9
AND y.year = n.year)
AND (o.year < 2007)
;
```

```
/* October                                                          */

INSERT INTO month_end_balance_fact
SELECT n.month_order_sk, n.product_sk, (n.month_order_amount +
       m.month_end_amount_balance), (n.month_order_quantity +
       m.month_end_quantity_balance)
FROM
  month_end_balance_fact m
,  month_end_sales_order_fact n
, month_dim o
, month_dim p
WHERE
    o.month = 9
AND p.month = 10
AND m.month_sk = o.month_sk AND n.month_order_sk = p.month_sk
AND o.year = p.year
AND m.product_sk = n.product_sk
AND (p.year < 2007)
;

INSERT INTO month_end_balance_fact
SELECT m.*
FROM
   month_end_sales_order_fact m
, month_dim n
WHERE
    n.month = 10
AND m.month_order_sk = n.month_sk
AND m.product_sk NOT IN (
 SELECT x.product_sk
 FROM month_end_balance_fact x, month_dim y
 WHERE x.month_sk = y.month_sk AND y.month = 9
 AND y.year = n.year )
AND (n.year < 2007)
;

INSERT INTO month_end_balance_fact
SELECT o.month_sk, m.product_sk, m.month_end_amount_balance,
       m.month_end_quantity_balance
FROM
  month_end_balance_fact m
, month_dim n
, month_dim o
WHERE
    n.month = 9
```

```
AND m.month_sk = n.month_sk
AND o.month = 10
AND n.year = o.year
AND m.product_sk NOT IN (
SELECT x.product_sk
FROM  month_end_sales_order_fact x, month_dim y
WHERE x.month_order_sk = y.month_sk AND y.month = 10
AND y.year = n.year)
AND (o.year < 2007)
;

/* November                                                   */

INSERT INTO month_end_balance_fact
SELECT n.month_order_sk, n.product_sk, (n.month_order_amount +
       m.month_end_amount_balance), (n.month_order_quantity +
       m.month_end_quantity_balance)
FROM
  month_end_balance_fact m
,  month_end_sales_order_fact n
, month_dim o
, month_dim p
WHERE
    o.month = 10
AND p.month = 11
AND m.month_sk = o.month_sk AND n.month_order_sk = p.month_sk
AND o.year = p.year
AND m.product_sk = n.product_sk
AND (p.year < 2007)
;

INSERT INTO month_end_balance_fact
SELECT m.*
FROM
   month_end_sales_order_fact m
, month_dim n
WHERE
    n.month = 11
AND m.month_order_sk = n.month_sk
AND m.product_sk NOT IN (
 SELECT x.product_sk
 FROM month_end_balance_fact x, month_dim y
 WHERE x.month_sk = y.month_sk AND y.month = 10
 AND y.year = n.year )
AND (n.year < 2007)
;
```

```
INSERT INTO month_end_balance_fact
SELECT o.month_sk, m.product_sk, m.month_end_amount_balance,
      m.month_end_quantity_balance
FROM
  month_end_balance_fact m
, month_dim n
, month_dim o
WHERE
    n.month = 10
AND m.month_sk = n.month_sk
AND o.month = 11
AND n.year = o.year
AND m.product_sk NOT IN (
SELECT x.product_sk
FROM  month_end_sales_order_fact x, month_dim y
WHERE x.month_order_sk = y.month_sk AND y.month = 11
AND y.year = n.year)
AND (o.year < 2007)
;

/* December                                                     */

INSERT INTO month_end_balance_fact
SELECT n.month_order_sk, n.product_sk, (n.month_order_amount +
      m.month_end_amount_balance), (n.month_order_quantity +
      m.month_end_quantity_balance)
FROM
  month_end_balance_fact m
,  month_end_sales_order_fact n
, month_dim o
, month_dim p
WHERE
    o.month = 11
AND p.month = 12
AND m.month_sk = o.month_sk AND n.month_order_sk = p.month_sk
AND o.year = p.year
AND m.product_sk = n.product_sk
AND (p.year < 2007)
;

INSERT INTO month_end_balance_fact
SELECT m.*
FROM
   month_end_sales_order_fact m
```

```
, month_dim n
WHERE
    n.month = 12
AND m.month_order_sk = n.month_sk
AND m.product_sk NOT IN (
 SELECT x.product_sk
 FROM month_end_balance_fact x, month_dim y
 WHERE x.month_sk = y.month_sk AND y.month = 11
 AND y.year = n.year )
AND (n.year < 2007)
;

INSERT INTO month_end_balance_fact
SELECT o.month_sk, m.product_sk, m.month_end_amount_balance,
       m.month_end_quantity_balance
FROM
  month_end_balance_fact m
, month_dim n
, month_dim o
WHERE
    n.month = 11
AND m.month_sk = n.month_sk
AND o.month = 12
AND n.year = o.year
AND m.product_sk NOT IN (
SELECT x.product_sk
FROM  month_end_sales_order_fact x, month_dim y
WHERE x.month_order_sk = y.month_sk AND y.month = 12
AND y.year = n.year)
AND (o.year < 2007)
;

/* end of script                                                    */
```

Testing the Initial Population Script

I know the **month_end_balance_initial.sql** script is a long one. However, you can run it by simply calling its file name.

```
mysql> \. c:\mysql\scripts\month_end_balance_initial.sql
```

To confirm that the initial population was successful, query the **month_end_sales_order_fact** and the **month_end_balance_fact** tables. Use this statement to query the first table.

```
mysql> select month_order_sk mosk, product_sk psk,
       month_order_amount amt,
    -> month_order_quantity qty from month_end_sales_order_fact
    -> order by month_order_sk, product_sk;
```

Here is the query result.

```
+------+------+----------+------+
| mosk | psk  | amt      | qty  |
+------+------+----------+------+
|   11 |    3 |  1000.00 | NULL |
|   12 |    1 |  1000.00 | NULL |
|   13 |    2 |  2000.00 | NULL |
|   14 |    3 |  2500.00 | NULL |
|   15 |    1 |  3000.00 | NULL |
|   16 |    2 |  3500.00 | NULL |
|   17 |    3 |  4000.00 | NULL |
|   18 |    1 |  4500.00 | NULL |
|   19 |    2 |  1000.00 | NULL |
|   20 |    3 |  1000.00 | NULL |
|   24 |    2 |  5000.00 | NULL |
|   24 |    3 |  4000.00 | NULL |
|   25 |    1 | 46500.00 |  420 |
|   25 |    2 | 25000.00 |  120 |
|   25 |    4 | 47000.00 |  275 |
|   25 |    5 | 27000.00 |   90 |
|   25 |    7 |  4000.00 |   40 |
+------+------+----------+------+
17 rows in set (0.00 sec)
```

To query the month_end_balance_fact table, enter the following on your console.

```
mysql> select month_sk msk, product_sk psk, month_end_amount_balance
       amt,
    -> month_end_quantity_balance qty from month_end_balance_fact
    -> order by month_sk, product_sk;
```

The query result is as follows.

```
+------+------+----------+------+
| msk  | psk  | amt      | qty  |
```

```
+------+------+----------+------+
|   11 |    3 |  1000.00 | NULL |
|   12 |    1 |  1000.00 | NULL |
|   12 |    3 |  1000.00 | NULL |
|   13 |    1 |  1000.00 | NULL |
|   13 |    2 |  2000.00 | NULL |
|   13 |    3 |  1000.00 | NULL |
|   14 |    1 |  1000.00 | NULL |
|   14 |    2 |  2000.00 | NULL |
|   14 |    3 |  3500.00 | NULL |
|   15 |    1 |  4000.00 | NULL |
|   15 |    2 |  2000.00 | NULL |
|   15 |    3 |  3500.00 | NULL |
|   16 |    1 |  4000.00 | NULL |
|   16 |    2 |  5500.00 | NULL |
|   16 |    3 |  3500.00 | NULL |
|   17 |    1 |  4000.00 | NULL |
|   17 |    2 |  5500.00 | NULL |
|   17 |    3 |  7500.00 | NULL |
|   18 |    1 |  8500.00 | NULL |
|   18 |    2 |  5500.00 | NULL |
|   18 |    3 |  7500.00 | NULL |
|   19 |    1 |  8500.00 | NULL |
|   19 |    2 |  6500.00 | NULL |
|   19 |    3 |  7500.00 | NULL |
|   20 |    1 |  8500.00 | NULL |
|   20 |    2 |  6500.00 | NULL |
|   20 |    3 |  8500.00 | NULL |
|   21 |    1 |  8500.00 | NULL |
|   21 |    2 |  6500.00 | NULL |
|   21 |    3 |  8500.00 | NULL |
|   22 |    1 |  8500.00 | NULL |
|   22 |    2 |  6500.00 | NULL |
|   22 |    3 |  8500.00 | NULL |
|   24 |    2 |  5000.00 | NULL |
|   24 |    3 |  4000.00 | NULL |
|   25 |    1 | 46500.00 |  420 |
|   25 |    2 | 30000.00 | NULL |
|   25 |    3 |  4000.00 | NULL |
|   25 |    4 | 47000.00 |  275 |
|   25 |    5 | 27000.00 |   90 |
|   25 |    7 |  4000.00 |   40 |
+------+------+----------+------+
41 rows in set (0.00 sec)
```

Note

The month surrogate key 11 is January 2006 and the month surrogate key 25 is March 2007, meaning the **month_end_balance_fact** table has been correctly populated with all month end sales order facts from January 2006 to March 2007. The balances are all populated correctly as well: The amounts and quantities are accumulated, rolled onto the next months.

Regular Population

You need two scripts for the regular population. The first script is for January population and is presented in Listing 24.3. The second script is for the other months and is given in Listing 24.4.

The January regular population script is similar to the January initial population in that the script must reset the month end balance. However, while the January initial population is part of the whole initial population script, the January regular population is a separate script from the other months. You run the January regular population script at the end of January.

The regular population for the other months (February to December) is also similar to the initial population in that they both have three Insert statements. However, while the initial population must load historical data from January 2006 to March 2007 all at once, the regular population loads the current month data only. The other difference is that the regular population does not have a specific year condition. You run the regular population at the end of every month (February to December).

Listing 24.3: January month end balance regular population script

```
/******************************************************************/
/*                                                                */
/* jan_month_end_balance_regular.sql                              */
/*                                                                */
/******************************************************************/

USE dw;

INSERT INTO month_end_balance_fact
SELECT m.*
```

```
FROM
  month_end_sales_order_fact m
, month_dim n
WHERE
    month = 1
AND m.month_order_sk = n.month_sk
AND n.year = YEAR(CURRENT_DATE)
;

/* end of script                                                    */
```

Listing 24.4: Month end balance regular population for all months except January

```
/******************************************************************/
/*                                                                */
/* month_end_balance_regular.sql                                  */
/*                                                                */
/******************************************************************/

USE dw;

INSERT INTO month_end_balance_fact
SELECT
  n.month_order_sk
, n.product_sk
, (n.month_order_amount + m.month_end_amount_balance)
, (n.month_order_quantity + m.month_end_quantity_balance)
FROM
  month_end_balance_fact m
, month_end_sales_order_fact n
, month_dim o
, month_dim p
WHERE
    o.month = MONTH(CURRENT_DATE) - 1
AND p.month = MONTH(CURRENT_DATE)
AND m.month_sk = o.month_sk
AND n.month_order_sk = p.month_sk
AND o.year = p.year
AND m.product_sk = n.product_sk
;

INSERT INTO month_end_balance_fact
SELECT m.*
FROM
  month_end_sales_order_fact m
```

```
, month_dim n
WHERE
n.month = MONTH(CURRENT_DATE)
AND m.month_order_sk = n.month_sk
AND m.product_sk NOT IN (
SELECT x.product_sk
FROM
  month_end_balance_fact x
, month_dim y
WHERE
    x.month_sk = y.month_sk
AND y.month = (MONTH(CURRENT_DATE)-1)
AND y.year = n.year )
;

INSERT INTO month_end_balance_fact
SELECT
  o.month_sk
, m.product_sk
, m.month_end_amount_balance
, m.month_end_quantity_balance
FROM
  month_end_balance_fact m
, month_dim n
, month_dim o
WHERE
    n.month = MONTH(CURRENT_DATE)-1
AND m.month_sk = n.month_sk
AND o.month = MONTH(CURRENT_DATE)
AND n.year = o.year
AND m.product_sk NOT IN (
SELECT x.product_sk
FROM
  month_end_sales_order_fact x
, month_dim y
WHERE
    x.month_order_sk = y.month_sk
AND y.month = MONTH(CURRENT_DATE)
AND y.year = n.year)
;

/* end of script                                                    */
```

As the regular population scripts are similar to the initial population script, you don't need to test the regular population.

Example Queries

In this section I use two queries (given in Listings 24.6 and 24.7) to show that the month end balance measure (which is an accumulated measure) must be used with caution as it is not fully-additive. A measure is not fully-additive across some of its dimensions, usually across the time dimension. A measure that is not fully-additive is semi-additive.

Additive Across Products

You can correctly add the accumulated balance (month end amount balance) across products as demonstrated by the query in Listing 24.6.

Listing 24.6: Across products

```
/**********************************************************************/
/*                                                                    */
/* balance_across_products.sql                                        */
/*                                                                    */
/**********************************************************************/

USE dw;

SELECT
  Year
, month
, SUM(month_end_amount_balance)
FROM
  month_end_balance_fact a
, month_dim b
WHERE a.month_sk = b.month_sk
GROUP BY year, month
ORDER BY year, month
;

/* end of script                                                      */
```

Run the script in Listing 24.6 using this command.

```
mysql> \. c:\mysql\scripts\balance_across_products.sql
```

You should see the following response.

```
Database changed
+------+-------+-------------------------------+
| year | month | SUM(month_end_amount_balance) |
+------+-------+-------------------------------+
| 2006 |     1 |                       1000.00 |
| 2006 |     2 |                       2000.00 |
| 2006 |     3 |                       4000.00 |
| 2006 |     4 |                       6500.00 |
| 2006 |     5 |                       9500.00 |
| 2006 |     6 |                      13000.00 |
| 2006 |     7 |                      17000.00 |
| 2006 |     8 |                      21500.00 |
| 2006 |     9 |                      22500.00 |
| 2006 |    10 |                      23500.00 |
| 2006 |    11 |                      23500.00 |
| 2006 |    12 |                      23500.00 |
| 2007 |     2 |                       9000.00 |
| 2007 |     3 |                     158500.00 |
+------+-------+-------------------------------+
14 rows in set (0.02 sec)
```

You can verify this result (the sum of amount balances of all products every month) against the previous initial population's query output.

Non-Additive Across Months

The query in Listing 24.7 adds the month end balances across months.

Listing 24.7: Across months

```
/******************************************************************/
/*                                                                */
/* balance_across_months.sql                                      */
/*                                                                */
/******************************************************************/

USE dw ;

SELECT
  product_name
, SUM(month_end_amount_balance)
FROM
  month_end_balance_fact a
, product_dim b
```

```
WHERE
a.product_sk = b.product_sk
GROUP BY product_code
ORDER BY product_code
;

/* end of script                                                    */
```

Run the script in Listing 24.7 by using this command.

```
mysql> \. c:\mysql\scripts\balance_across_months.sql
```

Here is the response.

```
Database changed
+--------------------------+-------------------------------+
| product_name             | SUM(month_end_amount_balance) |
+--------------------------+-------------------------------+
| Hard Disk Drive          |                     104000.00 |
| Floppy Drive             |                      83500.00 |
| LCD Panel                |                     116500.00 |
| Keyboard                 |                      27000.00 |
| High End Hard Disk Drive |                       4000.00 |
+--------------------------+-------------------------------+
5 rows in set (0.00 sec)
```

The query output is incorrect. The correct output should be the same as the result of the following query, which is a query against the source data (the **month_end_sales_order_fact** table).

```
mysql> SELECT product_name, sum(month_order_amount)
    -> FROM month_end_sales_order_fact a, product_dim b
    -> WHERE a.product_sk = b.product_sk
    -> group by product_code;

+--------------------------+-------------------------+
| product_name             | sum(month_order_amount) |
+--------------------------+-------------------------+
| Hard Disk Drive          |                55000.00 |
| Floppy Drive             |                36500.00 |
| LCD Panel                |                59500.00 |
| Keyboard                 |                27000.00 |
| High End Hard Disk Drive |                 4000.00 |
+--------------------------+-------------------------+
5 rows in set (0.00 sec)
```

In other words, the **month_end_balance** measure is additive across products, but not across months.

Summary

In this chapter you learned to implement an accumulated measure, the month end amount balance, and its initial and regular populations. You also learned that the accumulated measure is not fully-additive.

In the next chapter you will learn to implement a new dimension, a special dimension to enhance your data analysis

Chapter 25
Band Dimensions

This chapter, the last in this book, teaches you a technique for implementing band dimensions. A band dimension contains bands of continuous values. For example, an annual sales order band dimension might contain bands called "LOW", "MED", and "HIGH"; which are defined as 0.01 to 15000, 15000.01 to 30000.00, and 30000.01 to 99999999.99, respectively. For example, a sales order with an annual amount of 10000 falls into LOW.

A band dimension can store more than one set of bands. For example, you might have a set of bands for promotion analysis, another for market segmentation, and possibly yet another for sales territory planning. Your users define the bands; they are rarely available directly from the transaction source data.

In this chapter you also apply the multi-star development experience you learned previously to implement band dimensions.

Annual Sales Order Star Schema

In this section I explain how to implement an annual order segment band dimension. To do this, you need two new stars as shown in Figure 25.1. The fact tables of the stars use (relate to) the existing **customer_dim** table and a new **year_dim** table. The year dimension is a subset dimension of the date dimension. The **annual_customer_segment_fact** table is the only table that uses the **annual_order_segment_dim** table. The **annual_order_segement_dim** is the band dimension.

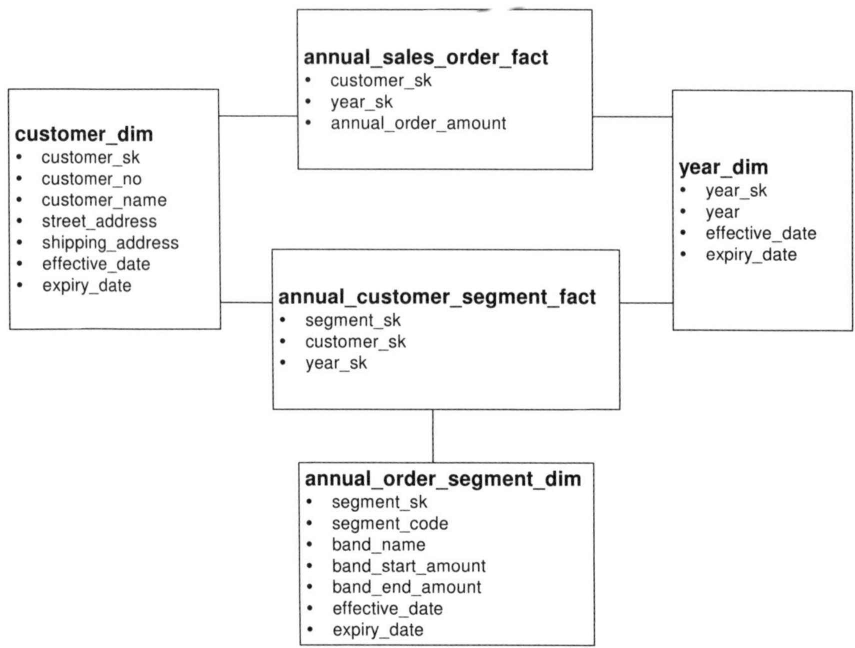

Figure 25.1: The annual sales order schema with the annual_order_segment_dim band dimension

The **annual_order_segment_dim** table stores more than one set of bands. In the example below you populate the table with two sets of bands "PROJECT ALPHA" and "Grid." Both sets are for segmenting customers based on their annual sales order amount.

PROJECT ALPHA has six bands and Grid has three bands. A sample of bands is shown in Table 25.1.

Segment Name	Band Name	Start Value	End Value
PROJECT ALPHA	Bottom	0.01	2500.00
PROJECT ALPHA	Low	2500.01	3000.00
PROJECT ALPHA	Mid-low	3000.01	4000.00
PROJECT ALPHA	Mid	4000.01	5500.00
PROJECT ALPHA	Mid-high	5500.01	6500.00
PROJECT ALPHA	Top	6500.01	99999999.99
Grid	LOW	0.01	3000.00

Grid	MED	3000.01	6000.00
Grid	HIGH	6000.01	99999999.99

Table 25.1: Marketing segment bands

Each band has a start value and an end value. The granularity of the band is the gap between the band to its next band. The granularity must be the smallest possible value of the measure, which in the case of the sales order amount is 0.01. The end value of the last band in a segment is the possible maximum value of the sales order amount.

The script in Listing 25.1 creates the **annual_order_segment_dim** band dimension and pre-populates the bands with the sample bands in Table 25.1.

Listing 25.1: Creating the band dimension

```
/******************************************************************/
/*                                                                */
/* band_dim.sql                                                   */
/*                                                                */
/******************************************************************/

USE dw;

CREATE TABLE annual_order_segment_dim
( segment_sk INT NOT NULL AUTO_INCREMENT PRIMARY KEY
, segment_name CHAR(30)
, band_name CHAR(50)
, band_start_amount DEC(10,2)
, band_end_amount DEC(10,2)
, effective_date DATE
, expiry_date DATE )
;

INSERT INTO annual_order_segment_dim VALUES
  (NULL, 'PROJECT ALPHA', 'Bottom', 0.01, 2500.00, '0000-00-00',
       '9999-12-31')
, (NULL, 'PROJECT ALPHA', 'Low', 2500.01, 3000.00, '0000-00-00',
       '9999-12-31')
, (NULL, 'PROJECT ALPHA', 'Mid-Low', 3000.01, 4000.00, '0000-00-00',
       '9999-12-31')
, (NULL, 'PROJECT ALPHA', 'Mid', 4000.01, 5500.00, '0000-00-00',
       '9999-12-31')
, (NULL, 'PROJECT ALPHA', 'Mid_High', 5500.01, 6500.00, '0000-00-
       00', '9999-12-31')
```

```
, (NULL, 'PROJECT ALPHA', 'Top', 6500.01, 99999999.99, '0000-00-00',
      '9999-12-31')
, (NULL, 'Grid', 'LOW', 0.01, 3000, '0000-00-00', '9999-12-31')
, (NULL, 'Grid', 'MED', 3000.01, 6000.00, '0000-00-00', '9999-12-
      31')
, (NULL, 'Grid', 'HIGH', 6000.01, 99999999.99, '0000-00-00', '9999-
      12-31')
;

/* end of script                                                    */
```

Run the script in Listing 25.1:

```
mysql> \. c:\mysql\scripts\band_dim.sql
```

You will see this on the console.

```
Database changed
Query OK, 0 rows affected (0.18 sec)

Query OK, 9 rows affected (0.05 sec)
Records: 9  Duplicates: 0  Warnings: 0
```

The script in Listing 25.2 creates the other new tables: **year_dim**, **annual_sales_order_fact**, and **annual_customer_segment_fact**.

Listing 25.2: Creating the annual tables

```
/******************************************************************/
/*                                                                */
/* annual_tables.sql                                              */
/*                                                                */
/******************************************************************/

USE dw;

CREATE TABLE year_dim
( year_sk INT NOT NULL AUTO_INCREMENT PRIMARY KEY
, year INT(4)
, effective_date DATE
, expiry_date DATE )
;

CREATE TABLE annual_sales_order_fact
( customer_sk INT
, year_sk INT
, annual_order_amount DEC(10,2) )
```

```
;

CREATE TABLE annual_customer_segment_fact
( segment_sk INT
, customer_sk INT
, year_sk INT)
;

/* end of script                                                    */
```

Run the script in Listing 25.2 using this command.

```
mysql> \. c:\mysql\scripts\annual_tables.sql
```

The following is the response on your console.

```
Database changed
Query OK, 0 rows affected (0.12 sec)

Query OK, 0 rows affected (0.10 sec)

Query OK, 0 rows affected (0.11 sec)
```

Initial Population

In this section I explain the initial population and show you how to test it. The script in Listing 25.3 initially populates the **year_dim** table with data from the **order_date** dimension (a view of the **date_dim** table), the **annual_sales_order_fact** table with data from **sales_order_ fact**, and the **annual_customer_segment_fact** table with data from **annual_sales_order_fact**. The script loads all previous years' data (historical data).

Listing 25.3: The initial population script

```
/******************************************************************/
/*                                                                */
/* band_ini.sql                                                   */
/*                                                                */
/******************************************************************/

INSERT INTO year_dim
SELECT DISTINCT
```

```
  NULL
, year
, effective_date
, expiry_date
FROM order_date_dim
;

INSERT INTO annual_sales_order_fact
SELECT
  b.customer_sk
, year_sk
, SUM(order_amount)
FROM
  sales_order_fact a
, customer_dim b
, year_dim c
, order_date_dim d
WHERE
    a.customer_sk = b.customer_sk
AND a.order_date_sk = d.order_date_sk
AND c.year = d.year
AND d.year < YEAR(CURRENT_DATE)
GROUP BY a.customer_sk, d.year
;

INSERT INTO annual_customer_segment_fact
SELECT
  d.segment_sk
, a.customer_sk
, c.year_sk
FROM
  annual_sales_order_fact a
, customer_dim b
, year_dim c
, annual_order_segment_dim d
WHERE
    a.customer_sk = b.customer_sk
AND a.year_sk = c.year_sk
AND year < YEAR(CURRENT_DATE)
AND annual_order_amount >= band_start_amount
AND annual_order_amount <= band_end_amount
;

/* end of script                                                    */
```

To test the initial population script, set your MySQL date to any date in 2006 to load year 2005 data. You load the 2006 sales orders later in the regular testing section.

Now run the script in Listing 25.3:

```
mysql> \. c:\mysql\scripts\band_ini.sql
```

You should get this as the response.

```
Query OK, 7 rows affected (0.10 sec)
Records: 7  Duplicates: 0  Warnings: 0

Query OK, 6 rows affected (0.05 sec)
Records: 6  Duplicates: 0  Warnings: 0

Query OK, 12 rows affected (0.06 sec)
Records: 12  Duplicates: 0  Warnings: 0
```

To confirm the initial population was successful, query the **annual_customer_segment_fact** table using this statement.

```
mysql> select a.customer_sk csk, a.year_sk ysk,
    -> annual_order_amount amt, segment_name sn, band_name bn
    -> from annual_customer_segment_fact a, annual_order_segment_dim
       b,
    -> year_dim c, annual_sales_order_fact d
    -> where a.segment_sk = b.segment_sk AND a.year_sk = c.year_sk
    -> AND a.customer_sk = d.customer_sk AND a.year_sk = d.year_sk
    -> order BY a.customer_sk, year, segment_name, band_name;
```

Here is the query result.

```
+------+------+---------+---------------+----------+
| csk  | ysk  | amt     | sn            | bn       |
+------+------+---------+---------------+----------+
|    1 |    1 | 8000.00 | Grid          | HIGH     |
|    1 |    1 | 8000.00 | PROJECT ALPHA | Top      |
|    3 |    1 | 4000.00 | Grid          | MED      |
|    3 |    1 | 4000.00 | PROJECT ALPHA | Mid-Low  |
|    4 |    1 | 4000.00 | Grid          | MED      |
|    4 |    1 | 4000.00 | PROJECT ALPHA | Mid-Low  |
|    5 |    1 | 6000.00 | Grid          | MED      |
|    5 |    1 | 6000.00 | PROJECT ALPHA | Mid_High |
|    6 |    1 | 6000.00 | Grid          | MED      |
|    6 |    1 | 6000.00 | PROJECT ALPHA | Mid_High |
```

```
|    7 |    1 | 8000.00 | Grid          | HIGH     |
|    7 |    1 | 8000.00 | PROJECT ALPHA | Top      |
+------+------+---------+---------------+----------+
12 rows in set (0.00 sec)
```

The query result proves that every customer who has placed at least one order in 2005 is assigned to a band of each of the two segments. You can verify that the assignments of the annual sales amounts on the bands are correct. You need to refer back to Table 25.1 to find out the definition of the bands.

Revising the Regular Population Script

In this section I explain the regular population script and how to test it. The regular population is similar to the initial population, except that the former does not need to load the **year_dim** table. The **annual_customer_segment_fact** table is populated with data form the **annual_sales_order_fact** table.

You schedule the regular population script in Listing 25.4 annually. The script loads the previous year sales order data.

Listing 25.4: The revised regular population script

```
/*****************************************************************/
/*                                                               */
/* band_regular.sql                                              */
/*                                                               */
/*****************************************************************/

INSERT INTO annual_sales_order_fact
SELECT
  b.customer_sk
, year_sk
, SUM(order_amount)
FROM
  sales_order_fact a
, customer_dim b
, year_dim c
, order_date_dim d
WHERE
    a.customer_sk = b.customer_sk
AND a.order_date_sk = d.order_date_sk
AND c.year = d.year
```

```
AND c.year = YEAR(CURRENT_DATE) - 1
GROUP BY
  customer_number
, c.year
;

INSERT INTO annual_customer_segment_fact
SELECT
  d.segment_sk
, b.customer_sk
, c.year_sk
FROM
  annual_sales_order_fact a
, customer_dim b
, year_dim c
, annual_order_segment_dim d
WHERE
    a.customer_sk = b.customer_sk
AND a.year_sk = c.year_sk
AND c.year = YEAR(CURRENT_DATE) - 1
AND annual_order_amount >= band_start_amount
AND annual_order_amount <= band_end_amount
;

/* end of script                                                    */
```

Testing

To test the regular population, set your MySQL date to a date in 2007 and run the **band_regular.sql** script:

```
mysql> \. c:\mysql\scripts\band_regular.sql
```

You should see this message on your console.

```
Query OK, 7 rows affected (0.06 sec)
Records: 7  Duplicates: 0  Warnings: 0

Query OK, 14 rows affected (0.05 sec)
Records: 14  Duplicates: 0  Warnings: 0
```

Query the **customer_order_segment_fact** table to confirm the regular population was successful.

```
mysql> select a.customer_sk csk, a.year_sk ysk,
    -> annual_order_amount amt, segment_name sn, band_name bn
    -> from annual_customer_segment_fact a, annual_order_segment_dim
       b,
    -> year_dim c, annual_sales_order_fact d
    -> where a.segment_sk = b.segment_sk AND a.year_sk = c.year_sk
    -> AND a.customer_sk = d.customer_sk AND a.year_sk = d.year_sk
    -> order BY a.customer_sk, year, segment_name, band_name;

+------+------+---------+---------------+----------+
| csk  | ysk  | amt     | sn            | bn       |
+------+------+---------+---------------+----------+
|    1 |    1 | 8000.00 | Grid          | HIGH     |
|    1 |    1 | 8000.00 | PROJECT ALPHA | Top      |
|    1 |    2 | 4000.00 | Grid          | MED      |
|    1 |    2 | 4000.00 | PROJECT ALPHA | Mid-Low  |
|    2 |    2 | 5500.00 | Grid          | MED      |
|    2 |    2 | 5500.00 | PROJECT ALPHA | Mid      |
|    3 |    1 | 4000.00 | Grid          | MED      |
|    3 |    1 | 4000.00 | PROJECT ALPHA | Mid-Low  |
|    3 |    2 | 2000.00 | Grid          | LOW      |
|    3 |    2 | 2000.00 | PROJECT ALPHA | Bottom   |
|    4 |    1 | 4000.00 | Grid          | MED      |
|    4 |    1 | 4000.00 | PROJECT ALPHA | Mid-Low  |
|    4 |    2 | 3000.00 | Grid          | LOW      |
|    4 |    2 | 3000.00 | PROJECT ALPHA | Low      |
|    5 |    1 | 6000.00 | Grid          | MED      |
|    5 |    1 | 6000.00 | PROJECT ALPHA | Mid_High |
|    5 |    2 | 2500.00 | Grid          | LOW      |
|    5 |    2 | 2500.00 | PROJECT ALPHA | Bottom   |
|    6 |    1 | 6000.00 | Grid          | MED      |
|    6 |    1 | 6000.00 | PROJECT ALPHA | Mid_High |
|    6 |    2 | 3000.00 | Grid          | LOW      |
|    6 |    2 | 3000.00 | PROJECT ALPHA | Low      |
|    7 |    1 | 8000.00 | Grid          | HIGH     |
|    7 |    1 | 8000.00 | PROJECT ALPHA | Top      |
|    7 |    2 | 3500.00 | Grid          | MED      |
|    7 |    2 | 3500.00 | PROJECT ALPHA | Mid-Low  |
+------+------+---------+---------------+----------+
26 rows in set (0.00 sec)
```

The query result shows that every customer who placed at least one order in 2005 and 2006 is assigned to a band of each of the two segments for each of the two years. You can verify that the assignments of the annual sales amounts on the bands are all correct. You need to refer back to Table 25.1 to find out the definition of the bands.

Summary

In this final chapter of the book you learned what a band dimension is and how to implement a customer segment band dimension

.

Appendix A
Flat File Data Sources

To test the examples in this book, you need the flat file data sources listed in Table B.1. All the files can be found in the ZIP file accompanying this book.

You should follow the instructions in the Instruction column carefully, especially when testing these three flat files, **customer.csv**, **factory.csv**, and **product.txt**.

No	File Name	Used In	Instruction
1	product2-1.txt	Chapter 2	Copy to the mysql\data\dw directory and rename to product.txt
2	product2-2.txt	Chapter 2	Delete product.txt, copy this file to mysql\data\dw directory, and change its name to product.txt
3	customer2.csv	Chapter 2	Delete customer.csv, copy this file to the mysql\data\dw directory, and change its name to customer.csv
4	customer8.csv	Chapter 8	Delete customer.csv, copy this file to the mysql\data\dw directory, and change its name to customer.csv
5	product8.txt	Chapter 8	Delete product.txt, copy this file to the mysql\data\dw directory, and change its name to product.txt
6	customer10.csv	Chapter 10	Delete customer.csv, copy this file to mysql\data\dw directory, and change its name to customer.csv
7	promo_schedule.csv	Chapter 11	

8	campaign_session.csv	Chapter 16	
9	ragged_campaign.csv	Chapter 16	
10	factory19.csv	Chapter 19	Copy to the mysql\data\dw directory and change its name to product.txt, and then change its name again to factory.csv
11	non_straight_campaign.csv	Chapter 20	
12	product21.txt	Chapter 21	Rename product.txt back to product8.txt, then rename this file to product.txt
13	zip_code.csv	Chapter 23	
14	customer23.csv	Chapter 23	Rename customer.csv back to customer10.csv, then rename this file to customer.csv
15	factory23.csv	Chapter 23	Rename factory.csv back to factory19.csv, then rename this file to factory.csv

Table B.1: Flat files data sources and usage instructions

Index